Leicester–Nottingham Studies in Ancient Society

Volume 3

THE CITY IN LATE ANTIQUITY

THE CITY
IN LATE ANTIQUITY

Edited by

JOHN RICH

London and New York

First published 1992
by Routledge
11 New Fetter Lane, London EC4P 4EE

Simultaneously published in the USA and Canada
by Routledge
a division of Routledge, Chapman and Hall Inc.
29 West 35th Street, New York, NY 10001

Reprinted in 1996

Typeset in Times on 10/12 point by
Witwell Ltd, Southport
Printed in Great Britain by
TJ Press (Padstow) Ltd, Padstow, Cornwall

British Library Cataloguing in Publication Data
The city in late antiquity. - (Leicester–Nottingham
   studies in ancient society; 3)
   I. Rich, John   II. Series
   307.7640937

Library of Congress Cataloguing in Publication Data
The City in late antiquity/edited by John Rich.
   p.   cm. — (Leicester–Nottingham studies in ancient society:
v. 3)
   Includes bibliographic references and index.
   1. Cities and towns. Ancient—Rome. I. Rich, John.
II. Series.
HT114.C525   1992
307.76′0937′6—dc20   91-36367

ISBN 0-415-14431-0 (pbk)

Contents

Contributors

Philip Dixon is Senior Lecturer in Archaeology at the University of Nottingham.

Jill Harries is Lecturer in Ancient History at the University of St Andrews.

Hugh Kennedy is Reader in Mediaeval History at the University of St Andrews.

Cristina La Rocca has a research post at the University of Padua.

Claude Lepelley is Professor of Roman History at the University of Paris X.

Wolfgang Liebeschuetz is Professor of Classics and Ancient History at the University of Nottingham and a Fellow of the British Academy.

Andrew Poulter is Lecturer in Archaeology at the University of Nottingham.

Richard Reece is Senior Lecturer in Archaeology at University College London.

John Rich is Lecturer in Classics at the University of Nottingham.

Preface

Between 1986 and 1988 a series of seminars and two conferences on the theme of 'The Ancient City' were jointly organized by the Classics Departments of the Universities of Leicester and Nottingham. This is the second of two volumes based on papers given at those meetings (the first, *City and Country in the Ancient World*, edited by Andrew Wallace-Hadrill and myself, was published in 1991 as volume 2 in the Leicester–Nottingham Studies in Ancient Society series). The 'Ancient City' series concluded in April 1988 with a conference at Nottingham on 'The End of the Ancient City?'. Six of the seven papers delivered at that conference appear, in substantially revised form, in this volume, along with two further papers (by Liebeschuetz and Dixon).

Liebeschuetz's paper is a synoptic study of the ancient city under the Later Roman Empire and during the Empire's disintegration, whereas the remaining papers deal with particular aspects of the subject and particular regions. The papers bring out the rich range of evidence – literary, documentary and archaeological – which is available, and the different perspectives which may be brought to bear on it by archaeologists and by historians. They also bring out the great diversity of the ancient city. In some regions, the classical city and its traditions survived only weakly, if at all, by the fourth century. In Britain this was because it had never put down more than shallow roots, as Reece and Dixon show. In the Danubian provinces, discussed by Poulter, cities had flourished in the Early Empire, but never really recovered from the third-century crisis. By contrast, in Africa the cities' institutions and culture retained exceptional vitality in the fourth century, as Lepelley shows. Yet here too they eventually succumbed, crushed by the Vandal and Arab invasions. However, if in many parts of the empire the cities went under, elsewhere they showed more staying-power. One factor making for continuity was Christianity, which was, as Liebeschuetz notes, on the whole 'city-friendly'; Harries explores this phenomenon in the context of Gaul. The last two papers, by La Rocca and Kennedy, show how in regions as diverse as northern Italy and Syria much of the physical fabric of the late antique cities and even something of their distinctive ideology could survive into mediaeval times.

The maps of northern Africa and the Danubian provinces (see pp. 53, 102) were drawn by David Taylor, of the Archaeology Department of Nottingham University, and are intended simply to identify towns and provinces mentioned in the text. I am very grateful to the many who assisted both in the organization of the seminar series and in the production of this volume, and in particular to the following: the Society for the Promotion of Roman Studies for a generous grant towards the costs of the seminar series; Andrew Wallace-Hadrill, co-organizer of the series; Ross Balzaretti, Wolf Liebeschuetz and Robert Markus for their advice; Bryan Ward-Perkins for assistance with the jacket illustration; and Adrienne Edwards and Pella Beaven for secretarial help.

Nottingham   J.W.R.
September 1991

Abbreviations

AE	*L'Année Épigraphique*
ANRW	*Aufstieg und Niedergang der römischen Welt*, ed. H. Temporini (Berlin and New York, 1972–)
Arch. Ért.	*Archaeologiai Értesitö* (Budapest)
BA	*Bibliothèque Augustinienne – Oeuvres de saint Augustin*
BAR	British Archaeological Reports
C.	*Corpus Inscriptionum Latinarum*, vol. iii
CCL	*Corpus Christianorum, series latina*
CIL	*Corpus Inscriptionum Latinarum*
CJ	*Codex Justinianus*
CSEL	*Corpus Scriptorum Ecclesiasticorum Latinorum*
CTh	*Codex Theodosianus*
IDR	*Inscripţiile antice din Dacia şi Scythia Minor*, ed. D.M. Pippidi and I.I. Russu (Bucharest)
IGBulg	*Inscriptiones Graecae in Bulgaria repertae*, ed. G. Mihailov (Sofia, 1958–70)
IGL	*Inscripţiile Greceşti şi Latine din secolele IV–XIII descoperite în Romania* (Bucharest, 1976)
ILCV	*Inscriptiones Christianae Latinae Veteres*, ed. E. Diehl, 2nd edn (Berlin, 1961)
ILJug	A. Šašel and J. Šašel, *Inscriptiones latinae quae in Yugoslavia inter annos MCMXL et MCMLX repertae et editae sunt* (Ljubljana, 1963)
ILS	*Inscriptiones Latinae Selectae*, ed. H. Dessau (Berlin, 1892–1916)
IMS	*Inscriptions de la Mésie Supérieure*, i: *Singidunum et le nord-ouest de la province*, ed. M. Mirkovich and S. Dušanich (Belgrade, 1976)
INMV	*Izvestiya na Narodniya Muzei Varna*
MAMA	*Monumenta Asiae Minoris Antiqua*

MGH	*Monumenta Germaniae Historica*
Not. Dig. Oc.	*Notitia dignitatum . . . in partibus Occidentis*, in O. Seeck (ed.), *Notitia dignitatum* (Berlin, 1876)
Not. Dig. Or.	*Notitia dignitatum . . . in partibus Orientis*
PL	*Patrologia Latina*, ed. J.P. Migne
PLRE	A.H.M. Jones, J.B. Martindale and J. Morris, *The Prosopography of the Later Roman Empire* (Cambridge, 1973–)
RAC	*Reallexicon für Antike und Christentum*
RE	*Realencyclopädie der classischen Altertumswissenschaft*
RIU	*Die Römischen Inschriften Ungarns*, ed. L. Barkóczi, A. Mócsy and S. Soproni, 3 vols (Budapest, 1972–81)
SC	*Sources chrétiennes*
SGLI	*Spätgriechische und spätlateinische Inschriften aus Bulgarien*, ed. V. Beshevliev (Berlin, 1964)
Sirmium I	V. Popović, *A Survey of the Topography and Urban Organization of Sirmium in the Late Empire* (Belgrade, 1971)
Sirmium III	V. Popović and E.L. Ochsenschlager, *Archaeological Investigations in Sirmium* (Belgrade, 1973)
Sirmium VII	N. Duval and V. Popović, *Horrea et thermes aux abords du rempart sud*, Collection de l'École française de Rome 29/1 (Paris, 1977)
Villes	*Villes et Peuplement dans l'Illyricum proto-byzantin*, Collection de l'École française de Rome 77 (Paris, 1984)

∞ 1 ∞

The end of the ancient city

Wolfgang Liebeschuetz

The ancient city: a centre of administration and a way of life

Many sites of ancient cities are occupied by flourishing cities today. Not a few of them have continuous histories since Antiquity. So the Ancient City can be said to have come to an end only in a special sense, the disappearance of those characteristics which distinguished the Graeco-Roman city from others. Of these the most spectacular and influential have been cultural. They involve a particular style of architecture, sculpture and town planning, and a very distinctive literary and intellectual tradition. But the origin of the Ancient City was political and administrative. Its essential feature was the creation of a political, religious and cultural centre ('the city' in the narrow sense) for a rural territory around it. The political centre together with its territory represented the city state, or 'city' in a wider sense. According to Thucydides the creation of the political centre was the essential action in Theseus' *synoikismos* of Athens: he suppressed the local councils of the small communities of Attica and created a common council for the whole territory at what was thereafter the city of Athens (Thucydides 2.15; cf. Cavanagh 1991). The legend expresses the historian's view that the origin of the Athenian city state was political and administrative. The subsequent history of the city in the Graeco-Roman world, not least in the Later Empire, shows that its political and administrative rôle remained central. For Thucydides the original and essential instrument for creating and maintaining the Athenian

city state was the council or *boulē*. In his own time this was just
one of the political institutions of democratic Athens, working
alongside a popular assembly, popular courts and numerous
directly elected magistrates. Under Roman rule popular institutions faded away,[1] and the self-government of territory and
urban centre was left in the hands of the council (*curia, boulē*), a
body whose size might vary from about eighty to six hundred men
according to the size of the city. Membership was lifelong and in
practice hereditary. Vacancies were made up by co-option from
men of property, above all landed property. The history of the
cities in the Roman Empire is closely linked with the history of the
city councils and the civic élite (*curiales, decuriones, bouleutai*)
which had come to monopolize membership of the ruling council.
In the Roman period possession of a council was considered the
essential qualification for city status (Jones 1964, 724; Garnsey
and Saller 1987, 29).

Classical cities were above all a means to living a particular kind
of good life. Philosophers might theorize about this in different
ways. Aristotle wrote that man was a political animal (*Politics*
1.2), that is, that man is designed to live in a city (*polis*), and he
proceeded to draw up a blueprint for a city which would enable its
inhabitants, or at least some of them, to live as nature intended
them to (*Politics* 7–8). This ideal was expressed in political
institutions, in art and entertainment, and in architecture. Town
planning, architecture, festivals and other public spectacles were
more than pure aesthetics. They formed the basis of a calendar of
urban ceremony, participation in which symbolized consent to the
social order at every level from the family to the Empire.
Inasmuch as ritual moulds and transmits attitudes, the ritual of
the classical city helped to unite different groups within the town,
inhabitants of the city and inhabitants of its territory, and the
hundreds of cities that made up the Empire, with a ruler whose
image was kept before his subjects by the imperial cult (Clavel-
Lévêque 1984; Price 1984; Wörrle 1988). Politics was becoming
the concern of ever fewer of the inhabitants of the city. But the
institutions which satisfied the aesthetic-architectural definition of
the city (Finley 1973, 124) – rectangular street plans, wide public

---

[1] On the disappearance of Greek democratic institutions see Ste Croix
1981, 300–26.

spaces and impressive public buildings, festivals, entertainments and baths – flourished exceedingly. The Romans had adopted the Greek ideal very early in their history, and they introduced it to large areas of western Europe and the Balkans where it had been unknown before (Drinkwater 1987a).

So the consolidation of the Roman empire saw a huge expansion of the classical city.[1] For the mass of the inhabitants the advantages were perhaps mainly intangible, the consciousness of participating in 'no mean city'. For the well-to-do the city provided not only amenities, but also a position of leadership which was guaranteed by the Romans. The Romans gained in that the cities provided a means of administering large territories which did not require a huge civil service.[2] So the provincial élite took up the Greek vision of urban life as modified by the Romans, and with the encouragement of the Roman authorities proceeded to build temples, assembly places (*fora*) and 'mansions' (Tacitus, *Agricola* 19), and to establish games and festivals.[3] Finance was provided largely by voluntary or semi-voluntary munificence. This was expensive, and performing administrative services like tax-collecting for the Romans was troublesome, but public spending made the councillors' wealth and power acceptable to poorer fellow citizens, while their administrative services ensured that the maintenance of the political *status quo* remained in the interest of the Roman government. Considerations of class-interest apart, there is no doubt that in the first and second centuries AD the pattern of life represented by the classical city had a very great, in fact almost irresistible, appeal. The climax of the physical development of the classical city was reached in some areas at the end of the second century, more generally, in the first two decades of the third century. After that the great flood of private munificence displayed in public buildings, banquets, distribution of money or food, games, statues and inscribed monuments subsided everywhere, and never recovered to anything

[1] Cf. Levick 1987, 377: between the first and the third centuries the number of coining cities in Asia Minor rose from 154 to 246.
[2] The best account of Greek cities' relationship with the Roman government is Jones 1940, 113–55. There is no comparable study for the Roman city.
[3] Jones 1940, 211–58, gives a survey, again seen from the Greek side.

remotely approaching its former level. The Empire was passing through the crisis of the third century, which marks the beginning of Late Antiquity, and the real starting point of this paper.[1]

A development which was hastened, if not caused, by the third-century crisis was the splitting of the Roman Empire into Eastern and Western halves. Socially as well as physically the lands to the south and south-east of the Mediterranean had of course always been very different from those to the north and north-east. But the Roman Empire and not least urbanization had made them seem more alike. After the third century the unifying pull of Rome was weaker, and in many respects developments in East and West began to diverge once more. Certainly the crisis affected cities in East and West – the dichotomy of course provides only a very rough classification – in different ways. However, the evolution of cities in East and West was not so much in opposite directions, as out of step. Over a perspective of centuries it will be seen that cities in East and West follow a similar pattern up to say 800, and this fact justifies the procedure of continuing to treat them as a single phenomenon.

The third-century crisis and the inscriptions of Aphrodisias

The crisis of the third century really did affect cities everywhere. The universality of its impact is shown by the fact that, paradoxically, it can be demonstrated most graphically in a city which was relatively little affected, Aphrodisias in Caria. Since Aphrodisias experienced quite exceptional continuity from the Early to the Late Empire, it continued to produce inscriptions at a time when most cities ceased to do so, and these inscriptions testify to profound changes.

The rate of production of inscriptions dropped dramatically. The three hundred years AD 250–550 have left 250 inscriptions whereas the previous three hundred years left 1500 (Roueché 1989a, 20). Among the later inscriptions there is a great and sudden reduction in the proportion honouring private benefactors. The men commemorated after the crisis were usually imper-

[1] On the crisis see King and Henig 1981; Drinkwater 1987b; Alföldy 1989a.

ial officials or the emperor. It is also significant that the inscriptions of the Later Empire are quite different stylistically. Verse epigrams tend to take the place of prose in honorific inscriptions. Inscriptions cease to take the form of a public record, and often seem to have been set up for their decorative value. Their appeal has become aesthetic and ceremonial rather than political.

The social development reflected by these changes in the inscriptional habit is the progressive weakening of local politics. Political initiative is in the hands of the imperial governor who has his headquarters at Aphrodisias. The institutions of political self-government decay. The last reference to the traditional chief magistrate is on an inscription dated between 284 and 301. The latest monumental honour put up in the name of council and people dates from the late 360s (Roueché 1989a, 42–3, no. 22). Acclamations replace debated and voted decrees (ibid., 121–36, no. 80–4). The urban élite no longer competes for office, and no longer attaches importance to the 'immortality' which consists of a statue with a laudatory inscription set in a public place where their fellow citizens could not fail to see it.

The rise and decline of the epigraphic habit at Aphrodisias is an exceptionally well-documented example of an Empire-wide phenomenon.[1] The evidence for underlying social changes is also Empire-wide, though change came at different rates to different areas of the Empire. That is the theme of much of this chapter.

The inscriptions of Aphrodisias reveal an unexpected episode. The fading out of private and civic commemorations in the third century was partially reversed in the fifth. We have a comparatively large number of inscriptions dating from the middle of the fifth to the middle of the sixth centuries commemorating private benefactions, or work undertaken by a new civic finance officer, the 'father of the city', *patēr tēs poleōs* (Roueché 1979). After this Indian summer secular inscriptions come to an end around AD 600. Later inscriptions are either ecclesiastical or funerary, and there are very few. We are approaching the end of Aphrodisias as a classical city.

This partial revival of civic activities at Aphrodisias in the late fifth and sixth centuries is an example of a phenomenon which has

[1] For the wider picture see Mrozek 1973; Liebeschuetz 1981, 485–92; MacMullen 1982 and 1986; Mann 1985.

been noted in widely separated areas of what had once been the Empire. For instance church building in Aquitaine, starting at a very low level in the fourth century, rose to a peak in the sixth and declined to nothing in the early seventh century (Rouche 1979, 295). It is perhaps not altogether a coincidence that the cathedral of Trier built in the reign of Gratian, and badly damaged in the invasions of the fifth century, was rebuilt by Bishop Nicetius about the same time as Justinian rebuilt St Sophia at Constantinople (Irsch 1931; Kempf 1964). Obviously the scale and quantity of building in the early sixth-century boom was much greater in the East, but peaks of activity nevertheless appear to have been achieved in the East and West at about the same time.

Factors transforming the city

Why the crisis of the third century had such immediate and lasting effects is a question to which there is no simple answer. Certainly an important factor was a transformation of the view held by the wealthy ruling group of the cities, the decurions, of their relations with their fellow town dwellers, and of their own rôle in the collective life of the community. An unmistakable symptom was the growing isolation of the élite, and the concentration of wealth in fewer hands. This was, of course, a long-term development which the financial hardships of the third century merely accelerated. But it looks as if in Late Roman towns the élite were not ashamed – or afraid – to display their riches in conspicuous consumption such as the building of large town houses, at the same time as they were becoming reluctant to use them in the traditionally accepted way by spending on behalf of fellow citizens (Brown 1978, 27–53).[1] Various explanations can be suggested. The Diocletianic reforms setting up a more elaborate central administration, smaller provinces, and a highly bureaucratic system of taxation, with taxes raised, and partly spent in kind,

---

[1] Large Late Roman town houses are found at, for example, Istrus and Callatis in Moesia, Antioch and Apamea in Syria, and Gerasa in Arabia (Claude 1969, 183–5), as also at Ostia (Meiggs 1973, 258–62), and in Britain at Silchester, Cirencester, Verulamium and Caerwent (Todd 1981, 222).

made much heavier demands on decurions. Henceforth they would not only be obliged to collect the taxes, but they would also have to spend a great deal of time administering the distribution of levies, the transport and storage of products of taxation, the paying out of salaries and the keeping of accounts (Jones 1964, 448–62). If things went wrong, decurions were liable to corporal punishment or to making up a deficit out of their own property.

In the smaller provinces they were now under continuous supervision by the provincial governors. In the East civic coinages came to an end in the third century (Howgego 1985). In the fourth century the estates and other sources of income of cities were taken over by the imperial *res privata*, and only a third of the revenue from these sources was allocated to civic expenses,[1] moreover only to such expenses as were approved by the governor, especially the building of walls (Liebeschuetz 1959). Walls – even for a reduced urban perimeter – involved a massive physical effort and great expense. That they had now become essential, to the point of becoming part of the definition of a city (see pp. 163–5), is a mark of the changed and more utilitarian role of cities in Late Antiquity.

The confiscation of two-thirds of the cities' income from property and local taxes, added to the great new expense of fortification, must have very much reduced city councils' ability to finance projects of the traditional kind, and even to maintain existing structures. Compared with their predecessors earlier in this century, historians of the present more democratic age have shown little sympathy for the decurions, focusing attention on opportunities for unjust profits rather than losses and punishments. The fact remains that the rôle of decurions had become more burdensome, hazardous and frustrating, so that there was a strong incentive for councillors to evade their curial duties if they could contrive to do so (Liebeschuetz 1972, 166–86). But the very circumstances which made curial service unbearable also provided opportunities for escape. The Diocletianic system required a great increase in the number of élite officials both at provincial and central levels of government as well as at a newly created

---

[1] The view of Durliat 1988, 38 n. 78, that the city's 'third' consisted of a third of not only of the former civic revenues but also all the tax revenue collected there, is refuted by *CTh* 5.14.35 (395).

intermediate diocesan level. Imperial service was rewarded with
honorific titles and legal privileges which might include personal
or even hereditary immunity from curial services (Jones 1964,
740–5; Millar 1983). After they had acquired their title, these men
might return to their own or some other city as *honorati*, to
occupy positions of prestige or power – for instance through
access to the imperial governor – above that of decurions who had
remained at home content to serve their cities (for examples from
Antioch see Liebeschuetz 1972, 186–92 and 197–200).

   The service of the church was another way out of the council.
After the conversion of Constantine most cities had a bishop, and
bishops came to be chosen to an increasing extent from the curial
class (Jones 1964, 925 n. 141; Eck 1978 and 1983). As bishops they
still served the inhabitants of a city, their own or another. But they
worked for an ideal which was not the 'good life' of the classical
city. In fact they would denigrate the traditional values of the civic
élite as the pursuit of 'vain glory'.

   The effects of these developments were clearly visible all over
the Empire, but they were considerably more conspicuous in the
West than in the East. The physical damage was worst in exposed
frontier areas, above all the Balkans (see chapter 4 in this volume),
the Rhineland and Northern Gaul.[1] But even there the
number of sites completely abandoned was not large. The building
of walls around a reduced perimeter, often leaving monumental
structures derelict outside the circuit, was the commonest
response (Johnson 1983; Wightman 1985, 223–33; Keay 1988,
178–81).

   An Empire-wide feature was a decline in the monumental and
aesthetic aspects of city life. Almost everywhere decurions ceased
to embellish their cities with the characteristic public buildings.
There was a great decline in the number of competitions and
festivals. The initiative in public building passed from councillors
to imperial governors. Different parts of the Empire were affected
to different degrees. In large areas of Britain, Gaul and the

---

[1] In the Rhineland cities shrank, and their fortifications now housed
both soldiers and civilians, but most survived until at least 450. Smaller
sites were much more vulnerable, and their abandonment began well
before the third-century crisis. See Petrikovits 1980, 239–43 and 297, and
on Gaul Wightman 1985, 243–6, and Van Ossel 1985.

Balkans it would scarcely be an exaggeration to say that the monumental and aesthetic ideal of the classical city was simply given up. In Italy and around the northern and western Mediterranean the classical pattern was maintained but on a reduced scale and showing signs of gradual decline (Mrozek 1978; Ward-Perkins 1984). The classical city continued most strongly, and without shrinkage of the built-up area, in north Africa and in the Greek East, particularly in cities that served as provincial capitals.[1]

Not all cities were worse off. The splitting of provinces meant that more cities enjoyed the profits of being centres of provincial administration (Roueché 1989b). The flourishing condition of Apamea in the fifth century illustrates how advantageous this could be (Balty 1980 and 1989). In such cases the gain was at the expense of the old capital of the undivided province, as is vividly, if rhetorically, described in letters of Basil pleading for Caesarea when that city had been deprived of half its province (*Epistles* 74–6).

The total number of cities was not reduced. There was a tendency for smaller centres to develop, and for a denser network of towns to come into being. This is striking in Roman Britain (Burnham and Wacher 1990; Millett 1990, 143–51), but also very evident in Gaul (Duby 1980, 109–17; Bekker-Nielsen 1989, 42, table 6.1). Large city territories were liable to be divided up (Wightman 1985, 204–5 on northern France and Belgium; Lepelley 1979, 123–5 on Tunisia) and this development continued through the fourth, and even the fifth, century. The splitting of a civic territory, of course, resulted in the strengthening of what had been a village at the expense of the old city centre. Thus splitting city territories had effects comparable to those which followed the splitting of provinces. People were certainly aware of the economic advantages of living in a provincial capital or to a lesser extent in the administrative centre of a rural territory. It is likely that political pressure to share this advantage was one of the reasons why provinces and civic territories continued to be divided.

[1] A wall cutting off a large area of the Hellenistic city of Side, in southern Asia Minor, was wrongly dated to the third century by Claude 1969, 244–5. The wall, and therefore the abandonment of the part of the city excluded by it, are seventh century (Foss 1977c, 172–80).

It is inevitable that the best-known Late Roman cities are those which were least affected by the changes which were making cities less distinguished. The great cities of the East, Ephesus (Foss 1979), Sardis (Foss 1976), Ancyra (Foss 1977b), and Antioch (Libanius, *Oration* 11.228; Downey 1961, 342–50 and 403–10), recovered from the ravages of the third century and received spectacular new buildings. The same was true of Trier and Carthage in the West. The most important factor making for urban prosperity seems to have been the presence of imperial or military administration. Imperial money raised by taxation, and spent on orders of the imperial governor, compensated for reduced income from curial munificence and civic property. In the Latin half of the Empire the cities of North Africa seem to have been affected much less by the third-century crisis than any other. The building and setting up of monuments came to an end in the mid-third century there as elsewhere. But there was a wave of public building under the Tetrarchy and another in the second half of the fourth century.[1] At least some of the city councils seem to have remained intact (Chastagnol 1978; Lepelley 1979, 243–92), and the titles which had been objects of intense competition everywhere before the crisis continued to be used, and presumably valued, in the cities of North Africa (see pp. 60–1). This was in spite of the fact that Christianity took very strong root in these cities. Part of the explanation might be exceptional wealth, derived from the export of African olive oil, which seems to have dominated markets in Italy and indeed all round the Mediterranean.

The apparent shrinkage of the inhabited core of so many – but not all – cities in the West[2] raises problems which are still unsolved. The obvious explanation of the phenomenon would be that the population of the sites had shrunk considerably. But other explanations are possible. It might be that even under the Early Empire some of the more extensive urban sites had contained only the substantial houses of the urban élite, and had never housed a large population of humbler people. It has been

---

[1] Lepelley 1979, 72–111. Civic building finally declined in Africa under Honorius and Valentinian III.

[2] See above (p. 8), and also Duval 1959; Duby 1980, 399–411 (noting as exceptions Autun, Fréjus, Trier and Toulouse).

suggested that this was true of many British cities (see chapter 5 in this volume). Alternatively, a Late Roman city might have a large population living in suburbs outside the circuit of walls (Février *et al.* 1980, 411 on Paris, Périgueux and Clermont; Sivan, forthcoming, on Bordeaux). Probably the answer has to be found separately for each city.

The question of population is related to that of changes in the importance and location of trade and manufacture. This topic can only be touched on here.[1] Towards the end of the second century the western provinces were becoming self-sufficient in the characteristic consumer items of Roman civilization such as fine pottery, silverware, glass, wine, olive oil and eastern spices.[2] Remote northern Britain seems to have become largely self-sufficient (Millett 1990, 159–63), even though it was, of course, incapable of growing its own olives, or, to any significant extent, vines. Shrinkage of imports may therefore be the reason why London, the principal port for continental trade, underwent considerable reduction of its built-up area (Hobley 1986). There certainly were important changes in the pattern of trade elsewhere. Amphora exports from Gaul and Spain to other Mediterranean areas seem to have come to an end during the fourth century (Keay 1984; Panella 1989, 131). In Asia Minor the pottery trade became regionalized in the fourth century (Abadie-Reynal 1989, 149).[3] These changes are likely to have had a detrimental effect on at least the cities on the older trade routes,

---

[1] For differing views see Finley 1973, 123–41; Hopkins 1978 and 1980; Garnsey and Saller 1987, 31–63.

[2] The theory of the commercial emancipation of the provinces is no longer held in the form proposed by Rostovtzeff 1957, but a trend to provincial self-sufficiency can be inferred from such indicators as the decline in the volume of shipwrecks from the peak period 200 BC–AD 200 (Hopkins 1980, 105–6, 123–4), the collapse of the slave-worked villa system in Italy in the second century, and the rise of African oil exports. See Wickham 1988.

[3] The network of pottery trade seems to have expanded again in the fifth and sixth centuries to include the whole coastal area from Gaza to Constantinople, perhaps 'on the back' of the *annona* of Constantinople (Abadie-Reynal 1989). There was also wide distribution of column capitals of Proconnesian marble during the fifth and sixth centuries, either under private or government direction, mainly in Byzantine-controlled areas (Sodini 1989, 163–86).

for instance between the mouth of the Rhône and the Rhineland and around the coast of Spain (Keay 1988, 176). A striking development was the great expansion of the African amphora trade which reached all shores of the Mediterranean (Panella 1989). It certainly reached Provence and the Rhône valley, but did not perhaps penetrate much more deeply into Gaul (Hitchner 1992).

The Diocletianic system of taxation certainly affected the condition of cities in as far as they were centres of distribution of economic resources. When the tax was raised in kind (Mazzarino 1951; Jones 1964, 448–62; Cerati 1975), the operations involved in bringing the supplies to the government employees – soldiers or civilians – who were to receive them were themselves made into a tax (Liebeschuetz 1961). The collectors were required not only to raise so much tax in kind or money, but also to deliver it to a particular group of recipients of government salaries (Gascou 1989, especially pp. 289–99). This may have meant that the provision of corn, meat, oil and the like for garrisons was taken out of the hands of traders working for payment and given to landowners working under government direction. As the quantity of supplies required by the army was enormous, the change would have affected a very large number of people. Unfortunately, it is very difficult to tell how far such a change actually happened. The decline of the inscriptional habit deprives us of the principal source of evidence for the class of people, mainly freedmen or their descendants, who had carried on transport and trade in cities like Ostia, Arles, Narbonne or Lyon (Schlippschuch 1974). But if this class had ceased to exist that would have made a big difference to the character of cities.[1]

The best-documented aspect of urban change is the decline of the institutions of civic self-government in the fourth century. Neither the emperor nor the councillors were whole-hearted in their defence. The emperor needed councils, but he also needed administrators who were most conveniently recruited from councillors. It was in the interest of councillors as a whole to keep

---

[1]   On the possible effect of tax changes in encouraging the development of small towns at the expense of *civitas* capitals see Millett 1990, 123–6 and 148–51. For merchants at Milan, an imperial capital, see Cracco Ruggini 1961, 84.

their city councils large, so that duties could be shared among many colleagues. On the other hand, pressure exerted by individual councillors seeking to gain the prestige and immunities of imperial posts was evidently very great indeed, to the point that the imperial authorities were induced to keep governors or equivalent officials in office for no more than a year when, from the point of view of efficiency of administration, as well as that of keeping councillors in their councils, far longer periods of office would have been desirable (Jones 1964, 374–83). So councils became even more oligarchical, and ordinary decurions came to be dominated by a small group of *principales*, who enjoyed legal privileges close to those of the ex-officials or *honorati* resident in the city (Liebeschuetz 1972, 171–4 and 181–2). As a class decurions were thoroughly demoralized, while the councils which they had considered 'the souls' of their cities came to be seen as nothing more than pieces of administrative machinery. After the fourth century curial status was not something which its holder would proudly proclaim, or his correspondents mention. It is clear that in many places councils were greatly depleted, and that this caused serious problems for the administration of the Empire, even at such prosperous cities as Antioch (ibid., 174–86).

The fourth century saw the first attempts to find alternative ways of organizing the tasks performed for the Empire by decurions. Valens and Valentinian, for a time and in some areas, attempted to collect taxes through *honorati* and former officials, or even members of provincial or other offices.[1] Nevertheless collection by decurions seems to have remained the rule.[2] In time the employment of alternatives to collection by decurions in many places became unavoidable, but in the fourth century arrangements of this kind appear to have been few. The numerous laws issued to keep decurions and their property in the councils (Jones 1964, 737–55) were not without effect. Many of the laws remained relevant long enough to be included in the Code of Justinian, and, as we shall see, councils survived in some form or other considerably longer still.

[1] *CTh* 12.6.4 (365, Africa), 5 (365, Cilicia), 7 (364, Illyricum), 9 (365–8, Illyricum, decurions excluded); 11.7.12 (383, Pontus, decurions to collect only from decurions).

[2] *CTh* 12.6.20 = *CJ* 10.72.8 (386, East); *CTh* 12.6.22 = *CJ* 10.72.4 (386, Africa).

As city councils were losing the capacity to represent their cities, bishops were growing into the rôle. The fourth century saw the beginning of the Christianization of cities (Claude 1969, 85–101; Dagron 1971; Ward-Perkins 1984, 51–84). This was on the whole a city-friendly development. Election by laymen continued to play a part in the making of a bishop (Jones 1964, 914–20), who thus came to be looked upon as the natural leader of the city especially in emergencies. This was the position of Synesius, Bishop of Ptolemais, while his city was under siege by nomads (Liebeschuetz 1986). This development gathered strength gradually as cities became more deeply Christianized, and especially as the imperial structure was weakened by barbarian settlement. Subsequently many cities owed their survival to the fact that they had a bishop (Rouche 1979, 290).

What happened to Christianity in Britain remains a problem. As it was still essentially an urban religion, the problem of the fall of Romano-British Christianity is linked to that of British cities. In the fourth century Britain certainly had a significant amount of Christianity (Thomas 1981), including bishops. But it seems to have had no monumental churches, and few churches of any kind, although these were features of Christianity in other provinces, even in areas where Christianity only became widespread after Constantine. British cities did not shrink to citadels, but the Roman way of life – not just monumental building – seems to have collapsed soon after 400, earlier and more completely than anywhere else in the Empire (Frere 1977; Hobley 1986; Millett 1990, ch. 6; see chapters 5 and 6 in this volume). Moreover the collapse seems to have happened well before large-scale invasion and barbarian settlement. This is unlikely to mean that all occupation on city sites ceased. The protection of walls was surely too useful to be wasted. There is indeed some, but not very much and not very impressive, evidence of occupation continuing into the fifth century.[1] In Gildas' summary account of the wars following the end of imperial military protection we are told in a general way that inhabitants abandoned fortified cities in the face

---

[1]   Barker 1975 (Wroxeter); Wacher 1975, 11 (Cirencester), 154 (Glouces-ter), 334–5 (Exeter). There is no evidence so far that the 'small towns' which flourished in the fourth century fared better than the *civitas* capitals in the fifth (Burnham and Wacher 1990, 314–19).

of an invasion by Picts and Scots (*The Ruin of Britain* 19.3), that revolting Saxon federates broke into all 'colonies' with battering rams and burnt or killed everything inside (24.3), and that at the time of writing, around 540, the cities were no longer inhabited but abandoned and destroyed (26.2).[1] But what seems to be significant is that Gildas, who as a Christian and writer of convoluted but rather correct Latin (Kerlouégan 1968) was surely an heir of Roman Britain, thought of himself as a Briton, but not at all as a Roman. As he saw it, the Romans had been protectors and rulers, but they had left. There is no awareness that not so long before the inhabitants of Britain had been Romans. Gildas the moralist is concerned with the morals and conduct of kings, probably Welsh kings, but he does not mention any city by name, whether as a centre of resistance or of government or as the see of a bishop. Neither Vortigern nor Ambrosius, nor even the legendary Arthur, is linked with a city. In Noricum, Bishops Paulinus of Tiburnia and Constantius of Lauriacum organized the defence of their cities under the guidance of the enigmatic hermit Severinus (Eugippius, *Life of Severinus* 25.2, 30.2; cf. Noll 1963; Enodius, *Life of Antonius* 9). By contrast, his biographer relates how St Germanus came to Britain, and won his 'hallelujah victory', but tells us nothing about any part played by British colleagues (Constantius, *Life of St Germanus* 16; Thompson 1984, 19ff). We know that some Christianity did survive, with bishops, until Gildas' day, whenever that may have been, but it survived without strength, and Augustine's mission in the South had to start conversion practically from scratch. The weakness of British cities and British Christianity are evidently interrelated, but it is impossible to say which caused the other.

The fifth century and after: the West

In the fifth century barbarian invasions and large-scale settlement of Goths or Vandals in different provinces of the West inevitably affected the cities, but perhaps less than might have been expected. The general effect was to accelerate trends which were already visible in the fourth century. Some cities were destroyed

---

[1] On Gildas see Davies 1968; Thompson 1979.

for ever. In some regions, for example, Rhaetia (Fischer and Riekhoff-Pauli 1982, 52 and 62–3), the depopulation of the surrounding country must have made it impossible to feed large urban populations. In Noricum and Pannonia the Roman population appears to have evacuated exposed frontier areas (Mócsy 1974, 352–4). One can list factors which made a city vulnerable: a small territory,[1] infertile soil, a weak manufacturing or distributive rôle, the absence of organs of civil, military or ecclesiastical administration or of a garrison. Simply, or in combination, these weaknesses might lead to the fading away of the population of a site, or to failure to rebuild and reoccupy a settlement that had been destroyed in war. Thus at Luni the city was gradually, although not totally, abandoned as its harbour silted up and the hinterland was occupied by Lombards (Ward-Perkins 1978). In some areas cities fared particularly badly, for example, in south-western France (Rouche 1979) and along the coast of Picenum in Italy (Alfieri 1977). However, as we have already observed in the case of Britain, permanent and total abandonment of a city site was rarer than would appear at first sight.[2] More often, occupation continued but with the city adapted to a changed and more utilitarian rôle as garrison, refuge, and, usually, residence of a bishop.[3] Sometimes the population was larger than is suggested by the smallness of the walled area, for on a number of sites evidence has been found of suburban settlements of simple houses, often grouped around a monastery beyond the walls surrounding the fortress and/or cathedral complex (Rouche 1979, 270–1, Aquitaine; Cüppers 1977, Trier). Poulter suggests that the poorer classes were actually excluded from fortress towns in the eastern Balkans (1990, 41–2, and see chapter 4 in this volume).

The fifth century raises in a more acute form the question of ruralization. To what extent did the civic élite move into the countryside? The Late Roman aristocrats of Gaul, Ausonius and his circle in the fourth century, Sidonius and his in the fifth, spent

---

[1] Alföldy 1989b. Their large territories enabled cities in Noricum to survive relatively well into the fifth century, but not beyond.
[2] For possible evidence of continued occupation at 'destroyed' Avenches (Aventicum) see Favrod and Fuchs (1990).
[3] However, the Rhineland cities were without bishops from *c.* 440 to the end of the fifth century (Petrikovits 1980, 297).

much time in villas,[1] but they also had strong links with cities. To what extent did they become country gentlemen? In time, the decline of secular literary education and progressive militarization must have favoured the ruralization of the aristocracy.[2] However, if there was a large-scale exodus of the urban élite into the countryside, it is not obvious where they went. It is by no means certain that villas continued to flourish in fifth-century Gaul elsewhere than in Aquitaine (Grünewald 1974; Percival 1992).

What happened to craftsmen and shopkeepers (Cracco Ruggini 1971; Petrikovits 1981)? Did they leave the urban centres to settle around villas (as proposed by Palladius, *De Re Rustica* 1.6; 7.8), or monasteries, or in some of the smaller settlements which seem to have flourished in Late Antiquity? Or did they become mobile? It seems that the end of the Roman period saw a great reduction in the quantity of artisan-produced material, but the development is difficult to date. Was it a cause or a consequence of the emptying of cities? Laws suggest that there was indeed some movement of artisans out of cities (Jones 1964, 762 n. 112; Rouche 1979, 270–1; Cracco Ruggini 1989, 260–1). A motive might have been to avoid the compulsory duties to which *collegia* of craftsmen were liable. We lack the evidence to estimate the scale of such movement. But it does seem to be the case that in northern France and the Rhineland the aristocracy eventually became rurally based and, when there was a revival of the crafts, it was not based on the old cities (Dhondt 1957).

Meanwhile cities continued to perform their Late Roman functions as centres of civil and/or ecclesiastical administration, refuges for the country population and bases for defending troops in time of war. A few became the residence of a Germanic king.

---

[1] Sidonius' senatorial correspondents Eutropius (*Epistles* 1.6) and Syagrius (8.8) were evidently well on the way to being based in the country. Maurusius spent at least autumn and winter in the country (2.14). On his way to Italy, Sidonius was put up by a succession of friends in residence in villas between Lyons and the Alps.

[2] Fixot 1980, 498–504, for Frankish Gaul. In northern Italy landowners remained fixed in the cities (Wickham 1981, 86–7). In Spain vast Late Roman villas may have been self-sufficient economic units (Gorges 1979), although many Spanish cities remained well populated (Keay 1988, 192–8).

Cities reduced to these rôles were found in the Balkans (see chapter 4 in this volume) and in northern Gaul (Wightman 1978 and 1985, 219–42 and 305–8; Horn 1987; Frézouls 1988). Among these the most outstanding were Trier, Metz, Soissons and Paris. In other areas, for instance Gaul south of the Loire (Sivan 1992; Loseby 1992), Spain (Taradell 1977), North Africa, at least in the early Vandal period (see chapter 2 in this volume; Humphrey 1980), and most of the eastern provinces (Patlagean 1977, 156–235), city life seems to have continued much as in the fourth century. In northern Italy and Tuscany, of some one hundred Roman *municipia* three-quarters still survived in AD 1000. Of those abandoned the majority had never had a bishop. By contrast, less than half of the cities of southern Italy, with their small and infertile hill territories, survived the troubles of the sixth and seventh centuries (Wickham 1981, 80). In Aquitaine the survival of cities as centres of considerable population was paralleled by the maintenance of a locally minted coinage, mainly in gold. It seems, although the evidence is not quite clear (King 1992), that Visigothic kings produced coins imitating imperial Roman issues. Then in the second half of the sixth century cities in Aquitaine began to mint coins of their own (Rouche 1979, 300–8; Hendy 1988).[1] The survival of full urbanism was evidently linked with the continuation of a money economy and trade.

In the fifth century bishops generally achieved a position of at least potential leadership in the West. Urban populations were now at any rate nominally Christian. The effect was profound. Many cities acquired a new Christian identity, founded on the cult of relics of a saint or saints, whose presence provided an ever-effective source of supernatural patronage and protection to those who worshipped at their shrine (Van Dam 1985, 230–300; see pp. 85–9 and 94–5). The saint brought glory to the city and prestige to the bishop. The church made provision for pilgrims, and these together with clerics travelling on church business maintained communications in a world which in the West tended towards greater regional self-sufficiency (Mathisen 1992). As temples were destroyed or fell into decay (Ward-Perkins 1984, 85–91),

---

[1] So, too, in Lombardy (Wickham 1981, 92) and at an unidentified mint north of the Loire (King 1992).

churches came to be the most prominent buildings in their cities. The prestige of the episcopal office gave territorial magnates who had freed themselves from institutionalized civic responsibilities an incentive for returning to the service of their city (e.g. Prinz 1973; Kopecek 1974; Mathisen 1984). Bishops were less involved in the regular secular administration of their cities under the Visigothic kings than under the Eastern emperors. (The same contrast is also found between Lombard and Byzantine Italy; Wickham 1981, 77–8.) However, wherever secular administration, whether urban or imperial, broke down, we find bishops left in charge. It was in the guise of the ecclesiastical diocese that the unity of city and territory, which was the essence of the Graeco-Roman city, survived longest. So the territory of the *civitas Agrippinensium* long survived as the diocese of the Bishop of Cologne (Ennen 1975, 38–91). City states surviving as ecclesiastical dioceses were numerous, particularly in Italy (Dilcher 1964).

Very extensive *civitates* were liable to break up into smaller ecclesiastical units. In the south of France, between 400 and 450 Nice, Carpentras, Toulon and Lizés were taken (or took themselves) out of the control of their *civitas* capital to receive a bishop of their own (Loseby 1992). Thus we observe in the sphere of ecclesiastical administration the continuation of a secular trend which had promoted secondary centres like Geneva, Grenoble, Gap and Sisteron. The phenomenon can also be seen in North Africa.

The rise of the bishop was not paralleled by the elimination of secular institutions of city self-government. Indeed the rôle of civic institutions was probably enhanced in areas under the control of Germans. Certainly the mere fact of the establishment of kingdoms by Goths and Vandals seems to have made little difference to the condition of cities in areas under their rule (Humphrey 1980; Clover 1982).

In 506 the Visigothic King Alaric II published a lawbook, the *Lex Romana Visigotorum* or *Breviarium Alarici*, for the benefit of at least the Romans among the subjects of his Gallic kingdom. This essentially consists of extracts from earlier Roman collections of laws, especially the *Codex Theodosianus* and the *Novellae* of Theodosius and his immediate successors. Most of the extracts are accompanied by an *interpretatio* which is not simply a paraphrase of the legal text, but introduces modifications adjusting the law to changes in society.[1] As a source for the social history of Visigothic Gaul, the *Breviarium* of Alaric has the serious disadvantage that, while we are provided with information about surviving Roman institutions, and, thanks to the *interpretationes*, about the modifications which they have undergone, we are not informed about institutions introduced by the Gothic kings themselves. It is nevertheless possible to recognize important developments. There has been a reduction in the administrative importance of the province and its governor, and a corresponding increase in that of city-based officials. Vicars and dioceses have disappeared. The praetorian prefect has become much less prominent. Provincial governors survive. They continue to exercise jurisdiction and are closely associated with the collection of taxes. But the ruler now has a representative in the city itself, the *comes civitatis* (Spandel 1957; Claude 1964), who also acts as a judge.[2] In Visigothic Gaul *comites* were appointed by the Visigothic king, but were not necessarily Goths (e.g. Attalus, *comes* of Autun: Sidonius, *Epistle* 5.18). The office was not a Germanic innovation, but is found, sometimes with different titles (prefect, tribune) all over the Empire (Declareuil 1910). In the West the *comes* ended by becoming country based, in fact a count (Claude 1964).

The decline in provincial government is not surprising. After all the presence of Gothic settlers not subject to the Roman governor must have made his rôle very difficult. But Novels of Justinian suggest that provincial government was weakened also in the East, where it was not obstructed by refractory German settlers with direct access to a German king. So this development was Empire-wide.

In the city decurions still had an essential rôle. The *Breviarium* retains many laws designed to prevent decurions from evading their duties. That decurions might escape into the imperial, or now the royal service, had become much less of a problem, but

---

[1]   The *interpretationes* are cited below by page references to Conrat 1903 and then by the laws as numbered in Mommsen's edition of the Theodosian Code and the associated *Novellae*.

[2]   It is often not clear whether a *iudex* mentioned in the *interpretatio* of a law is a governor (*iudex ordinarius*) or a civic judge (*iudex civitatis*), who might be the *comes* or the *defensor*.

decurions might go into hiding, move to another city (Conrat 1903, 736: *CTh* 12.1.2), marry their daughters to non-decurions (Conrat 1903, 737: *CTh* 12.1.7), refuse to have legitimate children (Conrat 1903, 737: *Novellae* of Theodosius 11.1.5–9), or enter the service of a magnate (Conrat 1903, 239–40: *Novellae* of Majorian 1.1.4–5). It seems that all decurions now had the rank of *honorati* and enjoyed the associated privilege of sitting with the judge when he was hearing a case (Conrat 1903, 773–4: *CTh* 1.15.1; 1.71; on the privilege see Liebeschuetz 1972, 190). The proliferation and devaluation of official titles was of course a characteristic of Late Roman society. Since the rank of an *honoratus* recognized service to the Empire, it had become meaningless in the territory of a Gothic king. But the use of senatorial titles by men who were not senators and lived in a provincial city was introduced in the East too sometime after 450 (Jones 1964, 528–9; Roueché 1989a, 131), yet another example of parallel development in the east and west of the divided Empire.[1] The code makes clear that apart from decurions there also existed a class of powerful landowners who were not liable to curial duties, but available as patrons and protectors of fugitive decurions. These presumably included Goths, but also descendants of the great senatorial families who had built up large estates in the last century of imperial rule, and were now consolidating their position in the service of Visigothic kings (Rouche 1979).

The Late Roman tax system survived, and, as long as it continued, it was necessary that the tax – which was after all a land tax – should be collected not only from the built-up area, but from the whole city territory. In this way the system of taxation preserved the unity of urban core and surrounding agricultural territory. There must have been great difficulties. The greatest landowners were presumably no longer able to claim privileges as members of the imperial senate – certainly these privileges have not been taken into the *Breviarium* – but their land-based power of obstruction and resistance was certainly greater than ever: they were on the way to becoming mediaeval barons, even if landholding in return for military service was still centuries away. Bishops

[1] Both East Roman and Visigothic governments were anxious that lower-ranking *honorati* should return to the service of their city (*CTh* 12.1.187 (436); *CJ* 12.1.15 (426–42)).

too protested about tax demands and succeeded in achieving immunity for ecclesiastical estates. So the public revenue diminished. But as late as 590 there is still evidence of *curiales* being involved in tax collection under the supervision of royal officials (Rouche 1979, 338–46). There is no reference to collection other than by *curiales*, but collection by officials eventually became the rule in Visigothic Spain (Edict of Erwig of 683, Zeumer 1902, 479ff; cf. Thompson 1969, 215).

It is not surprising to find evidence that amenities provided by cities have shrunk. Some laws of Book 11 of the Theodosian Code, dealing with public works, aqueducts and public shows, have been included in the *Breviarium*. The one law about public buildings shows that some public buildings might be repaired, with the public fisc contributing a third of the cost, but it also permits persons who have built homes on public land to keep them. Some aqueducts are still functioning, since existing water rights are confirmed, but the code includes no provision for maintenance of aqueducts. The *Breviarium* has no regulations for teachers or doctors or actors. Such literary education as survived was evidently provided by private tutors in senatorial houses.[1] The closing of schools and the declining prestige of literary culture removed one of the strongest incentives for landowners to reside in cities (Cassiodorus, *Var.* 8.31). Education became a matter for clergy and monks (see Riché 1973).

One function of the council has become very much more prominent, if it was not indeed new: the witnessing and recording in the municipal *gesta* of legal transactions such as wills, gifts, emancipation of slaves, adoptions, oaths and sales of property. This notarial rôle of the city council is attested by surviving *formulae* from Aquitaine (Bordeaux, Bourges, Cahors and Poitiers), Burgundy, and northern Gaul (Sens, Orleans, Tours, Le Mans, Paris), and also from Italy and Dalmatia. (The Gallic material is collected in Zeumer 1886.) These documents show that city councils, sometimes with *curatores* and *defensores*, survived in some places well into the eighth century. In Italy *gesta municipalia* disappear around 800. Significantly in some cities,

---

[1] A late fifth-century private (?) teacher at Arles: Pomerius, *PLRE* 2.896. The end of secular rhetorical culture as experienced by Gregory of Tours: Van Dam 1985, 221–6.

such as Naples and Amalfi, the professional notaries, who took on this work, assumed the title of *curiales* (Schmidt 1957, 122–4).

At this time the principal civic magistrate in Gaul, as elsewhere in the Empire, was the *defensor*. This office had been created by the imperial government, and in the Empire appointments were still at least formally made by the praetorian prefect. One object of the innovation had no doubt been to establish some direct control by the imperial government of civic administration at city level (Jones 1940, 150–1 n. 102). As had already been shown in the case of the older supervisory office of the *curator* (Burton 1979), the imperial government was not capable of maintaining so high a degree of centralization: the *defensor*, like the *curator* before him, soon ceased to be a delegate of the central authorities and became in fact a local magistrate. Since one of his original functions had been to protect both *plebs* and decurions from wrong at the hands of the powerful (Conrat 1903, 728: *CTh* 1.10.2), it is likely that he was normally chosen from the powerful himself. At first decurions were excluded, but later they became eligible. For all practicable purposes, in most parts of the Empire – perhaps North Africa was an exception – the *defensor*, often together with the *curator*, replaced the traditional curial magistrates (Liebeschuetz 1972, 167–70).

In Visigothic Gaul the *defensor* was elected by all citizens (*consensus civium, subscriptio universorum*). This procedure would seem to have been more popular than that followed in the East where appointment was by bishop, clergy, *honorati, possessores* and *curiales* (*CJ* 1.55.8). In cities which were inhabited principally by the bishop and a few magnates the participation of the people is likely to have been a formality. But Aquitaine, the area for which the *Breviarium* was principally designed, included cities with a considerable plebeian population, so that the part played by the citizens in choosing the *defensor* may well have been meaningful. In the northern Italian cities the people retained a genuine voice in the election of bishops, which thus did not become the exclusive concern of the clergy.

The *defensor* of Visigothic Gaul seems to have wider powers of jurisdiction than civic officials of the fourth century. He judges criminal actions involving offences against mobile or immobile property, and civil actions too can be started in his court (Conrat 1903, 729: *CTh* 2.1.8, 4.2). Guardians are required to make an inventory of their ward's property in the *defensor*'s presence (Conrat 1903, 730: *CTh* 3.17.3). The *defensor* is to assure punishment of robbers irrespective of who the robbers' patrons are (Conrat 1903, 731: *CTh* 1.10.3), and he is allowed to order a whipping – but not of the innocent (Conrat 1903, 732: *CTh* 2.1.10–12). The enhanced position of the *defensor* in Visigothic Gaul resembles that of the same office as defined by Justinian in seemingly quite different circumstances in the East (*Nov.* 15 (534)).

The administration of cities in Ostrogothic Italy seems to have resembled that in Visigothic Gaul and Spain. The *defensor* was the local head of the city, whose inhabitants were his clients (Cassiodorus, *Var.* 7.11). Theoderic was delighted when the *defensor* and the *curiales* of Catana in Sicily took the initiative of asking permission to restore the city walls using material from the ruined amphitheatre (*Var.* 3.49). It was the *defensor* and *curiales* that Theoderic addressed when he made demands on cities (*Var.* 4.45, transport; 5.14, tax collecting; 3.9, building material). The *defensor* was particularly responsible for fixing prices (*Var.* 7.11). Besides the *defensor* most, perhaps all, cities, had a *comes civitatis*, appointed by the Ostrogothic king for supervision, and above all to exercise jurisdiction (*Var.* 6.23, 26).

A fundamental change in the relations of city and country resulted from the fact that the countryside was becoming militarized. This was not only a result of German settlement. The great landowners of Gaul were themselves acquiring armed followings. The process can be observed in the case of one Ecdicius (*PLRE* 2, s.v. Ecdicius 3), who around 471 raised first a small troop, and later on an army to resist the Visigoths (Sidonius, *Epistles* 3.3.7–8). The Visigoths themselves made use of this capability and compelled Roman aristocrats and their men to fight for them (Sidonius, *Epistles* 5.12; Gregory of Tours, *Hist. Franc.* 2.3). This was a development of fundamental importance.[1] In the indepen-

---

[1]   Bachrach 1971; Rouche 1979, 350–2. In general on militarization in the West see Krause 1987, 131ff, who supplies a comprehensive survey of the evidence but tends to underestimate the scale of the development. On fortified hill-fort refuges, frequent in frontier zones, and fortified villas, for which there is some but not abundant evidence, see Johnson 1983, 226–44. In Italy militarization occurred both under the Lombards and Byzantines without ruralization (Wickham 1981, 72 and 76–7).

dent city state the peasants were the army, and they were called up by the city. Under the Empire peasants might be individually conscripted into the imperial army, and in the Late Empire landowners provided recruits as a tax, while themselves remaining civilians. That landowners should join the army at the head of their own armed tenantry is a fundamental departure from both the principle of the city state and the practice of the Empire. But that was the way of the future (*Leges Visigothorum* 9.2.8-9; cf. Thompson 1969, 262-6). Even the clergy became militarized (Prinz 1971). The gradual militarization of the landed aristocracy, together with the equally gradual breakdown of the Roman city-organized system of taxation did much to end the integration of urban centre and territory which had been a principal character-istic of the ancient city.

So power moved to the countryside. In the sixth century Bishop Nicetius of Trier had a castle on the Moselle in addition to his residence near the cathedral (Venantius Fortunatus 3.12). Not much later the Frankish *comites civitatis* and their families seem normally to have lived outside the fortifications of their city. The Carolingians abandoned the Roman system of taxation, and ceased to use city organization as a basis of their administrative system. If we look for an event which marks the transition from the Late Roman to the Early Mediaeval form of organization, it might be found in the Lombard invasion of Italy and the Arab invasion of Spain. The degree of physical and indeed demographic continuity between ancient and mediaeval cities of the former Western Roman Empire varies greatly from area to area (Ennen 1975, 27-45). It was strongest in and around the coast and above all in northern Italy, and weak to the point of insignificance in Britain and along the Danube.

The fifth century and after: the East

The cities in the East did not have invasions to cope with, and they remained part of a tight imperial system, which restricted their independence, but itself depended on the cities for its financial resources. Whatever may have been the demographic situation in the West, evidence such as the bringing into cultivation of marginal land, and the density of settlements, suggests that the population of the eastern provinces had been growing steadily from the mid-fourth century to reach a maximum at the limit of what the land could sustain in the early sixth century. Cities developed against that background (Patlagean 1977, 426; Tate 1989). As a rule it would seem that the physical structure of the cities in the East was still intact.

It is difficult to pinpoint economic factors which made for the maintenance of urban populations in the East at a time when these were shrinking in the West. It is, however, possible to show that cities in the East remained centres of high literary culture in the way Western cities did not. This was nothing new. Latin secular literature had always been to a remarkable extent a court-, that is Rome-, centred phenomenon. Greek literary culture was many centred. In the East in Late Antiquity there were notable centres of literary culture not only at Constantinople, but at Athens, Antioch, Gaza and Alexandria, and at different times notable literary figures practised at Pergamum, Aphrodisias, Apamea and elsewhere. The difference between the provision for higher education in East and West is made abundantly clear by Kaster's prosopography of Late Roman grammarians (Kaster 1988). That this literary culture extended even to small towns – at least in Egypt – is proved by the life and writings of Dioscorus of Aphrodito (MacCoull 1988). In the Thebaid in the sixth century social advancement and official patronage were still bound up with proficiency in rhetoric and intimate familiarity with Homer and other classical texts. The secular literary culture had been adapted and developed in a deeply Christianized society. The tradition of secular literacy helped to preserve civic traditions, not least in stories of mythological origins (Bowersock 1990). It certainly counteracted any tendency for members of the élite to move their residence away from their city.

But the civic institutions of the East showed signs of disintegration similar to those observed in the West. If anything, disintegration had gone further, thanks to the continuation of strong imperial administration. The councils had shrunk. The *curiales* had lost the social and political leadership in the cities to *principales* and *honorati* (Dagron 1980). Councillors no longer thought it worthwhile to commemorate their membership, and references to city councils are consequently very rare, whether in literary or in epigraphic sources. For the imperial administration this was a dangerous development. The civil service and army could be neither paid nor supplied without the resources levied by the cities, but the levying of resources was very difficult without the decurions. There was no adequate substitute. The fact that *curiales* lived in the cities, even needed permission to leave their city, and were forbidden to reside permanently on their estates (*CTh* 12.1.9, 143; 12.3.1; 12.8.1), made them exceptionally vulnerable to pressure by the government.

To compensate for the weakening of the *curiales*, the imperial government tried to re-involve the *honorati* in the running of cities, and so to keep alive self-government. Zeno ordered that civic revenues should not be administered by the provincial governor but should be paid intact to the city, there to be spent under the supervision of the *curator* (*CJ* 8.12.1 (485–6)). Subsequently we find an official called 'father of the city' (*patēr tēs poleōs*) in charge of civic finance in a number of Eastern cities (Roueché 1979 and 1989, 77–8; Dagron and Feissel 1987, 215–20; Sijpesteijn 1987). At this time only the highest-ranking members of the senatorial order, the *illustres*, retained full senatorial privileges, and the government attempted to induce lower-ranking members to resume residence in their ancestral city (Jones 1964, 524; *CTh* 12.1.187 (436); *CJ* 12.1.15 (426–42); *CJ* 12.2.1 (450)). There they were once more to take an active part in civic government. First the *defensor* (*CJ* 1.55.8 (409), 11 (505)), and later the corn-buyer (*CJ* 1.4.17 (491–505)), the *curator* (*MAMA* 3.197A) and the *patēr tēs poleōs* (Roueché 1979) were to be elected from all the notables, that is bishop, clergy, *honorati*, *possessores* and *curiales*. (The bishop's elected position and his direct contact with the population made him the natural leader of the city, and he regularly acted as such in emergencies, while in the East he also came to perform a key rôle in routine administration: Dagron 1980; Durliat 1982a and 1982b, 1984.) The working of the new system has not yet been systematically studied. It was certainly less uniform than the old system. There was both regional variation and piecemeal reform. Anastasius gave an important rôle in the collection of taxes to *vindices* (Chauvot 1987), but these did not become universal. A *vindex* was director of the finances of Alexandria (Justinian, *Ed.* 13). In some places, and at least for a time, *vindices* seem to have taken over tax collection from *curiales* (Euagrios 3.42), and their introduction was later described as marking the end of government of cities by city councils (Lydus, *De Magistr*. 3.42, 46, 49; Malalas 16, p. 400). But Justinian's Code does not mention *vindices*. Its compilers seem to have assumed that councils were still – or once again the principal collectors of taxes. Justinian's Novels, however, reveal that arrangements varied considerably from place to place (*Nov.* 128.5, 8).

As usual, the fullest documentation comes from Egypt. Gascou (1985) has argued that the large estates of great families and monasteries, which are a feature of sixth-century Oxyrhynchus, had come into existence since the fourth century.[1] In his view they were semi-public institutions which had been built up with the encouragement, or at least consent, of the imperial administration for the purpose of levying taxes in money or in kind and to provide other services. Perhaps the government connived at the enlargement of estates through patronage on condition that the patron assumed responsibility for all the fiscal obligations of the peasants whom he had taken under his protection. Henceforth, Gascou (1985) has argued, the collection and the liability for taxes and other government requirements such as the maintenance of the public post or the provision of policemen (*riparii*) was regularly shared among the great houses, who in one operation levied both rents and taxes from peasants, with the result that it is in fact impossible to distinguish public and private levies in their surviving papyrus accounts. This looks like the breaking up of the city organization by incipient feudalism, but in Gascou's view the privatization of tax collecting was not a usurpation, but a reform instigated by the imperial government. In any case it clearly did not take the fiscal tasks undertaken by the great houses out of a city-based system of administration. Decurions, usually described as *politeuomenoi*, continued to exist, but they scarcely figure on the documents studied by Gascou. Certainly there must have been some authority co-ordinating the contribution of the houses and controlling the duty-rota. In Egypt that rôle seems to have been performed by pagarchs who acted as directors of taxation, with personal financial liability (Gascou 1972; Liebeschuetz 1973 and 1974). This office was held by the great houses in turn. Sometimes

---

[1]   Bowman 1985 regards the very late development of the large estates as possible, but not certain.

the head of the house delegated a senior administrator to do the work. So the notorious Menas was an employee of the *gloriosissima* Patricia. Sometimes responsibility and liability were shared by two individuals from different houses. All, or nearly all, the holders had real or assumed honorary titles. The most distinguished of the houses were the Apions, a family several generations of which achieved positions of great power at Constantinople, and whose wealth was of the same order as that of Roman senators a century earlier.

We cannot tell to what extent the Egyptian system was applied in other provinces. It is, however, clear that elsewhere a reformed system of civic administration, making use of the services of 'notables', achieved some success. There was a revival of private munificence not only at Aphrodisias and at Athens, but even at Tomis on the Black Sea (see p. 128). It is likely that it was the class of civic notables that financed both teachers and pupils of the flourishing schools at Athens, Alexandria, Gaza and Berytus in the later fifth and early sixth centuries. It may well be that it was people like the Apions who made it possible for Anastasius to build up a large surplus, and for Justinian to finance campaigns of reconquest. But Justinian's campaigns were regularly hampered by lack of men and money, and the cause of this chronic inadequacy has been held to lie in a weakening of cities – at least in their rôle of instruments of control and exploitation of the countryside (Cameron 1985, 23; 1989, 180–4). As in the West, since the fourth century there was a weakening of the provincial organization, if for at least superficially different reasons. Whereas in the small Germanic kingdoms of the West provincial governors were dispensable, in the East they seem simply to have become ineffective. Nevertheless, some of the factors that made provincial government less effective in the East were significant in the West too. The laws which Justinian drew up to restore provincial government reveal disorder in large parts of central Asia Minor caused by bandits and powerful individuals. In Egypt Justinian noted that taxes paid by the taxpayers failed to reach their destination. Justinian's response was to strengthen the position of provincial governors by once again combining civil and military government. Justin II seems to have recognized the changed balance of power when he legislated that names of men who might be appointed provincial governors should be proposed by the provincial assemblies. Since at this time all the leading inhabitants of cities were entitled to attend the provincial assembly, this meant in effect that governors were to be appointed by the provincial élite (*Nov.* 149.1). Justinian had earlier laid down the same procedure in his Pragmatic Sanction for 'liberated' Italy (*Const. Pragm.* 12). Similar in spirit to it was the rule in Visigothic Gaul that the principal officers on a governor's staff, the *cancellarius* and the *domesticus*, should not be brought into his province by a newly appointed governor, but were to be designated by the king only after they had been elected by the citizens (Conrat 1903, 721–2; *CTh* 1.10.2).

The emperors claimed that they were principally concerned to protect the cities and their citizens from extortion by provincial governors, who were out to enrich themselves, or at least to recoup the large sums they had expended on buying the governor-ship (Jones 1964, 395). No doubt extortion by officials was still all too common. But as Justinian's laws uniting civil and military administration show, there had been a significant change in the position of governors since the fourth century. On the one hand, the weakening and, in many cities, the effective disappearance of the councils left a vacuum in the direction of the many services which the imperial administration still required to be organized at city level – not to mention the essential requirements of the cities themselves. So there was more need for intervention by governors. On the other hand, the new type of civic authorities, whether wealthy and well-connected notables like the Apions, or the bishop of a major city, were in a stronger position *vis-à-vis* a governor than curial officials of the old kind had been. Even if houses like the Apions who maintained *bucellarii* were the exception, it would certainly seem that pagarchs commanded considerably more coercive power than had ever been at the disposal of curial officers (Gascou 1972; Liebeschuetz 1973). It was a new factor that many cities now housed detachments of the army inside their walls (see chapter 4 in this volume; Remondon 1961; Liebeschuetz 1974). So the problem of coping with dis-ruptive or obstructive patronage by the local commander must have become much more acute than it had been when soldiers were stationed in forts in the countryside – though even then it had not been insignificant, as in the case of Abinnaeus (Bell *et al.* 1962; cf. the examples in Libanius, *Oration* 47). The exercise of control by provincial governors had become both more necessary and much more difficult. This accounts for the fact that Justinian tried to strengthen provincial government by once again combining military and civilian administration, at the same time as he tried to give greater cohesion to administration at city level by new regulations for the appointment and duties of the *defensores*.

It remains to enquire how far the cities themselves, the combination of urban centre and rural territory, remained unchanged. Cities certainly were losing the traditional symbols of unity and identity: the councils became insignificant, athletic and theatrical shows were being discredited morally, and civic shows were diminishing in frequency and in scale (Cameron 1973, 228–32). Makeshift shops built into the colonnades were narrowing the great monumental streets. Few monuments were put up to commemorate acts of munificence by local citizens, although there was a very limited return to this form of display in the early sixth century. The largest cities, like Antioch (Liebeschuetz and Kennedy 1988; see chapter 8 in this volume) and Ephesus, flourished into the sixth century. But there is evidence of prosperity in smaller cities too. Thus at Gerasa in Arabia there was much construction, especially of churches, in the fifth and sixth centuries, although the excavators noted comparatively shoddy building techniques and the use of spoil (Kraeling 1938; Claude 1969, 251–2). As a rule the built-up area had not shrunk and monumental centres were more or less intact (Claude 1969, 41–69). Visually cities were becoming strongly Christianized (Dagron 1971; Cormack 1990). Temples were destroyed and replaced by churches (Claude 1969, 85–100). Gymnasia and palaestra had gone and with them athletics and the physical education of youth (ibid., 76). But the provision and prestige of rhetorical education was as high – or almost as high – as ever (Roueché 1989a, 77–9).

Urban populations seem to have been growing. Certainly the largest and best-documented cities, Constantinople, Antioch and Alexandria, experienced a constant influx of immigrants from the countryside (Patlagean 1977, 179–81). Such cities included large numbers of unskilled workers, and crowds of beggars offered great scope to the charity of the organized Church and of urban ascetics (ibid. 181–96). The cities certainly included large numbers of artisans. Funeral inscriptions of the small city of Corycus in Cilicia illustrate the range of trades and the degree of specialization of individual craftsmen (*MAMA* 3. 200–788; Patlagean 1977, 156–70; Rey-Coquais 1977). There is evidence for the organization of trades into guilds in some cities, for example, Constantinople, Sardis and Antioch. The imperial government legislated to prevent guilds using their monopoly to raise prices. It remains uncertain how widespread guild organization was (Cracco Ruggini 1971 and 1976; Liebeschuetz 1972, 219–24; Patlagean 1977, 175–6).

Mass entertainments continued to be a regular feature of urban life, if not on the scale of the second century. In major centres of government the inhabitants were entertained by chariot races, and in most cities, in spite of the opposition of the church, by theatrical shows. Both were organized by Empire-wide organizations, the Blues and the Greens. Popular disturbances, started by fighting between the two groups of partisans, from time to time caused serious bloodshed and destruction. They are best documented at Constantinople and Antioch but occurred also in smaller towns, particularly in a wave of unrest in the reign of Phocas. These riots still lack an explanation in social terms (Cameron 1973 and 1976). The factions were only one element in a pattern of discontinuous but recurrent urban unrest (Patlagean 1977, 206–31; Gregory 1979). The impression is unavoidable: the cities of the East continued to have large urban populations.

As in the West the unity of urban centre and territory was maintained by the authority of the bishop which extended over both, and, again as in the West, Christianity also fostered centrifugal tendencies. In large rural territories the bishop was represented by *chōrepiscopoi* or *periodeutai* who tended to seek independence. The bishops resisted, eventually with success (Dagron 1979, 44–7). Even so some villages did acquire a bishop of their own, especially villages strengthened by a garrison. Thus large city territories broke up into smaller units. This process might help to account for some of the eighty cities of Achaea listed in the *Synecdemus of Hierocles*, and perhaps also for the existence of the very large number of small cities in Africa (Maier 1973).

It is a characteristic of the Late Empire that villages acquired monumental buildings, and so became archaeologically visible. They also became more prominent in literary sources, above all the Lives of Syrian or Mesopotamian ascetics who often settled in the neighbourhood of a village. Large villages have been noted in

Thrace. In Pisidia villagers refused to pay taxes (Justinian, *Nov.* 124.1, 3 (535)). Remains of solidly built villages are visible today in Isauria, in the Negeb, and in Cyrenaica. Libanius tells us of large self-sufficient town-like villages in the territory of Antioch, and over a wide area of northern Syria the ruins of numerous well-built villages survive to the present day (Tchalenko 1953–8).[1]

It is evident from the number and quality of village remains that more money – or at least more labour and craftsmanship – was expended on villages in Late Antiquity than earlier. There is, as far as I know, no evidence to establish how, and indeed whether, the terms of economic exchange (whether of rents or trade) between town and country had become more favourable to the countryside, but certain developments surely strengthened the bargaining power of villages against their traditional landlords, rulers or patrons from the city. In Syria at any rate very many villages came to include one or more monasteries. The patronage of the archimandrites and hermits must have helped villagers (Tchalenko 1953–8, 3.63–5; Sevcenko and Sevcenko 1984, 52–3, with Roueché 1989a, 140). It is significant for the emancipation of the countryside that the powerful and widespread religious movement that divided the East in the later fifth, sixth and seventh centuries, the anti-Chalcedonians or Monophysites, drew its strength from rurally situated monasteries in Mesopotamia, northern Syria and Egypt (Liebeschuetz and Kennedy 1988, 81ff).

It is likely that patronage of the commanders of rurally situated forts helped villagers to assert their independence from the city in whose territory they were situated. This is the situation described in Libanius' speech on patronage (*Oration* 47). The presence of a fort would favour secession: we know of a number of military stations that became separated from their city territory, at least to the extent of receiving a bishop of their own. In Egypt, these included Philae, Syene, Elephantine, and Babylon; in Syria, Sura, Barbalissus, Resapha, Euaria and Danata. The effect was to increase the number of cities but to weaken existing ones. Even when not garrisoned, villages in frontier areas were likely to be

---

[1] It has been suggested that apparently new rural settlements in the Fayum and around Oxyrhynchus in Egypt in the fifth and sixth centuries reflect not a growth of population, but a shift from town to country (Pruneti 1981; Rathbone 1990, 122).

fortified and this too surely made for independence (Ahrweiler 1962; Goodchild 1979, 173–85 and 195–209; Malalas 347 (Syria)).

In the West, as we have seen, cities were damaged by the fact that the great landowners became based in the countryside and eventually militarized. It is difficult to trace this development in the East. Magnates like Synesius or the Apions retained close connections with cities, but Synesius certainly (Liebeschuetz 1985, 158–9) and perhaps the Apions too were more loosely attached to city life than leading members of provincial society had been in earlier times. Synesius had a fortified estate centre which he defended successfully against nomad raiders (*Epistles* 130–3). In 420 the fortification of estates was legalized (*CJ* 8.10.10). It may or may not be relevant to the strength of cities that in the frontier areas of Syria and Palestine, as earlier in North Africa, the Roman government came to rely for defence on federates, respectively Arab or Moor chieftains and their tribesmen (Shahid 1984; Matthews 1989, 371–4). This would have created a situation comparable to the Gothic settlement in fifth-century Gaul. This is likely to have broken the administrative link between inland cities and their territories.[1]

During the sixth century the cities of the Greek East were hit by a series of severe blows: earthquakes (Brandes 1989, 176–81), Persian invasions (Foss 1990), and, perhaps most serious of all, successive waves of bubonic plague (Conrad 1986; Durliat 1989), the first in 541. This was followed in the seventh century by years of Persian occupation and by the Arab invasions. The effect was like the crisis of the third century.[2] In Syrian Bostra the latest dated inscription dates precisely from 540–1 (Sartre 1982).

The crisis of the sixth and seventh centuries had more far-reaching long-term consequences than that of the third century. This was no doubt partly because to the calamities of war and plague was now added the creation of a new frontier and a new political geography through the Arab conquest. The administrative and military system in which the cities had performed essential functions had been transformed. But the fact that the cities found it so difficult and often impossible to adapt to the new

---

[1]   In general on the shift from city to country, village, estate or monastery see Mango 1980, 60–73.

[2]   Brandes 1989, 81–141, gives a city-by-city survey for Asia Minor.

situation suggests that by the mid-sixth century at least they were suffering from real structural weakness. In Byzantine Asia Minor some cities disappeared. Those which survived shrank to small fortified cores, a development which had taken place much earlier in many parts of the West. From the middle of the seventh century the theme organization broke the administrative link between city and territory and marked the end of the traditional institutions of urban self-government.[1] Even Constantinople was reduced to a fraction of its former population (Mango 1985, 53–60). In the Arab East some cities disappeared, but many survived and recovered, often with a change in their relative importance. In Syria, Antioch lost ground relatively to Beroea (Aleppo) and Damascus, both nearer to the Arab heartland. In Apamea the mansions of city magnates seem to have been transformed into working farms (Balty 1980, 497–501). The development of cities under the Arabs is a big theme. In the present volume post-Roman Antioch stands as representative for them all (see chapter 8 in this volume).

The development of the Late Roman city in East and West is a story of infinite variety. Nevertheless we are dealing with a single cultural institution liable to the same vicissitudes. Even if these did not affect cities everywhere at the same time, the unity was manifest to the end. The Eastern urban revival of the late fifth and early sixth century of which there is evidence in the form of striking buildings at, say, Gerasa or Apamea, and of a rich munificent city-based upper class at Aphrodisias and Athens is paralleled – if on a more modest scale – by abundant church-building in remote western Aquitaine, and as far north as Trier and Cologne. This was followed from *c.* 540 by an age of disasters which was once again suffered over the whole area of the old Empire: Persian, then Arab invasions of the East, Slav invasions of the Balkans, Lombard advances into Italy, and internecine wars among the Franks (Hodges and Whitehouse 1983, 57–61). The latest mention of a city council and a *defensor* in Gaul occurs on a formula from Poitiers of 805. In Italy most councils seem to have disappeared by 700 leaving the bishop, now by far the

---

[1] The majority of sites in Asia Minor nevertheless kept some kind of urban continuity after the clasical city had come to an end (Vryonis 1971, 6–24).

greatest landowner, supreme in the city (Wickham 1981, 19). At
Naples the council survived to the tenth century (ibid. 75). Leo VI
(886–912) formally abolished city councils in the Byzantine
Empire (Justinian, *Nov.* 46–8). By then surviving councils had
long become an anachronism. When stability was restored by the
Carolingian dynasty in the West and by Leo III in the East
(Haldon 1990), their administration was no longer based on the
ancient city units, and urban centres no longer served as administrative centres for a rural civic territory. The end of the ancient
city involved the emancipation of the countryside.[1]

Bibliography

Abadie-Reynal, C. (1989), 'Céramique et commerce dans le
    bassin égéen', *Hommes et richesses dans l'empire byzantin* i,
    IVe–VIIe siècles (Paris), 143–59.
Ahrweiler, H. (1962), 'L'Asie mineure et les invasions arabes',
    Revue Historique 227, 1–32.
Alfieri, N. (1977), 'L'insediamento urbano sul litorale delle
    Marche', in Duval and Frézouls, 87–98.
Alföldy, G. (1989a), *Die Krise des römischen Reiches*
    (Stuttgart).
Alföldy, G. (1989b), 'Die regionale Gliederung in der römischen
    Provinz Noricum', in G. Gottlieb (ed.), *Die Raumordnung im
    römischen Reich* (Munich), 37–55.
Bachrach, B. S. (1971), *Merowingian Military Organisation
    481–751* (Minneapolis).
Balty, J.-C. (1980), 'Notes sur l'habitat Romain, Byzantin et
    Arabe d'Apamée: rapport de synthèse', in *Colloque Apamée
    de Syrie*, Musées Royaux d'Art et Histoire (Brussels), 471–
    501.
Barker, P. (1975), 'Excavations on the site of the baths at
    Wroxeter', *Britannia* 6, 106–17.
Barley, M. W. and Hanson, R. P. C. (eds) (1968), *Christianity
    in Britain 300–700* (Leicester).

[1] I am grateful to John Drinkwater, John Rich and Charlotte Roueché
for reading and commenting on an earlier version of this paper.

Bekker-Nielsen, T. (1989), *The Geography of Power: Studies in the Urbanisation of Roman North West Europe*, BAR Int. Ser. 447 (Oxford).

Bell, H. I., Martin, V., Turner, E. G. and Van Berchem, D. (1962), *The Abinnaeus Archive* (Oxford).

Blake, H. M., Potter, T. W. and Whitehouse, D. B. (eds) (1978), *Papers in Italian Archaeology* 1 (London).

Bowersock, G. W. (1990), *Hellenism in Late Antiquity* (Cambridge).

Bowman, A. K. (1985), 'Landholding in the Hermopolite Nome in the fourth century', *Journal of Roman Studies* 75, 137–63.

Brandes, W. (1989), *Die Städte Kleinasiens im 7 und 8 Jahrhundert* (Amsterdam).

Brown, P. (1978), *The Making of Late Antiquity* (Cambridge, Mass.).

Bruhl, C.-R. (1975), *Palatium und Civitas, Studien zur Profantopographie spätantiker Civitates* i, *Gallien* (Cologne and Vienna).

Burnham, B. C. and Wacher, J. (1990), *The Small Towns of Roman Britain* (London).

Burton, G. P. (1979), 'The *curator rei publicae*: towards a reappraisal', *Chiron* 9, 456–87.

Butler, R. M. (1959), 'Late Roman town walls in Gaul', *Archaeological Journal* 116, 25–50.

Cameron, Alan (1973), *Porphyrius the Charioteer* (Oxford).

Cameron, Alan (1976), *Circus Factions* (Oxford).

Cameron, Averil (1985), *Procopius and the Sixth Century* (London).

Cameron, Averil (1989), 'Gelimer's laughter', in F. M. Clover and R. S. Humphreys (eds), *Tradition and Innovation in Late Antiquity* (Madison), 171–90.

Cavanagh, W. G. (1991), 'Surveys, cities and synoecism', in J. W. Rich and A. Wallace-Hadrill (eds), *City and Country in the Ancient World* (London).

Cerati, A. (1975), *Caractère annonaire et assiette de l'impôt foncier au bas-empire* (Paris).

Charanis, P. (1955), 'The significance of coins as evidence for the history of Athens and Corinth in the seventh and eighth centuries', *Historia* 4, 163–7.

Chastagnol, A. (1978), *L'album municipal de Timgad* (Bonn).

Chauvot, A. (1987) 'Curiales et paysans en orient à la fin du Ve et au debut du VIe siècle: note sur l'institution du *vindex*', in E. Frézouls (ed.), *Sociétés urbaines, sociétés rurales dans l'Asie mineure et la Syrie hellénistique et romaine* (Strasbourg).

Chrysos, E. (1971), 'Die angebliche Abschaffung der städtischen Kurien durch Kaiser Anastasius', *Byzantion* 3, 97–8.

Claude, D. (1964), 'Untersuchungen zum frühfränkischen Comitat', *Zeitschrift für Rechtsgechichte* 81, 1–79.

Claude, D. (1969), *Die byzantinische Stadt im 6 Jahrhundert* (Munich).

Clavel-Lévêque, M. (1984), *L'empire en jeu* (Paris).

Clover, F. M. (1982), 'Carthage and the Vandals', in J. H. Humphrey (ed.), *Excavations at Carthage, 1978, conducted by the University of Michigan* 7.1–22.

Conrad, L. (1986), 'The plague in Bilad al-Sham in pre-Islamic times', in M. A. Bakhil and M. Asfour (eds), *Proceedings of the Symposium on Bilad al-Sham* (Amman), 2.143–63.

Conrat, M. (1903), *Breviarium Alarici* (Leipzig).

Cormack, R. (1990), 'The temple as the cathedral', in Roueché and Erim (eds), 75–88.

Cracco Ruggini, L. (1961), *Economia e società nell'Italia annonaria* (Milan).

Cracco Ruggini, L. (1964), 'Vicende rurali dall'Italia antica dall'età tetrarchica ai Langobardi', *Rivista Storia Italiana* 76, 261–86.

Cracco Ruggini, L. (1971), 'Le associazoni professionali nel mondo romano bizantino', in *Settimane di studio del Centro Italiano di Studi sull'Alto Medioevo* (Spoleto) 18, 59–193.

Cracco Ruggini, L. (1976), '*Collegium* e *corpus*: la politica economica nella legislazione e nella prassi, istituzioni giuridice e realtà politiche nel tardo Impero', *Atti del convegno di Firenze* (Milan), 63–94.

Cracco Ruggini, L. (1989), 'La città imperiale', in A. Momigliano and A. Schiavone (eds), *Storia di Roma* (Turin) 4.201–64.

Cüppers, H. (1977), 'Die Stadt Trier und verschiedene Phasen ihres Ausbaues', in Duval and Frézouls, 223–8.

Dagron, G. (1971), 'Le christianisme dans la ville byzantine', *Dumbarton Oaks Papers* 31, 3–25 (= Dagron 1984b, ch. 9).

Dagron, G. (1979), 'Entre village et cité: la bourgade rurale des
IVe–VIIe siècles en Orient', *Koinonia* 3, 29–52 (= Dagron
1984b, ch. 8).

Dagron, G. (1980), 'Two documents concerning mid-sixth
century Mopsuestia', in A. E. Laiou-Thomadakis (ed.),
Charanis Studies (New Brunswick), 19–30 (= Dagron 1984b,
ch. 6).

Dagron, G. (1984a), 'Les villes dans l'Illyricum protobyzantin',
in *Villes et peuplement dans l'Illyricum protobyzantin*,
Collection de l'École Française de Rome 77 (Paris), 1–19.

Dagron, G. (1984b), *La romanité chrétienne en Orient*
(London).

Dagron, G. and Feissel, D. (1987), *Inscriptions de Cilicie*
(Paris).

Davies, W. H. (1968), 'The church in Wales', in Barley and
Hanson (eds), 138–50.

Declareuil, J. (1910), 'Les comtes de la cité', *Revue Historique
du Droit Français et Étranger* 34, 794–836.

Dhondt, J. (1957), 'L'essor urbain entre Meuse et mer du Nord
à l'époque mérovingienne', *Studi in onore di A. Sapori*
(Milan), 1.55–78.

Dilcher, G. (1964), 'Bischof und Stadtverfassung in Oberitalien',
Zeitschrift für Rechtsgeschichte, Germ. Abt. 81, 225–66.

Dölger, F. J. (1959), 'Die frühbyzantinische und byzantinisch
beeinflusste Stadt', *Atti del 3 congresso internazionale di
studi sull'alto medioevo* (Spoleto), 66–100.

Downey, G. (1961), *A History of Antioch in Syria* (Princeton).

Drinkwater, J. F. (1987a), 'Urbanization in Italy and the
Western Empire' in Wacher (ed.), 345–79.

Drinkwater, J. F. (1987b), *The Gallic Empire: Separatism and
Continuity in the Northwestern Provinces of the Roman
Empire AD 260–74*, *Historia* Einzelschrift 52 (Stuttgart).

Drinkwater, J. F. and Elton, H. (eds) (1992), *Fifth-Century
Gaul: a Crisis of Identity* (Cambridge).

Duby, G. (ed.) (1980), *Histoire de la France urbaine* i, *La ville
antique des origines au IXe siècle* (Paris).

Durliat, J. (1982a), 'Taxes sur l'entrée de marchandises dans la
cité Carales (Cagliari) à l'époque byzantine, 582–602',
Dumbarton Oaks Papers 36, 1–14.

Durliat, J. (1982b), 'Les attributions civiles des évêques

byzantines: l'exemple du diocèse d'Afrique 533–709',
Jahrbuch der österreichischen Byzantinistik 32.2, 73–84.

Durliat, J. (1984), 'L'administration civile du diocèse byzantin
d'Afrique (533–703)', *Rivista di Studi Byzantinei e Slavi* 4,
149–78.

Durliat, J. (1988), 'Le salaire de la paix sociale dans les
royaumes barbares (Ve–VIe siècles)', in H. Wolfram and A.
Schwarcz (eds), *Anerkennung und Integration*,
Österreichische Akademie, Phil. Hist. Kl. Denkschriften 193
(Vienna).

Durliat, J. (1989), 'La peste du 6e siècle' in *Hommes et richesses
dans l'empire byzantin* i, *IVe–VIIe siècles* (Paris), 107–25.

Duval, P.-M. (1959), 'Une enquête sur les enceintes gauloises',
Gallia 17, 37–62.

Duval, P.-M. and Frézouls, E. (eds) (1977), *Thèmes de
recherches sur les villes antiques d'occident* (Paris).

Eck, W. (1978), 'Der Einfluss der konstantinischen Wende auf
die Auswahl der Bischöfe im 4 und 5 Jahrhundert', *Chiron* 8,
561–85.

Eck, W. (1983), 'Der Episkopat im spätantiken Africa',
Historische Zeitschrift 236, 265–95.

Eck, W. (1989), *Religion und Gesellschaft in der römischen
Kaiserzeit* (Cologne and Vienna).

Ennen, E. (1975), *Die europäische Stadt des Mittelalters*
(Göttingen).

Ensslin, W. (1961), 'Vindex', *RE* IX.A1, 25–7.

Favrod, J. and Fuchs, M. (1990), 'Avenches de 260 à l'époque
mérovingienne', *Museum Helveticum* 47, 163–80.

Fentress, E. (1988), 'Sétif, les thermes du Ve siècle', in A.
Mastino (ed.), *L'Africa Romana*, (Sassari), 320–37.

Finley, M. I. (1973), *The Ancient Economy* (London).

Fischer, H. T. and Riekhoff-Pauli, S. (1982), *Von den Römern
zu den Bajuvaren* (Munich).

Fissall, D. and Kaygusuz, I. (1985), 'Un mandement impérial du
VIe siècle', *Travaux et Mémoires* 9, 397–419.

Foss, C. (1975), 'The Persians in Asia Minor and the end of
Antiquity', *English Historical Review* 90, 721–47 (= Foss
1990, ch. 1).

Foss, C. (1976), *Byzantine and Turkish Sardis* (Cambridge,
Mass.).

Foss, C. (1977a), 'Archaeology and the "twenty cities of Asia" ',
American Journal of Archaeology 81, 469–86 (= Foss 1990,
ch. 5).

Foss, C. (1977b), 'Late antique and Byzantine Ankara',
Dumbarton Oaks Papers 31, 27–87 (= Foss 1990, ch. 6).

Foss, C. (1977c), 'Attius Philippus and the Walls of Side',
Zeitschrift für Papyrologie und Epigraphik 26, 172–80 (=
Foss 1990, ch. 8).

Foss, C. (1979), *Ephesus after Antiquity: a Late Antique,
Byzantine and Turkish City* (Cambridge).

Foss, C. (1990), *History and Archaeology of Byzantine Asia
Minor* (Aldershot).

Frere, S. S. (1977), 'Verulamium and Canterbury', in Duval and
Frézouls (eds), 189–95.

Frézouls, E. (1988), *Les villes antiques de la France* ii
(Strasbourg).

Fulford, M. J. (1980), 'Carthage: overseas trade and the
political economy, *c.* AD 400–700', *Reading Medieval Studies*
6, 68–80.

Garnsey, P. and Saller, R. (1987), *The Roman Empire:
Economy, Society, Culture* (London).

Gascou, J. (1972), 'La détention collegiale de l'autorité
pagarchique dans l'Égypte byzantine', *Byzantion* 43, 60–72.

Gascou, J. (1976), 'Les monastères pachomiens et l'état
byzantin', *Bulletin de l'Institut Français d'Archéologie
Orientale* 76, 157–8.

Gascou, J. (1985), 'Les grands domaines, la cité et l'état en
Égypte byzantine', *Travaux et Mémoires* 9, 1–90.

Gascou, J. (1989), 'Le tableau budgetaire d'Antaeopolis', in
Hommes et richesses dans l'empire byzantin i, *IVe–VIIe
siècles* (Paris), 279–313.

Goodchild, R. (1979), *Libyan Studies*, ed. J. Reynolds
(London).

Gorges, J.-G. (1979), *Les villas hispano-romaines* (Paris).

Gregory, T.E. (1979), *Vox Populi: Popular Opinion and
Violence in the Religious Controversies of the 5th Century
A.D.* (Columbus, Ohio).

Grünewald, M.E.G. (1974), *Spätantike Herrschaftsvillen in den
nordwestlichen Provinzen des römischen Reiches* (Vienna).

Haldon, J.F. (1990), *Byzantium in the Seventh Century* (Cambridge).

Hendy, M. (1985), *Studies in the Byzantine Monetary Economy* (Cambridge).

Hendy, M.F. (1988), 'From public to private: the western barbarian coinages as a mirror of the disintegration of late Roman state structures', *Viator* 19, 29–78.

Hendy, M.F. (1989), *The Economy, Fiscal Administration and Coinage of Byzantium* (Northampton).

Hitchner, R.B. (1992), 'Meridional Gaul, trade and the Mediterranean economy in Late Antiquity', in Drinkwater and Elton (eds), 121–31.

Hobley, B. (1986), *Roman and Saxon London: a Reappraisal* (London).

Hodges, R. and Whitehouse, D. (1983), *Mohammed, Charlemagne and the Origins of Europe* (London).

Hopkins, K. (1978), 'Economic growth and towns in classical antiquity', in P. Abrams and E.A. Wrigley (eds), *Towns in Societies* (Cambridge), 35–7.

Hopkins, K. (1980), 'Taxes and trade in the Roman Empire (200 BC–AD 400)', *Journal of Roman Studies* 70, 101–25.

Horn, H.G. (ed.) (1987), *Die Römer in Nordrhein-Westfalen* (Stuttgart).

Howgego, C.J. (1985), *Greek Imperial Countermarks* (London).

Humphrey, J.H. (1980), 'Vandal and Byzantine Carthage', in J.G. Pedley (ed.), *New Light on Ancient Carthage* (Ann Arbor), 85–120.

Irsch, N. (1931), *Der Dom zu Trier* (Dusseldorf).

Johnson, A.C. and West, L.C. (1949), *Byzantine Egypt: Economic Studies* (Princeton).

Johnson, S. (1983), *Late Roman Fortifications* (London).

Jones, A.H.M. (1940), *The Greek City from Alexander to Justinian* (Oxford).

Jones, A.H.M. (1960), 'Church finance in the fifth and sixth centuries', *Journal of Theological Studies* n.s. 11, 84–94.

Jones, A.H.M. (1964), *The Later Roman Empire 284–602* (Oxford).

Kaster, R. (1988), *Guardians of Language: the Grammarian and Society in Late Antiquity* (Berkeley).

Keay, S.J. (1984), *Late Roman Amphorae in the Western Mediterranean: the Catalan Evidence*, BAR Int. Ser. 196 (Oxford).

Keay, S.J. (1988), *Roman Spain* (London).

Kempf, K. (1964), 'Untersuchungen am Trierer Dom 1961–63', *Germania* 42, 126–41.

Kerlouégan, F. (1968), 'Le latin du *De Excidio Britanniae* de Gildas', in Barley and Hanson (1968), 151–68.

King, A. and Henig, M. (1981), *The Roman West in the Third Century*, BAR Int. Ser. 198 (Oxford).

King, C.E. (1992), 'Roman, local and barbarian coinages in fifth-century Gaul', in Drinkwater and Elton (eds), 184–95.

Kirsten, E. (1954) 'Chorbischof', *RAC* 2.1105–14.

Kneppe, A. (1979), *Untersuchungen zur römischen Plebs des vierten Jahrhunderts* (Bonn).

Kopecek, T.A. (1974), 'The Cappadocian fathers and civic patriotism', *Church History* 43, 293–303.

Kraeling, C. (1938), *Gerasa* (New Haven).

Krause, J-V. (1987), *Spätantike Patronatsformen im Westen des römischen Reiches* (Munich).

Leclercq, H. (1948), 'Chorévêques', in Cabrol and Leclercq, *Dictionnaire d'archéologie chrétienne et de liturgie* iii, 1423–52.

Lemerle, P. (1979), *The Agrarian History of Byzantium from the Origins to the Twelfth Century* (Galway).

Lepelley, C. (1979), *Les cités de l'Afrique romaine au Bas-Empire*: i, *La permanence d'une civilisation municipale* (Paris).

Levick, B. (1987), 'Urbanization in the Eastern Empire' in Wacher 1987, 329–44.

Liebeschuetz, W. (1959), 'The finances of Antioch in the fourth century AD', *Byzantinische Zeitschrift* 52, 344–56 (= Liebeschuetz 1990, ch. 12).

Liebeschuetz, W. (1961), 'Money economy and taxation in kind in Syria in the fourth century', *Rheinisches Museum für Philologie* 104, 242–56 (= Liebeschuetz 1990, ch. 13).

Liebeschuetz, W. (1972), *Antioch: City and Imperial Administration in the Later Roman Empire* (Oxford).

Liebeschuetz, W. (1973), 'The origin of the office of the pagarch', *Byzantinische Zeitschrift* 66, 34–46.

Liebeschuetz, W. (1974), 'The pagarch: city and imperial administration in Byzantine Egypt', *Journal of Juristic Papyrology* 18, 163–8 (= Liebeschuetz 1990, ch. 18).

Liebeschuetz, W. (1981), 'Epigraphic evidence on the Christianisation of Syria', *Akten des XI Internationalen Limes Kongresses* (Budapest), 485–508 (= Liebeschuetz 1990, ch. 8).

Liebeschuetz, W. (1985), 'Synesius and municipal politics in Cyrenaica in the 5th century AD', *Byzantion* 55, 146–64 (= Liebeschuetz 1990, ch. 14).

Liebeschuetz, W. (1986), 'Why did Synesius become bishop of Ptolemais?', *Byzantion* 56, 180–95 (= Liebeschuetz 1990, ch. 15).

Liebeschuetz, W. (1990), *From Diocletian to the Arab Conquest: Change in the Late Roman Empire* (Great Yarmouth).

Liebeschuetz, W. and Kennedy, H. (1988), 'Antioch and the villages of Northern Syria in the 4th–6th centuries AD', *Nottingham Medieval Studies* 32, 65–90.

Loseby, S. (1992), 'Bishops and cathedrals: order and diversity in the fifth-century urban landscape of Southern Gaul', in Drinkwater and Elton (eds), 144–55.

Lotter, F. (1971), 'Antonius von Lerins und der Untergang Ufernorikums: ein Beitrag zur Frage der Bevölkerungs Kontinuität im Alpen-Donau-Raum', *Historische Zeitschrift* 212, 265–315.

MacCoull, C.S.B. (1988), *Dioscorus of Aphrodito: His Work and His World* (Berkeley).

MacKenzie, M.M. and Roueché, C. (1989), *Images of Authority: Papers Presented to Joyce Reynolds on her 70th birthday* (Cambridge).

MacMullen, R. (1982), 'The epigraphic habit in the Roman Empire', *American Journal of Philology* 103, 243–5.

MacMullen, R. (1986), 'Frequency of inscriptions in Roman Lydia', *Zeitschrift für Papyrologie und Epigraphik* 65, 237–8.

Maier, J.-L. (1973), *L'épiscopat de l'Afrique romaine, vandale et byzantine* (Rome).

Mango, C. (1980), *Byzantium: The Empire of New Rome* (London).

Mango, C. (1985), *Le développement urbain de Constantinople IVe-VIIe siècles* (Paris).

Mann, J.C. (1985), 'Epigraphic consciousness', *Journal of Roman Studies* 75, 204–6.

Martin, J. and Quint, B. (eds) (1990), *Christentum und antike Gesellschaft* (Darmstadt).

Mathisen, R.W. (1984), 'The family of Georgius Florentius Gregorius and the bishops of Tours', *Medievalia et Humanistica* n.s. 12, 83–95.

Mathisen, R.W. (1992), 'Fifth-century visitors to Italy: business or pleasure' in Drinkwater and Elton (eds), 228–38.

Matthews, J. (1989), *The Roman Empire of Ammianus* (London).

Mattingly, D.J. (1988), 'Olive cultivation and the Albertini tablets', in A. Mastino (ed.), *L'Africa Romana* (Sassari), 403–15.

Mazzarino, S. (1951), *Aspetti Sociali del Quarto Secolo* (Rome).

Meiggs, R. (1973), *Roman Ostia*, 2nd edn (Oxford).

Millar, F. (1983), 'Empire and city, Augustus to Julian: obligations, excuses and status', *Journal of Roman Studies* 73, 76–96.

Millett, M. (1990), *The Romanization of Britain* (Cambridge).

Mitford, T.B. (1950), 'Some new inscriptions from early Christian Cyprus', *Byzantion* 20, 128–32.

Mócsy, A. (1974), *Pannonia and Upper Moesia* (London).

Mrozek, S. (1973), 'À propos de la répartition chronologique des inscriptions latines dans le Haut Empire', *Epigraphica* 35, 113–18.

Mrozek, S. (1978), 'Private *munificentia* in Italien während der späten Kaiserzeit', *Historia* 27, 355–68.

Noll, R. (1963), *Das Leben des heiligen Severin* (Berlin).

Panella, C. (1989), 'Gli scambi nel mediterraneo occidentale', in *Hommes et richesses dans l'empire byzantin* i, *IVe-VIIe siècles* (Paris), 130–41.

Patlagean, E. (1977), *Pauvreté économique et pauvreté sociale à Byzance, 4e-7e siècles* (Paris).

Percival, J. (1992), 'The fifth-century villa: new life or death?', in Drinkwater and Elton (eds), 156–64.

Petrikovits, H.V. (1980), *Rheinische Geschichte*: i, *Altertum* (Dusseldorf).

Petrikovits, H.V. (1981), 'Die Spezialisierung des römischen Handwerks: 2, Spätantike', *Zeitschrift für Papyrologie und Epigraphik* 43, 285-306.

Poulter, A. (1990), 'Nicopolis', *Current Archaeology* 121, 37-42.

Price, S. (1984), *Rituals and Power: the Roman Imperial Cult in Asia Minor* (Cambridge).

Prinz, F. (1971), *Klerus und Krieg im frühen Mittelalter* (Stuttgart).

Prinz, F. (1973), 'Die bischofliche Stadtherrschaft im Frankenreich vom 5 bis zum 7 Jahrhundert', *Historische Zeitschrift* 217, 1-35.

Pruneti, P. (1981), *I centri abitati dell'Ossirinchite: repertorio toponomastico* (Florence).

Rathbone, D. (1990), 'Villages and population in Graeco-Roman Egypt', *Proceedings of the Cambridge Philological Society* 36, 100-42.

Rémondon, R. (1961), 'Soldats de Byzance d'après un papyrus trouvé à Edfou', *Recherches de Papyrologie* 1, 41-93.

Rey-Coquais, J. (1977), 'Inscriptions découverts dans les fouilles de Tyr', *Bulletin du Musée de Beyrouth* 29.

Riché, P. (1957), 'La survivance des écoles publiques en Gaule au Ve siècle', *Le Moyen Âge* 63, 421-36.

Riché, P. (1965), 'L'enseignement du droit en Gaule du VIe au XIe siècle', *Ius Romanum Medii Aevi* 1.5b, 1-21.

Riché, P. (1973), *Éducation et culture dans l'occident barbare* (Paris).

Riley, J.A. (1981), 'The pottery from the cistern 1977.1, 1977.2, and 1977.3', in J.H. Humphrey (ed.), *Excavations at Carthage, 1977, conducted by the University of Michigan* (Ann Arbor), 85-124.

Roques, D. (1987), *Synésios de Cyréne et la Cyrénaique du Bas-Empire* (Paris).

Rostovtzeff, M. (1957), *The Social and Economic History of the Roman Empire*, 2nd edn (Oxford).

Rouche, M. (1979), *L'Aquitaine des Wisigoths aux Arabes 418-781* (Paris).

Roueché, C. (1979), 'A new inscription from Aphrodisias and the title *patēr tēs poleōs*', *Greek, Roman and Byzantine*

Studies 20, 173–85.

Roueché, C. (1989a), *Aphrodisias in Late Antiquity* (London).

Roueché, C. (1989b), 'Floreat Perge', in MacKenzie and Roueché (eds), 205–28.

Roueché, C. and Erim, K.T. (eds) (1990), *Aphrodisias Papers* (Ann Arbor).

Russell, J. (1987), *The Mosaic Inscriptions of Anemurium* (Vienna).

Ste Croix, G.E.M. de (1981), *The Class Struggle in the Ancient Greek World* (London).

Sartre, M. (1982), *Inscriptions Grecques et Latines de la Syrie* 13.1, *Bostra* (Paris).

Schlippschuch, O. (1974), *Die Händler im römischen Kaiserreich in Gallien, Germanien, und den Donau provinzen* (Amsterdam).

Schmidt, H.F. (1957), 'Das Weiterleben und die Wiederbelebung antiker Institutionen im mittelalterlichen Städtewesen', *Annali di storia del diritto* 1, 85–135.

Schubert, W. (1969), 'Die rechtliche Sonderstellung der Dekurionen Kurialen in der Kaisergesetzgebung des 4–6 Jhs' *Zeitschrift für Rechtsgeschichte*, Röm. Abt. 86, 287–331.

Sevcenko, I. and Sevcenko, N. (1984), *The Life of Nicholas of Sion* (Brookline, Mass.).

Shahid, I. (1984), *Byzantium and the Arabs in the Fourth Century* (Washington).

Sijpesteijn, P. (1987), 'The title *patēr tēs poleōs* and the papyri', *Tyche* 2, 171–4.

Sivan, H. (1992), 'Town and country in late antique Gaul: the example of Bordeaux', in Drinkwater and Elton (eds), 132–43.

Sodini, J.-P. (1989), 'Le commerce des marbres à l'époque protobyzantine', *Hommes et richesses dans l'empire byzantin* i, *IVe–VIIe siècles* (Paris), 163–86.

Spandel, R. (1957), 'Dux und Comes in der Merowingerzeit', *Zeitschrift für Rechtsgeschichte* 74, 41–84.

Taradell, M. (1977), 'Les villes romaines dans l'Hispania de l'est', in Duval and Frézouls (eds), 97ff.

Tate, G. (1989), 'Les campagnes de Syrie du Nord', in *Hommes et richesses dans l'empire byzantin* i, *IVe–VIIe siècles* (Paris), 163–86.

Tchalenko, G. (1953–8), *Villages antiques de la Syrie du Nord: le massif du Bélus à l'époque romaine*, 3 vols (Paris).

Thomas, C.A. (1981), *Christianity in Roman Britain to AD 500* (London).

Thompson, E.A. (1969), *The Goths in Spain* (Oxford).

Thompson, E.A. (1979), 'Gildas and the history of Britain', *Britannia* 10, 203–26.

Thompson, E.A. (1984), *St Germanus of Auxerre and the End of Roman Britain* (Wadebridge).

Thompson, E.A. (1990), 'Ammianus Marcellinus and Britain', *Nottingham Medieval Studies* 34, 1–15.

Todd, M. (1981), *Roman Britain 55 BC–AD 400* (London).

Van Dam, R. (1985), *Leadership and Community in Late Antique Gaul* (Berkeley/London).

Van Ossel, P. (1985), 'Quelques apports récents à l'étude de l'habitat rural gallo-romain dans la région mosane', *Les Études Classiques* 53, 79–96.

Velkov, V. (1962), 'Les campagnes et la population rurale en Thrace aux IVe–VIe siècles', *Byzantinica Bulgarica* 1, 31–66.

Vryonis, S. (1963), 'An Attic hoard of Byzantine gold coins (668–741) and the numismatic evidence for the urban history of Byzantium', *Mélanges Ostrogorsky* (Belgrade), 291–300.

Vryonis, S. (1971), *The Decline of Medieval Hellenism in Asia Minor and the Process of Islamisation from the Eleventh through the Fifteenth Century* (Berkeley).

Wacher, J. (1975), *The Towns of Roman Britain* (London).

Wacher, J. (ed.) (1987), *The Roman World* (London and New York).

Waldherr, G. (1989), *Kaiserliche Baupolitik in Nordafrika: Studien zu den Bauinschriften der diokletianischen Zeit und ihrer räumlichen Verteilung in den römischen Provinzen Nordafrikas* (Frankfurt am Main).

Ward-Perkins, B. (1978), 'Luni, the decline and abandonment of a Roman town', in Blake, Potter and Whitehouse (eds), 313–21.

Ward-Perkins, B. (1984), *From Classical Antiquity to the Middle Ages: Urban Building in Northern and Central Italy AD 300–850* (Oxford).

Wickham, C. (1981), *Early Medieval Italy* (London).

Wickham, C. (1988), 'Marx, Sherlock Holmes and Late Roman

commerce', review of A. Giardina (ed.), *Società romana e impero tardoantico:* iii, *Le merci. Gli insediamenti, Journal of Roman Studies* 78 (1988), 183–93.

Wightman, E.M. (1978), 'The towns of Gaul with special reference to the North-East', in M.W. Barley (ed.), *European Towns, Their Archaeology and Early History* (London).

Wightman, E.M. (1985), *Gallia Belgica* (London).

Wörrle, M. (1988), *Stadt und Fest im kaiserlichen Kleinasien: Studien zu einer agonistichen Stiftung aus Oinoanda* (Munich).

Zeumer, K. (1886), *Formulae Merowingici et Karolini Aevi, MGH Legum sectio* 5 (Hanover).

Zeumer, K. (1902), *Leges Visigothorum, MGH Leges* 1.1 (Hanover).

∞ 2 ∞

The survival and fall of the classical city in Late Roman Africa

Claude Lepelley

In his great book *Saint Augustin et la fin de la culture antique*, published in 1938, Henri Marrou states that his original purpose was to examine the emergence, from what he regarded as the decline of classical civilization, of the mediaeval culture on which Augustine left so profound an impression. In the event, his study evokes the power of tradition far more than the birth of a new world. 'In the culture of St Augustine', wrote Marrou, 'I have thrown into light the inheritance of a tradition of remarkable continuity, homogeneity and fixity. Augustine is an ancient man of letters, a pupil of Cicero, a remote disciple of Isocrates' (Marrou 1938, 543). Marrou then regarded this very continuity as a form of sclerosis: 'I have not attempted to hide', he said, 'the impoverishment and ossification of this ancient tradition', as it was received by this 'man of letters from a decadent age' (ibid., iii–iv, xi–xiv and 543–4). In 1949, Marrou published his *Retractatio*, in which he vigorously rejected those 'peremptory assertions', 'the judgements', he said, 'of an ignorant and presumptuous young barbarian', blind to the beauty and the subtlety of this rhetorical culture, both in what it had inherited and in the new refinements added by the distinctive sensibility of late antiquity (Marrou 1949, 663–6).

I underwent a similar experience in my work on the cities of late Roman Africa (Lepelley 1979 and 1981a). At the outset, I thought that I was entering a new world, profoundly different from that of the classical city. There were, indeed, new elements, for instance the heavy yoke of the bureaucratic central government, whose oppressive legislation severely restricted municipal independence, or the increasing Christianization, which rendered obsolete the old religious base of civic life, and set alongside the traditional sources of authority the swelling new power of the Church. However, as my research progressed, I became more and more impressed by the continuities from the cities of the classical era, manifested not only in municipal institutions, but also in the daily life of the cities, in education, culture and social structures. The conviction grew upon me that life in the African cities of Augustine's day cannot be understood without constant reference to the same cities two centuries earlier, as they are revealed to us by the evidence of inscriptions, law and archaeology.

Marrou was the forerunner of the radical re-evaluation of Late Antiquity conducted in our own time by scholars from every part of the world. Marrou revealed the quality and vitality of Late Roman culture, creative, but still rooted in the classical tradition. But may not this rich and brilliant cultural life have depended on a favourable social context, in particular on prosperous cities, whose élites were still able to afford such education and still set store by the preservation of the traditional intellectual values which it transmitted?

The posing of questions like this has cast doubt on the old orthodoxy about Late Roman cities. The study of the cities was particularly badly affected by the prejudices which distorted our predecessors' interpretation of Late Antiquity. Disregarding the archaeological evidence, they declared that in every region of the Empire the cities were in full decline. The one-sided use of the legal texts preserved in the Theodosian Code led them to believe that municipal self-government had been completely destroyed and the decurions had become proletarianized, reduced to the unpaid, impoverished and terrorized agents of the tyrannical imperial government. In the view of these historians, the essential elements of the classical city – civic institutions, social structure, ideological tradition – had effectively disappeared.[1] However, a

---

[1]   Rostovtzeff 1957, 535–41; Abbott and Johnson 1926, 197–231. These authors were heavily influenced by the views and assumptions of Mommsen 1887–8, developed by Liebenam 1900.

remarkable wealth of documentation is available, and, when analysed, undermines these received ideas, especially in the case of Africa.[1]

Ubique res publica, 'everywhere the city!', exclaimed Tertullian (De Anima 30.3), thus evoking the triumph of the Roman municipal system in Africa under the Severi at the beginning of the third century, the rapid growth of hundreds of cities, and the major rôle which they played in the political, social and cultural life of the province of Africa Proconsularis. Two centuries later, the imperial government had certainly deprived those cities of much of their autonomy and revenue, but they remained vigorously alive. In the dark days of the Vandal invasions, Quodvultdeus, Bishop of Carthage, echoed Tertullian's phrase. 'Where is Africa', he lamented, 'which was like a garden of delights for the whole world? . . . Where are those great and most splendid cities?'[2]

It was the work of archaeologists which first prompted the radical re-evaluation of Late Roman Africa which has taken place in the last quarter of a century. All recent studies of Africa in the fourth century and at the beginning of the fifth show a quite remarkable degree of agreement in their insistence on the vitality and prosperity of the region, both in the cities and in the countryside. Numerous excavations and surveys have shown that in most cases the area of urban settlement in the early imperial period remained fully occupied under the Late Empire, and in some cities, like Cuicul (Djemila), Sitifis (Sétif) and Thamugadi (Timgad), new built-up areas were constructed in the fourth century, attesting a population increase (Février 1964; Lassus 1969; Duval 1982a and 1982b). Aristocratic houses in Cuicul and Carthage, when examined by sophisticated archaeological techniques, have turned out to have a long and complex history, extending over several centuries and incorporating several phases of reconstruction or restoration (Lassus 1971; Blanchard-Lemée

---

[1]   A much more judicious interpretation was presented by Jones 1964, 712–66. Warmington 1954, a regrettably brief work, offered rich new perspectives on Africa.
[2]   Quodvultdeus, Sermo II de tempore barbarico 5.4 (CCL 60.476–7): ubi est Africa, quae toto mundo fuit uelut hortus deliciarum, . . . ubi tantae splendidissimae ciuitates?

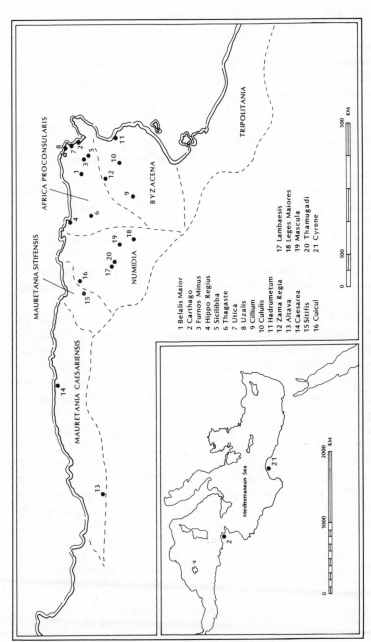

Late Roman Africa

AFRICA PROCONSULARIS

MAURETANIA SITIFENSIS

MAURETANIA CAESARIENSIS

NUMIDIA

BYZACENA

TRIPOLITANIA

1 Belalis Maior
2 Carthago
3 Furnos Minus
4 Hippo Regius
5 Sicilibba
6 Thagaste
7 Utica
8 Uzalis
9 Cillium
10 Cululis
11 Hadrumetum
12 Zama Regia
13 Altava
14 Caesarea
15 Sitifis
16 Cuicul

17 Lambaesis
18 Leges Maiores
19 Mascula
20 Thamugadi
21 Cyrene

Mediterranean Sea

0   100   500 KM

0   1000   2000 KM

1975; Beschaouch *et al.* 1977; Anselmino *et al.* 1986). The study of mosaics has played an important rôle in this enquiry. Specialists in this field have made an important revision of dating, based both on stylistic and stratigraphic criteria. The upshot is that dates have been generally lowered: many mosaics formerly assigned to the early imperial period are now dated to the fourth or fifth centuries, and others, previously attributed to the fourth century, are now dated to the Byzantine period. These results attest the long survival of an art of high quality, and show the luxury of upper-class homes and so the wealth of the city élites in the late period.[1]

In essence, the chronological revision, by which buildings which used to be considered earlier are now dated to the Late Empire, is the consequence of a major archaeological advance: the establishment of a typology of African red slip ware. An essential stage in this research was the publication in 1972 of John Hayes' now classic work, *Late Roman Pottery*. The evolution of the successive types of this pottery, from the end of the first century to the high mediaeval period, has now been established with certainty.[2] This addition to our knowledge has great and wide-ranging implications. Besides leading to a revision of stratigraphic datings in Africa and elsewhere, the pottery itself provides important evidence for economic history. The abundance of African red slip ware all round the Mediterranean has refuted the common notion that African wealth was based solely on the export of agricultural products. From the second century this semi-luxury pottery was produced on an industrial scale. From the age of Hadrian and Antoninus Pius, African pottery dominated the western Mediterranean market. It penetrated the East in the third century, and enjoyed a monopoly until the 330s. Thereafter, it had to compete with eastern products, but retained a major share in the Mediterranean market. Its position was only partially damaged by

---

[1]   Alexander *et al.* 1974 and 1976; Blanchard-Lemée 1975; Darmon 1980. Ennabli 1986 has revealed the magnificent mosaics adorning the private baths of a large mansion near Sicilibba, about 40 km south-west of Carthage. The pottery underneath enables these mosaics to be dated to the end of the fourth or the beginning of the fifth century.
[2]   Hayes 1972 and 1980; Carandini 1981; Tortorella 1986. On variations in the volume of exports, see Fentress and Perkins 1987.

the Vandal invasion, and exports continued until the Byzantine period. To the production and export of this pottery, one must add that of African amphoras (Zevi and Tchernia 1969; Panella 1983 and 1986). Thus the trade routes from Africa were busy and important.

Although African pottery production was significant, the wealth of the region derived above all from agriculture. Field surveys confirm that African agriculture was flourishing in the late period. A particularly significant survey is that directed by B. Hitchner in the region of Kasserine (ancient Cillium) in Byzacena, which shows that that region was cultivated and devoted to intensive olive-growing in the period from the second to the sixth centuries. Before and after that period, the region was exploited by nomadic pastoralism.[1] A preliminary report has just appeared of the Segermes valley survey conducted by a Danish team under the direction of J. Carlsen. In this northern region of Africa Proconsularis, 'the surface sherd scatters appear to indicate that the flourishing period for the countryside was in the third and fourth century AD, with a decline beginning before the Arab conquest' (Carlsen and Tvarnø 1990, 813). One may note at this point that the third-century crisis does not constitute a significant break in the archaeological record of the African countryside.[2] This observation is valid also for the urban scene: in the African cities, the third century is not marked by a regression or interruption comparable to those which can be detected in other regions.[3] These archaeological observations provide one of the strongest arguments of those historians who believe that the crisis had little impact on Africa, and that, protected from invasion by the Mediterranean, the region did not suffer difficulties comparable in magnitude to those by which Europe was afflicted.[4] The

[1] Hitchner 1988 and 1990; Mattingly 1988. Peyras 1983 detects a similar pattern of exploitation in the valleys of the northern tributaries of the lower Medjerda.
[2] This persistence of agricultural prosperity was noted by Lepelley 1967. Whittaker 1978 lays strong emphasis on the continuity in the patterns of agricultural exploitation.
[3] Mahjoubi 1978 and 1984 detects continuity from the second to the fourth centuries and subsequent change at the little town of Belalis Maior (Henchir el Faouar) in northern Tunisia.
[4] Mauretania suffered two serious revolts by Berber tribes, in 253–60 and 290–3 (Bénabou 1976, 214–40). The first also affected Numidia, but the

breach with the early imperial period was less brutal and less marked there than elsewhere. This is one of the main reasons for the persistence there in the fourth century of numerous traditions of the classical city, attested by the epigraphic and literary sources.

The archaeological evidence at which we have just glanced prevents us from claiming that these continuities were merely a cultural phenomenon, like that studied by Marrou. In particular, it cannot be said that the inscriptions reveal nothing but language used as a kind of classical decoration to express completely different political and social realities: the prosperity of the cities and the maintenance of their classical traditions undoubtedly had an economic base.[1] The inscriptions, like the excavations, attest an aspect of the material life of the cities: the huge effort which they expended to maintain and enhance the monumental heritage which was the concrete expression of the Roman civic ideal. The legacy of public buildings inherited from the Early Empire was restored and added to in the fourth century, the work being paid for sometimes from the cities' resources, sometimes by the generosity of individual members of the city élites.[2] In my book I listed 332 inscriptions attesting the erection or restoration of public buildings in African cities in the period from Diocletian to the Vandal invasions,[3] and new instances are frequently discovered. Thus were built or repaired a multitude of baths, porticoes, basilicas, theatres, triumphal arches, aqueducts and public fountains. The significance

heart of Roman Africa was not threatened. Similarly, in the fourth century, only Tripolitania was affected by the razzias of Saharan nomads (363–7) and only Mauretania by the war of Firmus (371–5). The fact that most of the cities of Proconsularis, Byzacena and even Numidia did not erect fortifications in the third and fourth centuries proves that they believed themselves to be secure until the arrival of the Vandals.

[1]   I completely share the view expressed by C. R. Whittaker in the discussion following the presentation of the original version of this paper at the Nottingham conference: 'The extraordinary boom in Late Antique Africa – in Proconsularis and Byzacena at least – has by now become axiomatic as a result of proper pottery dating. . . . Under these circumstances, might one not at least hazard the view that the conservatism of urban institutions in the fourth century was related to a stable economy?'

[2]   Much more rarely by imperial generosity, as at Utica under Constantine (*CIL* 8.1179).

[3]   Lepelley 1979, 112–20, gives a complete list of these inscriptions. All the texts are reproduced and discussed in Lepelley 1981a.

of such a phenomenon is rich and complex. It attests first of all to the continuance of economic prosperity, but the financial effort involved is evidence too of a resolute determination to preserve the material fabric of the classical city, at whatever cost, as an amenity for the inhabitants, and also, from local patriotism, to exalt the glory of the 'most splendid cities'.

Two texts from southern Numidia may be cited as examples of this epigraphic treasure trove. The first of these inscriptions comes from Mascula (the modern Khenchela), and was erected in the years 364–7 (*AE* 1911, 217; Marcillet-Jaubert 1987; *AE* 1987, 1082):

> *Aureis ubique temporibus dd(ominorum) nn(ostrorum)*
> *Valentiniani et Valen/tis perpetuorum [Au]gg(ustorum),*
> *statum desperata recipiunt, ami/ssa renouantur, ruinarum*
> *deformitatem decor nouit/atis excludit. Iamdudum igitur*
> *thermarum aestiual/ium fabulam factam depellens faciemque*
> *restituens,/ Publi(li)us C(a)eionius C(a)ecina Albinus u(ir)*
> *c(larissimus), consularis [s(ex)]f(ascalis) p(rouinciae)*
> *N(umidiae) C(onstantinae)],/ ad splendorem tam patriae*
> *quam prouinciae restituit,/ perfecit, dedicauit[que], omni*
> *nisu(?) [cur]antib[us] Aemilio Flauiano, Fabio Praetexta[to,*
> *F]lau[i]o/ Innocentio, Mario Secundino, [- - - io*
> *E]xcu[s]antio fl(aminibus) p(er)p(etuis). B(onis) b(ene)!*

In the golden times, everywhere prevailing, of our Lords Valentinian and Valens, perpetual Augusti, what was derelict recovers stability, what was abandoned is renovated, beautiful new monuments replace ugly ruins. Therefore, dispelling the long-standing ill repute of the summer baths and restoring their beauty, Publilius Caeionius Caecina Albinus, most distinguished man, consular governor with six *fasces* of the province of Numidia Constantina, has restored, completed and dedicated this building, for the glory of the homeland and of the province. The work was carried out, with every effort (?),[1] by the perpetual *flamines* Aemilius Flavianus, Fabius Praetextatus, Flavius Innocentius, Marius Secundinus, and – – – ius Excusantius. Happiness for such righteous men!

---

[1] *Omni nisu* is Marcillet-Jaubert's conjecture. The text is only known from a copy made in 1910.

The second inscription was found at Lambaesis (Lambèse), and was erected in the years 379–83 (*ILS* 5520):

> *Aureis temporibus/ ddd(ominorum) nnn(ostrorum) Gratiani
> Va/lentiniani et Theo/dosi(i) perpetuorum/ et diuinorum
> princi/pum, non solum labsa reparantur sed et noua/ pro
> felicitate con/struuntur; curia igi/tur ordinis quam maio/res
> nostri merito tem/plum eiusdem ordinis uo/citari uoluerunt,
> uetustate/ immo incuria u(e)terum in odiu* (sic) *foeda[ta]
> iacuisse [u]ide/batur, qua(e) nunc ex nouo opere in eodem
> solo egregi/ae* (sic) *cognoscitur; nam etiam in tam
> sple(n)didissima ciuitate/ meatus fluentorum deesse ui/
> debatur qui ex integro opere ad usum utilitatemque
> eiusde(m)/ urbis exstructus uidetur; quae/ omnia pro
> splendore felicis/sim(a)e urbis, sub fascibus Luci(i) Ae/mili(i)
> Metopi(i) Flauiani clarissimi uiri, consularis sexfascalis/
> p(rouinciae) N(umidiae), perfecta sunt, curante L(ucio)
> Silicio Rufo du/ouiralic(io), cu(ratore) r(ei) p(ublicae),/
> sumpto proprio.*

In the golden times of our Lords Gratian, Valentinian and Theodosius, eternal and divine Princes, not only are decayed buildings restored, but new ones are erected for the happiness of all. Therefore the *curia* of the order of decurions, rightly called by our ancestors the temple of the same order, which appeared collapsed, defaced and despised through age or rather through the unconcern of our elders, has been restored to beauty on the same site through new works. At the same time, the flow of running water of which this most splendid city was deprived, has been re-established for the use and benefit of this same city, by complete new works. All of this has been achieved to the glory of this most happy town under the *fasces* of Lucius Aemilius Metopius Flavianus, most distinguished man, consular governor with six *fasces* of the province of Numidia, through the care of Lucius Silicius Rufus, former duumvir, curator of the city, at his own expense.

In the second example, it is expressly stated that the works were carried out through the largesse of a municipal dignitary, while he was holding office.[1] The exaltation of the *curia*, or council

---

[1] The Mascula inscription does not indicate the source of finance. Doubtless the funds used came from the city treasury, or, more precisely, from the revenues of municipal lands which had been confiscated by the

chamber of the decurions, 'rightly called by our ancestors the temple of the . . . order', is a perfect expression of municipal patriotism rooted in the classical tradition: we remember that the Roman senate could meet in a temple, and that its usual meeting place, the Roman Curia, was regarded as a sanctuary.[1] The grandiose style of these inscriptions forms a striking contrast with the sober epigraphic language of the Early Empire: they express the love of tradition in the distinctive tones of Late Antiquity.

Another instance of concern for the fabric of the ancient city is to be found on four statue bases, discovered in the great baths of Caesarea (Cherchel), the capital of the province of Mauretania Caesariensis. On two of them dedications to Hercules and to Juno Regina were inscribed under the Principate. Beneath these dedications, in lettering of the late period, come the words *translata de sordentibus locis*, 'transferred from sordid places'.[2] Originally these were cult statues from temples. When the temples were closed in accordance with the anti-pagan decrees passed by the Christian emperors at the end of the fourth century, those sanctuaries fell into decay and became 'sordid places'. The city authorities then had the statues transferred to the great baths, which had become a sort of museum – a fine example of respect for the heritage of previous centuries.[3]

From the inscriptions we know of more than eighty instances of

imperial *res privata* and were later partially restored to the city. Laws providing for such restitution are recorded in 362, 374 and 395 (*CTh* 10.3.1; 15.1.18, 32).

[1] The sacred character of the Roman Curia led to the long controversy over the Altar of Victory. Attachment to the *curia* also finds expression in a recently published inscription of the second half of the fourth century from Leges Maiores (Henchir Gousset) in Numidia (Marcillet-Jaubert 1979; *AE* 1982, 961; Jacques 1985). This records that at his own expense, in honour of his father's flaminate, a perpetual *flamen* has restored the city *curia*, which he calls 'ancestral' (*curia genitalis*).

[2] *CIL* 8.20963, 20965. The same formula (*translata de sordentibus locis*) occurs on two other bases, where the god's name does not appear.

[3] Italian inscriptions record similar measures, at Verona between 379 and 383, at Liternum in Campania in the same period, and at Beneventum in 425 or later (*ILS* 5363, 5478–9). A law issued by Honorius in 399 (*CTh* 16.10.18) forbade the destruction of disused temples and ordered statues to be transferred elsewhere without being destroyed. Identical measures were enacted in 407 (*CTh* 16.10.19) and in 458 by Majorian (*Novel.* 4).

benefactions to the African cities taking the form of building works (listed by Lepelley 1979, 304–14). One must remember too the gifts of games, whose frequency and importance Augustine so often deplored. As Augustine remarked, many members of the city élites continued to compete for civic honours and incurred heavy expense in order to outdo the largesses of their rivals. 'The worldly man', he said in a sermon, 'prays to God for riches; if he gets them, he seeks empty honours from men, and, to obtain them, he offers indecent games . . . and public bear hunts. He gives his patrimony to the professional hunters of the arena, while Christ, in the person of the poor, goes hungry.'[1] Texts like these provide a decisive refutation of the view, held by so many modern historians, that the Late Empire saw a systematic flight from municipal obligations on the part of the supposedly impoverished and oppressed *curiales*.

The vitality of the old traditions in Late Roman Africa is just as evident in many other aspects of the life of the cities. Take for example the titulature of the cities. The extension of Roman citizenship to almost all the inhabitants of the Empire in 212 not only removed an important status distinction between individuals, but led to the levelling down of the cities, since the privileged categories of colonies and *municipia* lost their significance. The distinctions between colonies, *municipia* and peregrine cities in fact disappear in the course of the third century, and only one form of city is envisaged in fourth-century legislation.[2] However, the African cities always keep their old titles under the Late Empire, both on inscriptions and in literary texts. Africa is the only region for which the titles of *colonia* and *municipium* are retained in the Antonine Itinerary, the Peutinger Table and the Ravenna Cosmography. The Polish historian Tadeusz Kotula has counted eighty-two cities with the title of *municipium* and sixty-two with the title of *colonia* in post-235 documents (Kotula 1974). In Augustine's time Carthage was still referred to as a *colonia* and

---

[1]   Augustine, *Serm.* 32.20 (*CCL* 41.407). For other passages in which Augustine mentions the games see *Contra Academicos* 1.2 (*BA* 14.16–9); *Serm.* 21.10 (*CCL* 41.285–6); *En. in ps.* 80.7, 149.10 (*CCL* 39.1119, 40.2184).
[2]   There were, however, a good number of promotions of African cities to the rank of *colonia* or *municipium* during the third century, notably under Valerian and Gallienus (253–68); cf. Gascou 1982.

Thagaste as a *municipium* (Augustine, *Confessions* 6.7.11, 9.8.17). In the mid-fourth century, grandiose archaic designations for the 'most splendid cities' were still much in favour. For instance, under Constantine the citizens of Zama Regia styled themselves *coloni coloniae Aeliae Hadrianae Augustae Zamae Regiae,*[1] while in the 360s those of Thamugadi (Timgad) rejoiced in the title of *coloni coloniae Traianae Marcianae Thamugadensis,* thus evoking the memory not just of Trajan, the founder of the colony, but also of his sister Marciana.[2] Such titles betoken a vigorous local patriotism, a form of 'municipal snobbery', to use Kotula's phrase: recalling the antiquity of a city's Roman status served to enhance its prestige.

Personal names tell us the same story. The leading modern student of Roman onomastic practice, the Finnish scholar Iro Kajanto, has asserted that under the Late Empire the Roman world reverted to using a single name to designate its citizens. In archaic Rome, the single name was the *praenomen*; in the late period, it was usually the *cognomen*. Under the Late Republic and Early Empire, Roman citizens were distinguished from non-citizens by their use of three names, the *tria nomina*. The first name, the *praenomen*, began, so Kajanto claims, to fall out of use as early as the third century, while in the fourth century a strong tendency to drop the middle name, the *gentilicium*, can be observed (Kajanto 1963 and 1965). With qualifications, these generalizations may be broadly valid for some parts of the Roman world, but they do not apply to Africa. In fact, on thousands of late inscriptions large numbers of inhabitants of Roman Africa are named by both *gentilicium* and *cognomen*. These include members of the city élites, but are not confined to them: many of the texts are funerary inscriptions for persons of more modest social status.[3] It is especially significant that this practice

[1] *ILS* 6111c, a patronage tablet found at Rome, offered by Zama Regia to Q. Aradius Valerius Proculus, former governor of Byzacena.

[2] *AE* 1913, 25 = *ILCV* 387 (patronage tablet of Aelius Julianus).

[3] The *gentilicium* dropped out of use in everyday life, but was retained on official documents, and so for the names of dignitaries on inscriptions, not only in Africa but throughout the West. Thus its use became a mark of social distinction (cf. Pflaum 1977), although in the great Roman senatorial families it was obliterated from the fourth century by a complex polyonymy. The distinctive feature of African practice is the very frequent appearance of the *gentilicium* on late funerary inscriptions.

survived in remote towns, far from the coast and the great cultural centres. Thus at Altava, an isolated city from Mauretania Caesariensis, dated inscriptions attest Julii, Ulpii, and Aurelii living in the sixth century. The latest such text is the epitaph of one Aurelius Montanus who died in 599. Up to the beginning of the seventh century, these people persisted in recalling, by the use of these *gentilicia*, the memory of remote ancestors who, from four to six centuries earlier, had been granted Roman citizenship by emperors bearing those names.[1]

Similar observations may be made about city institutions. The old magistracies subsisted in the Late Empire: *duumviri* and *aediles* are frequently mentioned on inscriptions of the period.[2] Christian sources, such as the documents relating to the Diocletianic persecution and the Donatist quarrel, prove that the *duumviri* retained their judicial responsibilities, sharing them with the *curator rei publicae*.[3] Most remarkable of all is the fact that the traditional official priesthoods continued to be filled until the beginning of the sixth century, despite Christianization and the prohibition of pagan worship. Augurs and pontiffs are attested up to the 360s, and hundreds of *flamines* of the imperial cult are mentioned on late inscriptions (Lepelley 1979, 165–7 and 362–9), the latest being Flavius Geminius Catullinus, mentioned nineteen times on the Albertini Tablets at the end of the fifth century (Courtois *et al.* 1952, nos 3–57). Provincial priests (*sacerdotales*) still existed in the Vandal kingdom. The imperial cult, celebrated by municipal *flamines* and provincial priests, was to some extent secularized during Constantine's reign; reduced to a solemn tribute to the imperial majesty, it was henceforth performed without sacrifices.[4] Christians now regarded themselves as eligible to assume such positions. Eight late inscriptions are known from Africa, in which the subject's Christian faith is mentioned

[1]   Marcillet-Jaubert 1968, nos 222–4, the epitaphs of Ulpius Marturius, Iulius Germanus and Aurelius Montanus, who died in 592, 593 and 599 respectively. The dates are given by the provincial era of Mauretania.
[2]   Fifty-one duumvirs or *duumuiralicii* are listed in Lepelley 1979, 152–7.
[3]   Lepelley 1979, 161–3. See the *Acta purgationis Felicis* (Optatus Milevitanus, Appendix, *CSEL* 26.197–8).
[4]   This secularization of the imperial cult is attested by an inscription from Hispellum in Umbria, reproducing a rescript of Constantine dating to the years 333–5 (*ILS* 705).

without embarrassment alongside his tenure of an originally pagan priesthood.[1]

The municipal album of Timgad, which can be dated to the reign of Julian, gives a complete list of the decurions and dignitaries of the city, and is a vivid expression of the institutional traditionalism of Late Roman Africa.[2] This long document may be divided into four sections:

1 Senior dignitaries, above the order of decurions: senators, *perfectissimi* (high-ranking *equites*), patrons and provincial priests.
2 The first part of the list of decurions, i.e. those currently holding a municipal post, both magistracies and priesthoods.
3 The other decurions.
4 Christian clergy and imperial officials from decurional families.

Let us examine the second section, the list of magistrates and priests. It is headed by the *curator rei publicae*, who, at this period, bore the main responsibility for the administration of a city. A *curator* held office for a year, and was still appointed by the emperor, although in practice the choice was now made by the order of decurions, to which the *curator* himself belonged.[3] Next come the *duumviri*, the senior magistrates, although at this period subordinate to the *curator*. They are followed by the official priests: a large group of perpetual *flamines*, four pontiffs and four

[1] On these documents and their significance see Chastagnol and Duval 1974. To the six inscriptions discussed there should be added the patronage tablet of the Timgad *flamen* Aelius Julianus, which bears the chi-rho symbol, and *CIL* 8.25810, from Furnos Minus, as re-edited by N. Duval, *AE* 1978, 877 and 1982, 934.
[2] Chastagnol 1978 provides an edition of the album with commentary, which supersedes the older editions (*CIL* 8.2403, 17903; Leschi 1948).
[3] On the *curatores* see Lepelley 1979, 168–93, listing the 151 known from Late Roman Africa. Under the Early Empire, the *curator rei publicae* was an imperial appointee, despatched to a city which had fallen into financial difficulties (cf. Jacques 1984). In the fourth century the institution became general, and the *curatores* acquired wide powers, no longer limited to finance, but, instead of being sent in from outside, they were now chosen from within the local *curia* (a development already clearly perceived by Lucas 1940).

augurs. Last come the aediles and a quaestor.[1] The position of
the priests between the duumvirs and the other magistrates is of
great interest. It corresponds exactly to the way in which posts are
arranged in the inscriptions from the Principate recording
senatorial careers. In these one generally finds the consulate at the
head, then priesthoods, whatever their chronological place in the
honorand's career, and then his other magistracies and posts,
listed in either direct or inverse chronological order. In a Roman
city, the duumvirs held a position corresponding to that of the
consuls at Rome, and, like the consuls, they held the major
auspices and performed sacrifices, and so enjoyed supreme
religious authority during their term of office. The survival,
revealed by the album, of this hierarchical order of precedence at
Timgad in about 362 is an astonishing instance of institutional
conservatism, even though contemporaries may no longer have
clearly understood its religious significance.

We may note finally that the very limited degree of democracy
which was originally general in Roman cities survived to an extent
in Africa, when it had disappeared everywhere else. The best
evidence is a law addressed in 325 by Constantine to Tiberianus,
comes Africae (*CTh* 12.5.1). The Emperor required the authorities
to ensure that persons lacking the proper qualifications were not
appointed duumvirs as a result of the practice by which 'in Africa
nomination is traditionally made also by popular election' (*populi
quoque suffragiis nominatio in Africa ex consuetudine cele-
bretur*). This custom was not universal in Africa: the appointment
of magistrates by the decurions alone is attested on inscriptions.
However, in some cities a form of popular vote still played a rôle,
and this archaic survival was left undisturbed by the imperial
authorities.[2]

The claims made above for the survival of the classical city in
Africa are based on a very wide range of literary, epigraphic and
archaeological evidence. Yet numerous historians hold the apparently contradictory view that the Romanization of Africa was

---

[1]   The appearance of only one quaestor, not two, on the album may be an
oversight or due to a temporary vacancy.
[2]   This text is discussed by Jacques 1984, 385–8, who shows that the word
nominatio here denotes the election itself as well as the nomination of
candidates, and that a genuine procedure of popular election took place in
certain cities, alongside the choice by the *curia*, to which *quoque* refers.

limited and superficial. How, these writers enquire, could the disappearance of all traces of Roman civilization during the Middle Ages be explained, if the region had undergone a thorough Romanization, deeply rooted in the Latin tradition? What survived of the classical city under the Late Empire was, they claim, only a veneer, a fragile superstructure destined to crumble at the first shock, for it affected only the upper class of a society which at its roots was faithful to its pre-Roman traditions. Berber customs and tribal structures remained very strong in the mountains of Mauretania and in the steppes and deserts of the south. The peasants around Hippo Regius in Augustine's day showed little trace of Romanization: they still spoke a Neo-Punic dialect.[1] The religious troubles provoked in fourth-century Africa by the Donatist schism have often been seen as the expression of anti-Roman feeling.[2] Many scholars have insisted in this way on the fragility of Roman culture in Africa. This was the principal theme of the classic studies of William Frend and Christian Courtois, and their views have recently been upheld by Brent Shaw.[3]

In fact, the two views are not mutually exclusive. Systematic Romanization and urbanization only took place in what is now the eastern Maghreb, that is, northern and central Tunisia and eastern Algeria. Elsewhere, the phenomenon was much more limited, and the Roman cities were isolated enclaves in the still foreign world of the Berbers.[4] In the eastern zone, however, the

[1] Augustine speaks of *Punica lingua* and gives examples of Semitic words. The language in question is thus Neo-Punic, as shown by Green 1951, rather than Berber, as supposed by Frend 1952, 57–9.
[2] This view of Donatism as a kind of anti-Roman Berber separatist movement or as a social revolt by oppressed peasants was argued above all by Frend 1952, a remarkable work, but one which pushed its thesis too far. A better guide is Brown 1972, 237–59, who shows the fragility of these theories. On the history of Donatism see the excellent recent discussion of Birley 1987.
[3] Frend 1952; Courtois 1955; Shaw 1980 and 1983, with the judicious reply of Fentress 1983.
[4] This regional differentiation is a fact of fundamental importance, and it is essential not to generalize to the whole of North Africa observations which apply to some of its districts. The fact that it was only in the northeastern Maghreb that urbanization and Romanization went deep was actually a serious weakness, as became apparent in the sixth century, when tribes from outside attacked the heart of Roman Africa.

persistence in the late period of many of the traditions of the classical city is not merely an ideological and cultural phenomenon, but also reflects the survival of political and social structures. The break produced by the third-century crisis, which was so pronounced elsewhere, was here much less sharp. A similar continuity may undoubtedly be detected in other parts of the Roman world, for example in peninsular Italy, where rich epigraphic evidence reveals similar patterns (see Appendix pp. 70–2). The excessive specialization by which scholars have tended to concentrate either on the Early or on the Late Empire has led them to exaggerate the contrasts between the two periods at the expense of the continuities, and, in consequence, to stress unduly the links between Late Antiquity and the Middle Ages. In my view, a reconsideration has been necessary, to give its due place to what survived from the Early to the Late Empire, without concealing what changed.

Changes certainly happened, and a fixed and static view of this period would be unacceptable. Some of these developments are described in Peter Brown's brilliant work, *The Making of Late Antiquity*. One of the chief themes of that book is Eastern monasticism. Brown interprets the monks' way of life and thought from an anthropological point of view, and regards it as the most significant element in a new civilization. This has naturally led him to lay heavy stress on the contrast between the world he is evoking and the classical tradition (Brown 1978, especially pp. 27–53). However, this approach, perceptive and stimulating as it is, seems to me not altogether to do justice to the omnipresence in the Roman world of the fourth and fifth centuries of this classical tradition, above all in the life of the cities. A mediaevalist could, of course, object that monasticism, which began at this period, had a long and brilliant future, while the classical city had no future and would disappear – a legitimate observation, and one which strongly reflects Peter Brown's point of view. When we consider the doom of the classical city, we should try to explain it and to find in Late Antiquity the causes and initial symptoms of the city's fate, without falling back on the obsolete Gibbonian theory of decline. What we should be studying is not internal decay, but the birth, the formation and growth of new political, social and cultural structures, which competed with the classical city and eventually replaced it. I shall conclude by touching briefly on some aspects of this process.

The Early Empire succeeded in governing a huge territory with a surprisingly limited number of officials. A few hundred senators and *equites* administered the whole Empire, helped by imperial slaves and freedmen. Such a system could only work because all local government was left to the cities, whose leaders enjoyed both great prestige and considerable power over the common people, a power which they used both for good and ill. During the fourth century the emperors created a huge bureaucracy, composed of freeborn officials, who constituted a powerful new élite. Many city *curiales* succeeded in obtaining such positions, despite the imperial laws prohibiting them from doing so.[1] This development shows that these posts, with their power and privileges, could seem much more attractive than the situation of the leaders of the cities. The best-known example of this comes from Africa: it is that of the young Augustine and his friends, who in the 380s sought to escape their municipal obligations in order to enter the upper ranks of government or the liberal professions.[2]

Many people, nevertheless, remained strongly attached to the classical civic tradition: both the city élites, who still regarded their municipal magistracies as an important element in their social prestige, and the lower classes in the cities, who continued to benefit from the largesses of their leaders and the traditional amenities of a Roman town. However, such a structure was very expensive. The continued flourishing of the African cities and the maintenance of their classical traditions was linked, as we have seen, to very favourable economic circumstances, and was highly

---

[1] A large number of these laws are reproduced in *CTh* 12.1. Lepelley 1979, 243–79, assesses the extent of this development.

[2] Augustine took a teaching post in 375, which was a legal way of escaping his municipal obligations (*Confessions* 3.1–3; 4.7.12; 5.8.14). Later, at Milan, he sought to enter the upper ranks of the imperial administration as a provincial governor (*Confessions* 6.11.19), an ambition to which his conversion in 386 put an end. Alypius became a barrister and a legal adviser to senior government officials in Italy about 383–5 (Augustine, *Confessions* 6.8.13, 10.16). Another citizen of Thagaste, Evodius, the future Bishop of Uzalis, about the same time became *agens in rebus* at the imperial palace in Milan (Augustine, *Confessions* 9.8.17). Brown 1978, 45–53, has justly characterized the period as 'an age of ambition'.

vulnerable to shifts in the economic climate. It is no accident that few instances survive in the African epigraphical record of public buildings or benefactions made in the dark years of the third-century crisis, or under Constantine and his sons, when city revenues suffered heavily from confiscations. The same happened in the fifth century. Every reduction in the income either of private individuals or of the cities led to the disappearance of many features of the classical municipal system.

Theodoret of Cyrrhus described in his letters the arrival in the East in 439 of noble Carthaginian refugees, who had fled from the Vandal invaders.[1] Vandalic warriors who had seized the estates of these aristocrats in Africa Proconsularis had no intention of taking their place as defenders of a civic tradition which was totally foreign to them. Genseric certainly retained many Roman administrative institutions, considering them effective instruments for the government of his kingdom, but he never evinced any concern for the classical tradition itself, as Theodoric later did in Ostrogothic Italy. Vandal rule undoubtedly brought about the rapid and drastic decline, not of the towns themselves, but of the classical municipal system. The literary and epigraphic evidence for the Vandal period has nothing to say on this topic, and this silence may itself be taken as proof of a profound change. In the Byzantine period the typical African town huddled around a fortress and some churches, which had often been built with stones taken from ancient public monuments. We are now far from the world of the classical city, although reminders of it are sometimes to be found. An instance is afforded by an inscription, recently discovered by D. Pringle and published by J. Durliat, from Aïn-Djelloula (the ancient Cululis) in Byzacena. On this inscription, which dates to the years 539–44, a Byzantine official declares that, after the defeat of the Moors, he has restored the town on the orders of the patrician Solomon, returning to it 'census, stability, citizens, law, walls and lists of magistrates' (*censuram, statum, ciues, ius, moenia, fastus*).[2]

---

[1]   Theodoret of Cyrrhus, *Letters* 1.23; 2.29, 31, 33 (*SC* 40.94; 98.86, 90–2, 94). See also Victor Vitensis, *Historia persecutionis* 1.6 (*CSEL* 7.4, 23).
[2]   Durliat 1981, 37–42; Duval 1983, 167–70. On the site see Pringle 1981, 196–7. *Fastus* here probably implies merely that magistracies were revived.

Augustine had no wish to substitute the power of the church and the bishop for that of the state authorities, whether at imperial, provincial or municipal level. He regarded his own proper rôle as a form of patronage, and this led him to intervene with the authorities and the men of power for the protection of his congregation, particularly the poor, who were so easily oppressed (Markus 1970; Lepelley 1979, 389–408). Nevertheless, the church did undeniably come in various ways to take the place of the classical city. Two typical episcopal careers may serve to illustrate this process. Alypius, Augustine's disciple and friend, was a close relative of Romanianus, the rich leader, patron and benefactor of the city of Thagaste. Augustine describes Romanianus as a typical municipal aristocrat, popular thanks to his largesses, despite his undisputed local power and his enormous fortune. Alypius left for Italy, where he became a lawyer, thus escaping the municipal career which he did not want. Converted with Augustine in 386, he came back to Thagaste and lived with his master and their friends as a religious community. About 395, he became Bishop of his birthplace, Thagaste. Thus the family's leadership was carried on there, but in a new fashion.[1] Our second example comes from the Greek-speaking part of Africa. Synesius of Cyrene, born between 365 and 375, belonged to one of the leading families of the Pentapolis. He became a member of the council of Cyrene, and in 399 served as ambassador of the Pentapolis to the imperial court at Constantinople. In 410, the people of Ptolemais elected him as their bishop. His popularity as a brilliant and cultivated aristocrat had been enhanced first by the success of his embassy to Constantinople, where he had obtained a remission of taxes, then by the active part he took in organizing military resistance to invasion by the tribes of the Sahara (*PLRE* 2.1048–50, Synesius 1). It would seem, then, that the people of cities like Ptolemais felt that it was no longer now as magistrates, but as bishops that members of noble families, like Alypius and Synesius, could most effectively assume their traditional rôle of leadership and protection. There is an ambivalence in this process: on the one hand, the continuity by which local leadership remains with the aristocrats;

---

[1] Cf. Mandouze 1982, 53–65 and 994–7. On Romanianus as a benefactor see Augustine, *Contra Academicos* 1.2.

on the other, the radical change by which their power is exercised through a totally different institution. This marks a break with the classical city and the appearance of the episcopal city of the Middle Ages.[1]

This study has perhaps come to resemble the celebrated 'double discourses' of the Greek sophists, in which the cases for and against a proposition were argued with equal effectiveness. The argument of the second half of my paper is more orthodox, and might be considered the more convincing by a mediaevalist. Yet it cannot cancel out the argument presented in the first half, which constitutes a re-evaluation, prompted by archaeological discoveries of fundamental importance and confirmed by a large body of written evidence. We must, therefore, note and accept the co-existence of two realities: the survival of the classical city, and the slow emergence of new structures, which competed with it and very gradually took its place. The historian of Late Antiquity must take account of both these elements.[2]

Appendix: analogies and contrasts between Africa and the rest of the Roman world

Huge differences certainly existed from one city to another, and from one region to another. In Africa itself, a marked contrast can be observed between the eastern provinces of Proconsularis,

---

[1]   The development is well attested in fifth-century Gaul, where the best-known example is Sidonius Apollinaris, an Arvernian aristocrat who became Bishop of Clermont in 469 (cf. *PLRE* 2.115–8, Apollinaris 6). One may also add from the Africa of Augustine's day two unsavoury, but significant examples of brigand bishops, who acquired an illegal but absolute power: the Donatist Optatus of Timgad, who exercised a virtual tyranny there from 388 to 398 (Mandouze 1982, 797–802, Optatus 2; Lepelley 1981a, 471–3), and the Catholic Antoninus, who around 420 sacked his own see, the village of Fussala in the region of Hippo Regius (see no. 20* of the letters of Augustine recently discovered by J. Divjak, *BA* 46 B, 292–343).

[2]   I am very grateful to Wolfgang Liebeschuetz, Robert Markus, John Rich and Dick Whittaker for their comments on an earlier draft of this paper, and to John Rich for the English translation.

Byzacena and Numidia, which constituted the heartland of
Roman Africa, and the Mauretanias in the West. It would be
absurd to imagine that the situation reflected by the municipal
album of Timgad was repeated all over the Empire. Ammianus
(27.7) speaks of cities where not even three decurions could be
found. Late imperial laws envisage situations in which municipal
authorities were non-existent or had been reduced to insignificance (e.g. the eastern law of 415 cited in *CTh* 8.12.8). By contrast,
a law of Honorius passed in 397 rejoiced in the prosperity of the
African *curiae* 'rich in the desired number of decurions' (*CTh*
12.5.3).

The one region where one encounters a situation comparable to
that in Africa is peninsular Italy, above all Campania and
Samnium. There abundant epigraphic evidence bears witness to
the traditional magistracies, benefactions, extensive work on
public buildings, and the survival of ancient institutions (Lepelley,
forthcoming). In the East the situation is more complex. The
fulminations of the Church Fathers against the games and the
benefactors who gave them convey a very traditional picture of
civic life, but the epigraphic record is thin in this regard. This
emerges clearly from the Aphrodisias documents, which Charlotte
Roueché has so admirably edited. The epigraphic evidence for the
city's life is exceptionally rich for the Early Empire, but much
more limited thereafter. As a result, Aphrodisias' institutions and
activity in that period are poorly known, and eclipsed by the
governors of Caria, although the city remained populous and
flourishing. The same is true at Antioch, where Libanius' writings
certainly attest grave difficulties (e.g. *Or.* 48.3, according to which
the *boulē*, which formerly had six hundred members, numbered
no more than sixty in 381; cf. Petit 1955, 323; Liebeschuetz 1972).
Yet all archaeological studies show that Syria in the Late Roman
period enjoyed a level of prosperity comparable to that of Africa.
Allowance must be made for the vagaries of epigraphic fashion: it
is possible that in some regions the practice of commemorating
civic events on inscriptions was abandoned, without the resultant
silence having real significance. This possibility was canvassed by
Robert (1960), in a discussion of the passages in the Church
Fathers dealing with the city games and the benefactors who gave
them. Only a rigorous and systematic study of all the evidence on
city life in each part of the Empire would enable us to form a clear

picture of regional differences. The need for such a study was remarked, for the West, by Jones (1964, 1295).

Bibliography

Abbott, F. and Johnson, A. (1926), *Municipal Administration in the Roman Empire* (Princeton).

Alexander, M., Ennaifer, M., Dulières, C. and Besrour, S. (1973, 1974, 1976), *Corpus des mosaiques de Tunisie, Utique,* 3 vols (Tunis).

Anselmino, L., Panella, C., Santagelli, R. and Tortorella, S. (1986), 'Cartagine', in Giardina (ed.), iii.163–96.

Benabou, M. (1976), *La résistance africaine à la romanisation* (Paris).

Beschaouch, A., Hanoune, R. and Thébert, Y. (1977), *Les ruines de Bulla Regia* (Rome).

Birley, A.R. (1987), 'Some notes on the Donatist schism', *Libyan Studies* 18, 29–41.

Blanchard-Lemée, M. (1975), *Maisons à mosaïques du quartier central de Djemila (Cuicul)* (Aix-en-Provence).

Brown, P. (1972), *Religion and Society in the Age of Saint Augustine* (London).

Brown, P. (1978), *The Making of Late Antiquity* (Harvard).

Carandini, A. (1981), *Enciclopedia dell'arte antica, classica e orientale. Atlante delle forme ceramiche, I, Ceramica fine romana nel bacino mediterraneo (medio et tardo impero)* (Rome). (Includes contributions by C. Pavolini, L. Sagui, S. Tortorella and E. Tortorici.)

Carlsen, J. and Tvarnø, H. (1990), 'The Segermes valley archaeological survey (region of Zaghouan). An interim report', *L'Africa Romana* 7.2 (Convegno di 1989) (Sassari), 803–13.

Chastagnol, A. (1978), *L'album municipal de Timgad* (Bonn).

Chastagnol, A. and Duval, N. (1974), 'Les survivances du culte impérial en Afrique du Nord à l'époque vandale', *Mélanges William Seston* (Paris), 87–118.

Courtois, C. (1955), *Les Vandales et l'Afrique* (Paris).

Courtois, C., Leschi, L., Perrat, C. and Saumagne, C. (1952), *Tablettes Albertini, actes privés de l'époque vandale* (Paris).

Darmon, J.-P. (1980), *Nympharum Domus: les pavements de la maison des Nymphes à Neapolis (Nabeul, Tunisie) et leur lecture* (Leiden).

Durliat, J. (1981), *Les dédicaces d'ouvrages de défense dans l'Afrique byzantine* (Rome).

Duval, N. (1982a), 'L'urbanisme de Sufetula (Sbeitla)', *ANRW* 2.10.2.596–632.

Duval, N. (1982b), 'Topographie et urbanisme d'Ammaedara', *ANRW* 2.10.2.633–71.

Duval, N. (1983), 'L'état actuel de recherches sur les fortifications de Justinien en Afrique', *XXX Corso di Cultura sull'arte ravennate e bizantina* (Ravenna), 149–204.

Ennabli, A. (1986), 'Les thermes du thiase marin de Sidi-Ghrib (Tunisie)', *Monuments et Mémoires publiés par l'Académie des Inscriptions, Fondation Piot* 68 (Paris), 1–59.

Fentress, E. (1983), 'For ever Berber?', *Opus* 2, 161–75.

Fentress, E. and Perkins, P. (1987), 'Counting African Red Slip Ware', *L'Africa Romana* 5, 205–14.

Février, P.A. (1964), 'Notes sur le développement urbain en Afrique du Nord: les exemples comparés de Djemila et de Sétif', *Cahiers Archéologiques* 14, 1–26.

Frend, W.H.C. (1952), *The Donatist Church: A Movement of Protest in Roman North Africa* (Oxford).

Gascou, J. (1982), 'La politique municipale de Rome en Afrique du Nord. II, Après la mort de Septime Sevère', *ANRW* 2.10.2.230–320.

Giardina, A. (ed.) (1986), *Società romana e impero tardo antico*, 4 vols (Rome and Bari).

Green, W.M. (1951), 'Augustine's use of Punic', *Semitic and Oriental Studies presented to W. Popper, University of California Publications in Semitic Philology* 11, 179–90.

Hayes, J.W. (1972), *Late Roman Pottery* (London).

Hayes, J.W. (1980), *A Supplement to Late Roman Pottery* (London).

Hitchner, R.B. (1988), 'The Kasserine Archaeological Survey, 1982–6', *Antiquités Africaines* 24, 7–41.

Hitchner, R.B. (1990), with contributions by E. Ellis, A. Graham, L. Neuru and D. Mattingly, 'The Kasserine Archaeological Survey, 1987', *Antiquités Africaines* 26, 231–60.

Jacques, F. (1984), *La privilège de liberté. Politique impériale et autonomie municipale dans les cités de l'Occident romain (161–244)* (Rome).

Jacques, F. (1985), '*Genitalis curia*, l'hérédit du décurionat revendiquée dans une inscription de Numidie', *Zeitschrift für Papyrologie und Epigraphik* 59, 146–50.

Jones, A. H. M. (1964), *The Later Roman Empire* (Oxford).

Kajanto, I. (1963), *Onomastic Studies in the Early Christian Inscriptions of Rome and Carthage* (Helsinki).

Kajanto, I. (1965), *The Latin Cognomina* (Helsinki).

Kotula, T. (1974), 'Snobisme municipal ou prospérité relative: le statut des villes nord-africaines sous le Bas-Empire romain', *Antiquités Africaines* 8, 111–31.

Lassus, J. (1969), *Visite à Timgad* (Algiers).

Lassus, J. (1971), 'La maison à sept absides de Djemila (Cuicul)', *Antiquités Africaines* 5, 193–207.

Lepelley, C. (1967), 'Déclin ou stabilité de l'agriculture africaine au Bas-Empire? À propos d'un loi de l'empereur Honorius', *Antiquités Africaines* 1, 135–44.

Lepelley, C. (1979), *Les cités de l'Afrique romaine au Bas-Empire*: i, *La permanence d'une civilisation municipale* (Paris).

Lepelley, C. (1981a), *Les cités de l'Afrique romaine au Bas-Empire*: ii, *Notices d'histoire municipale* (Paris).

Lepelley, C. (1981b), 'La carrière municipale en Afrique romaine sous l'empire tardif', *Ktèma* 6, 333–47.

Lepelley, C. (forthcoming), 'Permanences de la cité classique et archaïsmes municipaux en Italie au Bas-Empire', *Mélanges d'histoire de l'Antiquité tardive offerts à A. Chastagnol* (Rome).

Leschi, L. (1948), 'L'album municipal de Timgad et l'*ordo salutationis* du consulaire Ulpius Mariscianus', *Revue des Études Anciennes* 50 (1948), 73–100.

Liebenam, W. (1900), *Städteverwaltung im römischen Kaiserreich* (Leipzig).

Liebeschuetz, W. (1972), *Antioch: City and Imperial Administration in the Later Roman Empire* (Oxford).

Lucas, C. (1940), 'Notes on the *curatores rei publicae* of Roman Africa', *Journal of Roman Studies* 30, 56–74.

Mahjoubi, A. (1978), *Recherches d'histoire et d'archéologie* à Henchir El-Faouar (Tunisie): la cité des Belalitani Maiores (Tunis).

Mahjoubi, A. (1984), 'La cité des Belalitani Maiores: exemple de permanence et de transformation de l'urbanisme antique', *L'Africa Romana* 1, 63–71.

Mandouze, A. (ed.) (1982), *Prosopographie chrétienne du Bas-Empire* i, *Afrique* (Paris).

Marcillet-Jaubert, J. (1968), *Les inscriptions d'Altava* (Aix-en-Provence).

Marcillet-Jaubert, J. (1979), 'Coloni loci Legum Maiorum', *Epigraphica* 41, 70–2.

Marcillet-Jaubert, J. (1987), 'Sur des *flamines* perpetuels de Numidie', *Zeitschrift für Papyrologie und Epigraphik* 69, 207–23.

Markus, R.A. (1970), *Saeculum: History and Society in the Theology of Saint Augustine* (Cambridge).

Marrou, H.I. (1938), *Saint Augustin et la fin de la culture antique* (Paris). 2nd edn with the *Retractatio* (Paris), 1958.

Marrou, H.I. (1949), *Retractatio*, 1st edn (Paris).

Mattingly, D.J. (1988), 'Oil for export? A comparison of Libyan, Spanish and Tunisian olive oil production in the Roman Empire', *Journal of Roman Archaeology* 1, 33–56.

Mommsen, T. (1887–8), *Römisches Staatsrecht*, 3rd edn (Leipzig).

Panella, C. (1983), 'Le anfore di Cartagine: nuovi elementi per la ricostruzione dei flussi commerciali del Mediterraneo in et à imperiale romana', *Opus* 2, 57–75.

Panella, C. (1986), 'Le anfore tardoantiche: centri di produzione e mercati preferenziali', in Giardina (ed.), iii.253–69.

Petit, P. (1955), *Libanius et la vie municipale à Antioche au IVe siècle* (Paris).

Peyras, J. (1983), 'Paysages agraires et centuriations dans le bassin de l'oued Tine (Tunisie du Nord)', *Antiquités Africaines* 19, 209–53.

Pflaum, H.G. (1977), Intervention on 'L'usage du gentilice dans l'élite sociale de langue latine au Bas-Empire', in *Actes du colloque 'L'onomastique latine'* (Paris), 435.

Pringle, D. (1981), *The Defence of Byzantine Africa from Justinian to the Arab Conquest*, BAR Int. Ser. 99.1–2 (Oxford).

Robert, L. (1960), '*Tropheus* et *Aristeus*', *Hellenica* 11–12, 569–76.

Rostovtzeff, M. (1957), *The Social and Economic History of the Roman Empire*, 2nd edn (Oxford).

Roueché, C. (1989), *Aphrodisias in Late Antiquity* (London).

Shaw, B.D. (1980), 'Archaeology and knowledge: the history of the African provinces of the Roman Empire', *Florilegium* 2, 28–60.

Shaw, B.D. (1983), 'Soldiers and society: the army in Numidia', *Opus* 2, 133–60.

Tortorella, S. (1986), 'La ceramica fine da mensa africana dal IV al VII secolo d. C.', in Giardina (ed.), iii.211–25.

Warmington, B.H. (1954), *The North African Provinces from Diocletian to the Vandal Conquest* (Cambridge).

Whittaker, C.R. (1978), 'Land and labour in North Africa', *Klio* 40, 331–62.

Zevi, F. and Tchernia, A. (1969), 'Amphores de Byzacène au Bas-Empire', *Antiquités Africaines* 3, 173–214.

∞ **3** ∞

Christianity and the city in Late Roman Gaul

Jill Harries

Despite the ravages of the third-century barbarian invasions and only partial recovery in the fourth century, cities, *civitates*, in fifth-century Gaul were still the main centres for the activities of local careerists and Christian leaders. The spread of Christianity in Gaul caused profound changes in the physical appearance of cities, which reflected both the emerging power of a new Christian élite and a shift in the identities of cities themselves. But despite the transformation of the urban landscape brought about by new church buildings, elements of continuity with the past remained. Bishops expressed a city's Christian identity often in terms of its past glories or present secular status. At Arles, for example, newly elevated to the status of provincial capital in 407 (Chastagnol 1973), a series of bishops sought, with mixed success, to assert a corresponding pre-eminence in the ecclesiastical sphere (Griffe 1966, 146–64). Conversely, for cities without secular status or economic power, the problems of decline or political impotence could be alleviated by the acquisition of the relics of saints or the skilful promotion of a local dead bishop, such as Martin of Tours (d. 397) or Germanus of Auxerre (d. 448).

Cities in Gaul should not be envisaged as homogeneous entities. Differences of geography precluded uniformity: for example, the *civitates* of Narbonensis I with their great urban centres and extensive territories, such as Narbonne, Béziers or Nîmes, could not but differ profoundly in social environment and economic opportunities from the tiny valley *civitates* of the Alpes Maritimes (Février 1977, 318). Such considerations also prevented equality of opportunity among bishops, as clearly bishops of the provincial capital at Narbonne had a better chance of achieving eminence and reputation than products of obscure mountain settlements like Barcelonnette or Glandève (Alpes Maritimes).

Moreover, the nature of the laity to which the bishop was answerable was determined by a city's character as port town, route centre, university city or administrative capital, and his response to them would have varied accordingly. In ways now largely lost to us, the laity must have ensured (despite the formal power of the clergy in elections) that they got the bishop they deserved, and the bishop in return would have reflected their aspirations – and exerted control when necessary. The supreme political skills and sometimes abrasive strength of character of Hilary of Arles (428–49), for example, were ideally suited to handling the proud prefects and imperial courtiers who crowded into his churches, as well as to subduing bishops who challenged his authority as metropolitan. By contrast, others compensated for secular decline and military threat by a flair for publicity. Euphronius, Bishop of the remote city of Autun, counteracted the terminal decline of its once famous school of rhetoric by literary promotion of his obscure local martyr, Symphorian, while Perpetuus of Tours, whose city was under threat from the Goths in Aquitaine to the south and the Franks to the north, used the talents of gifted friends to relaunch the cult of St Martin in the 460s, thus provoking a counter-offensive in support of Germanus of Auxerre in the late 470s. Local patriotism and the urge to substitute a positive Christian status for an increasingly doubtful secular standing combined with real Christian piety to promote saints and, with them, the cities with which they were most closely identified.

Given the wide disparities between one *civitas* and another, what made one urban centre and its surrounding territory a *civitas*, and another not? Under the Early Empire, the answer would have been simple: the existence of a *curia* and *civitas* magistrates. But even then, petitioners for *civitas* status would be likely to mention other features, such as water-supply, fertile territory, or splendid buildings, including city walls, which proved that the settlement could exist independently. It was presumably such criteria as these which procured the elevation of Grenoble and Geneva to *civitas* status at some point in the fourth century; they had hitherto been *vici* dependent on Vienne.

By the sixth century there was a connection between the presence of a bishop and the idea of a *civitas*. In practice, bishops in Gaul had been established in *civitates* first, and by the time of Gregory of Tours in the late sixth century it was natural to assume that *civitates* would, by definition, be places with bishops, although that was not invariably the case. But when Gregory (*Hist. Franc.* 3.19) considered the case of Dijon, a *castrum* dependent on Langres and without a bishop of its own, the reasons for his belief that it should be a *civitas* are similar to those advanced for elevation to *civitas* status under the Roman Empire: it had a large and fertile plain, several rivers, an impressive city wall thirty feet high and fifteen thick, and vineyards, the produce of which put the wines of Chalons-sur-Saône to shame. But Gregory, of course, was not concerned with Dijon receiving a *curia* but a bishop, and his priorities, although 'Roman' in a Christian sense, were not those of the Roman Empire.

The Changing City

In the aftermath of severe economic difficulties in some areas in the late second century and the Germanic invasions of the mid- to late third century, the physical structure of many cities underwent drastic alteration. At Lyon, for example, the upper city was gradually abandoned, perhaps because the four aqueducts which supplied water to the plateau through lead piping were plundered and fell into disuse (Audin 1956, 161–3). But the most striking general change was the creation, for many *civitates* and some other strong points as well, of walls with short circuits enclosing comparatively small areas. Some cities, such as Tours on the Loire, had never been fortified under the Early Empire, while others had built themselves long and impressive circuits: the early imperial wall of Vienne had a length variously estimated at between 5 and 7.3 km (Blanchet 1907, 145; Pelletier 1982, 104). By the end of the third century, fortified *castra* had become increasingly common. At Tours the inhabited centre under the Early Empire comprised, probably, some 30 ha and the *suburbium* perhaps twice as much again (Pietri 1983, 340); but the late imperial *castrum* covered a mere 9 ha, with a wall measuring 1.5 km (ibid., 344). At Vienne the fourth-century *castrum* on the 'colline de Pipet' had a wall reckoned to be 1.92 km long, enclosing some 36 ha, less than a fifth of the area fortified under the Early Empire (Pelletier 1974, 50–3).

The new, small *castra* do not in themselves prove a decline in population, although that may have been the case; on one assessment, the population of Tours may have dropped from about six thousand in the second century AD to some two thousand in the fourth (Boussard 1948, 328). Not all the urban dwellers who remained would have been housed within the *castrum* and, although evidence for fourth-century occupation is unevenly dispersed, there are scattered indications of continuing settlement outside the fortified areas. But many Gauls, none the less, would have passed their lives among the ruins of a more opulent past. Ammianus Marcellinus' (15.11.12) report of Avenches (Aventicum) as 'a *civitas* now abandoned but of no small distinction in former days, as the buildings, though half-ruined, even now testify' says nothing of people still living there, but in the 380s it still featured in the official list of provinces and cities (Harries 1978, 36), even though it may not have rated a bishop at that time.

Appreciation of the significance of this transformation of the physical city is essential for grasping the relationship of Christianity to the *civitas*. The city of the pagan past was often one of crumbling, disused walls and neglected monuments, ready to be remoulded by church-building bishops. For the inhabitants of many of these reduced urban centres there was no guarantee that prosperity could be rebuilt in a stable or secure environment. The effect of the third-century Germanic invaders on material prosperity and psychological security in some areas was underlined by continuing raids on the exposed eastern frontier regions in the fourth century and, in the fifth, by settlements of federate Goths in Aquitaine from 418, Burgundians in the Geneva area and later in the Rhône corridor from 443, and Franks progressively over the whole north. Although usually in name allies of Rome and often with close personal ties with Gallo-Roman aristocrats, the Germanic kings controlled what were *de facto* autonomous, and often threatening, political and military powers. To a laity feeling itself under threat, bishops could offer the other-worldly permanence of the *civitas Dei*, combined with a range of religious activities (with buildings to match) designed to underscore the power of the Church in the *civitas* of this world.

By contrast with new religious edifices, to which we shall turn in more detail later, we hear far less from the sources about what should have been more pressing needs, the building or upkeep of city walls, drains, streets or, where applicable, aqueducts. What seems to us essential was apparently peripheral to the writers of the time and the builders. However, it could be argued that our perceptions are distorted by the accidents of source survival. The social viewpoints offered us are mainly those of the priest Salvian, a native of north-eastern Gaul who migrated to Lérins and Marseille; of the prefect-turned-bishop, Sidonius Apollinaris; and, from over a century later, of Gregory of Tours. Naturally these, along with the other, lesser, literary works of churchmen or devout laymen, tend to emphasize what chiefly concerned them, namely the achievements of bishops, churches and the relics and celebration of saints. But churches, necropoleis and Christian inscriptions, usually funerary, predominate in the archaeological evidence too. The change in the physical appearance, and with it the very function, of the city was real.

Silence about city walls need not mean that they were allowed to fall into disrepair. The Huns were held up at Orleans in 451 long enough for the Roman army to arrive and raise the siege; and the walls of Sidonius' Clermont were adequate to withstand a series of Gothic sieges between 471 and 474, despite being in a semi-ruinous state (or so Sidonius claimed). The fortifications of the *castra*, the enclosed strong-points in the urban centres, aimed at being functional, not prestigious, and much of their financing, even when the central power was available to help, may have been local. The standard practice, under the Empire, seems to have been for walls to be financed partly by imperial grant and partly by local funds and labour (Ward-Perkins 1984, 193-4). However, in north-eastern Gaul the imperial presence would have been felt, in the fourth century, mostly at Trier and therefore perhaps comparatively little elsewhere. Certainly the scale of construction and maintenance at Trier, where an area of 285 ha was enclosed by a circuit 6 km in length dating from not later than the mid-third century (Wightman 1970, 92-8), was vastly different from that found elsewhere. These splendid walls suited the convenience and status of the imperial court in residence at Trier, but its withdrawal at the end of the fourth century left the Treveri with walls which were impressive, but indefensible by the remaining population; four recorded sacks by barbarian peoples followed in quick succession. Short city walls were better adapted to military and economic realities and their upkeep was probably continual, but unobtrusive. But, if the sources do reflect a broader social reality, credit and prestige went to the builders of churches, not the maintainers of walls.

City topography and episcopal power

The physical alteration in the appearance of the urban centres and the prevailing, if sporadic and regional, insecurity, combined with the decreasing effectiveness of Roman rule from Italy in the fifth century, offered opportunities for Christian leaders. But the situation of bishops could also be precarious. As learned Gauls knew, Christianity was late in arriving in Gaul (Sulpicius Severus, *Chron.* 2.32) and the episcopal organization of the Gallic provinces in 314, the date of the First Council of Arles, was widespread but superficial. Thereafter the number of bishops steadily increased but the rate of increase depended heavily on local circumstances. In some areas it is possible to detect expansion resulting from bishops' responses to an imperial initiative: for example in Valentinian I's newly recreated province of Narbonensis II and the neighbouring province of the Alpes Maritimes, new metropolitan sees were created at Aix-en-Provence and at Embrun, the provincial capital of the Alpes Maritimes, and various other sees may have been created in the area at the same time (Palanque 1949 and 1951). However, the powers of bishops and opportunities to expand church organization depended more on individual initiatives by such bishops as Martin of Tours, or Victricius of Rouen, who actively evangelized not only within his own province but also, presumably with the co-operation of other bishops, outside it (Harries 1978, 30–1). The importance in practice of local initiatives meant that the distribution of sees in Gaul was probably uneven throughout the fourth and fifth centuries, especially in the north. Although the evidence is disputable and full of pitfalls, the episcopal organization of the north which continued into the Middle Ages seems to have been largely the creation of the church under the Merovingians in the sixth and seventh centuries. There the prosperity even of Trier had declined steeply by the late fifth century (Gauthier 1980, 136–8), although it was to revive in the sixth, and other, lesser settlements found it hard to maintain continuity at all. While it is true that continuity on a site seems to have been best ensured by the previous existence of a church and a bishop, some form of economic base and fortifications (Wightman 1977, 308), there are many sees for which no bishop is attested before the early seventh century. One suspects that in many parts of the Frankish kingdom the survival or re-establishing of bishoprics would have been the work of dominant individuals.

By contrast, in the Mediterranean south and the Rhône corridor, Rome had been a presence since the second century BC, when the colony of Narbo was founded in *c*. 120; citizens from Narbonensis, such as Valerius Asiaticus from Vienne, Sex. Afranius Burrus from Vaison and Domitius Afer from Nîmes, had taken a prominent part in Roman imperial politics and public life, and under the Later Empire family links between southern Gaul and northern Italy were numerous and strong. In this area, Christianity was able to take root by the mid-second century, at Lyon and Vienne and probably at other points along trade-routes from the east. Lyon in particular was to benefit from the fact of an early foundation: she acquired martyrs of her own in 177, whose sufferings were broadcast to other churches through the letter on the subject preserved, and publicized, in Eusebius' *Ecclesiastical History*; and her late second-century bishop, Irenaeus, won a reputation of a different kind as a champion against heretics. Both the martyrs and Irenaeus were conspicuous presences in Lyon cult in the fifth century.

Southern Gaul in the fifth century had one further advantage: the barbarian presence was less intrusive. The resultant comparatively greater political and economic stability enabled the leaders of Christian communities in the south to expand their influence through building and the encouragement of new monastic and liturgical activity. How effectively this was done depended on the personality, energy and commitment of each individual bishop. Many a prominent bishop – Eucherius and Patiens at Lyon,

Mamertus at Vienne and Perpetuus at Tours – turned his personal rôle to serve the interests both of his own city and of the Gallic churches as a whole.

That personal rôle was played out in the context of the particular situation and character of a city and its relationships with other cities. Vienne, some 30 km south of Lyon in the Rhône valley, is a case in point. In pre-Roman times Vienne was the capital of the Allobroges and under the Empire it became the main urban centre of a large *territorium* extending from the middle valley of the Rhône to the shores of Lake Geneva and encompassing the lesser settlements of Geneva and Grenoble (Remy 1970). But the story of the city in the late fourth and fifth centuries is one of political decline. Geneva and Grenoble went their own ways, even acquiring bishops of their own, and from 407 onwards Arles was the dominant city by virtue of its new status as the seat of the Gallic prefecture.

In the first part of the fifth century secular rivalries found expression in the ecclesiastical sphere, as both Vienne and Arles claimed hegemony over the cities of the province still called Viennensis. At the Council of Turin (398 or 417, probably the latter), the secular province of Viennensis was split for ecclesiastical purposes between Arles and Vienne, with the latter retaining control over her historical dependencies, Geneva and Grenoble, and two other cities. But bishops of Arles, most notably Hilary (428–49) and his successor Ravennius, continued to expand their influence and in 450 the metropolitan rights of Vienne were again restricted by papal decree.

Nor was Arles the only rival. The tension between the cities of Lyon and Vienne was long-standing and perhaps inevitable, given their proximity and the contrast in character between a city whose prosperity was based on a large territory, and a commercial centre with a small territory, a large immigrant population and wealth based on trade (although Lyon also had an influential landowning aristocracy, which included Sidonius' family with their country estates and town house, and the consular family of the Syagrii). In ecclesiastical terms the rivalry reasserted itself in the fifth century, when Eucherius of Lyon (434–48) began to take an active interest in the Vienne dependency Geneva. There, he muscled in with a literary celebration of the martyrs of Agaune, who were rightfully the property of Geneva: this may have been with the consent and

even at the invitation of the bishop, Isaac, who received a
courteous mention in Eucherius' preface, and who may have
lacked the literary talent to do the job himself, but it was clear that
Eucherius intended to be the patron anyway. In 440 or earlier,
Eucherius' sway over Geneva was confirmed with the consecration
as bishop there of his son, Salonius. The ties continued into the
sixth century, when we find members of the same senatorial
family, Florentinus and his son Nicetius, being consecrated
bishops in respectively Geneva and Lyon.

These manoeuvres contained elements of co-operation as well
as competition. The influence of Lyon had expanded due to the
efforts of Eucherius but it was still possible for the rivals to
combine as patron cities of an historical dependent-city. One
indication of the harmony that could coexist with rivalry emerges
from the dedications of Salvian's literary works: as tutor to
Salonius, Salvian dedicated to him his work, *On the Government
of God (De Gubernatione Dei)*; and his *Commentary on
Ecclesiastes* Salvian offered to Salonius' metropolitan, Claudius
of Vienne.

Faced with a challenge that came, not in the first instance
from barbarians, but from friendly competitors in the shape of
other bishops, the Christian leaders of Vienne responded from
the late fourth century on with the creation of a sort of rampart
of saints, at once a source of protection and a focus for pilgrimage and devotion. Because of the continuity of occupation
on the site from antiquity to the Middle Ages – a continuity
which applies to most cities in modern France – certainty from
archaeological evidence is difficult and the picture is further
complicated by the fact that many cults are not attested before
the Middle Ages, although they may have originated earlier. It is
clear that, from the late fourth century on, a number of sites for
burial *ad sanctos*, close to the relics of saints, were developed
outside the city walls (i.e. the walls of the *castrum*) with sacred
buildings to match, although not much is known about them
(Pelletier 1974, 66–89; Descombes 1978). South-east of the city
was the *memoria* of the Milan martyrs, Gervasius and Protadius,
present thanks to Ambrose of Milan and a coterie of Gauls,
which included Martin of Tours, Victricius of Rouen and the
senatorial ascetic, Paulinus of Nola (Paul. Nol., *Ep.* 18): this is
known from the burial inscription of Foedula (*CIL* XII, 2115),

whom Martin had baptized. South-west of the Late Roman wall
was the basilica of the Apostles, later abbreviated to St Pierre,
which was probably the main church in the 'episcopal complex'
and which was the burial church for bishops from Mamertus on.
To the north there was another basilica which, according to a
later tradition, was dedicated to St Stephen, the first martyr, by
the priest Severus; the same tradition refers to Severus' foundation of an oratory to St Laurence. The existence of these cults at
Vienne in the fifth century is plausible, as both are attested
elsewhere and the spread of the cult of Stephen, as the first
martyr, was especially wide. Two other cults, also only attested
late, may have arrived at this time: Blandina, one of the Lyon
martyrs, would have been a natural early import from Lyon; and
Romanus had received a poem from Prudentius early in the fifth
century (*Peristephanon* 10), which celebrated him as a peculiarly
garrulous martyr (who continued to confess the faith even after
his tongue had been cut out). The existence of Laurence,
Blandina and Romanus is not, however, supported by any
archaeological evidence.

The activities of the Christian builders also extended to within
the late Roman walls. In the south-west corner of the *castrum*
was built, probably in the fifth century, a small, apparently
rectangular church measuring some 23 m by 16 m (75 ft × 52 ft).
This move from the suburbs, where Christian structures were
usually erected, to the very core of the city symbolized the
change in status of the now dominant religion. It was, in every
sense, no longer peripheral. And the presence of Christianity
within the *castrum* was further asserted, probably at some point
in the fourth or late fifth century, with the conversion of the
former temple of Augustus and Livia into a church.

There was also one further site, with which Mamertus of
Vienne (460s–470s) was especially associated. This was the burial
place of the martyrs Ferreolus and Julian of Brioude, which lay
to the north-west of Vienne and was reached by crossing the
Rhône, and proceeding northward along the Lyon road on the
west bank. An earlier structure dedicated to Ferreolus had been
too close to the river and had been undermined by the current.
Mamertus built a new basilica, which has been partly excavated
(Reynaud 1978). It was some 50 m long by 18.5 m wide (163 ft ×
60 ft) and had a large apse to the east and a single nave.

Mamertus, who, as we shall see, was a liturgical innovator, would clearly have made the most of processions from the city to the site to honour the cult. The presence of Julian of Brioude, by rights the property of Clermont, well illustrates the combination of competition and co-operation which featured in episcopal relations. Sidonius Apollinaris wrote, as Bishop of Clermont, to Mamertus in 473 (*Ep.* 7.1) to tell him how he had taken over Mamertus' idea of the Rogations, at Mamertus' suggestion. This, wrote Sidonius, was only his due, as Mamertus had 'translated' (from the old basilica to the new) the whole body of Ferreolus 'with the addition of the head of our Julianus'. The Arverni of Clermont therefore 'demand as compensation' that 'a share of patronage' should come from Mamertus, seeing that 'a share of our patron' had gone to him. Sidonius does not accuse Mamertus of stealing the relic but he makes clear that Julian was a possession of Clermont and that Mamertus' acquisition of Julian's head had put him in Sidonius debt. At the same time, however, Sidonius made no attempt to recover the relic and clearly felt that acquiescence was likely to prove more profitable than confrontation.

Many other cities in Gaul for which the evidence is available witnessed a similar explosion of church-building in the late fourth and fifth centuries. At Lyon, a church dedicated, like that at Vienne, to the Maccabees, dates from before the early fifth century, when the first burials *ad sanctos* are attested (Le Blant 1856, 41 and 53). Another church seems to have been dedicated to St Stephen by an obscure bishop, Alpinus, in the 420s (Reynaud 1973). Sidonius was commissioned to write a wall poem for yet another church, this one built by Patiens in the 460s within hailing distance of the Rhône (Sidonius, *Ep.* 1.10.5, *Carm.* 28–30). Outside the walls to the south was raised the church of St Laurence at Choulans in the late fifth or early sixth century (Reynaud 1976): St Laurence's cult we have already seen perhaps paralleled at Vienne, and he is known certainly to have received churches at Tours in the mid-fifth century and Clermont slightly later (Gregory of Tours, *Hist. Franc.* 2.20).

Lyon also shows the development of episcopal cult in its early stages, perhaps resulting from the fact that Lyon had a longer episcopal history than most Gallic cities could reliably claim. Bishop Iustus, who abandoned his flock at Lyon in the 380s to become an ascetic in Egypt, was brought back in death to Lyon and interred in the church of the Maccabees, which soon began to be called that of St Just. Similarly the two Lyon martyrs Epipodius and Alexander, whose relics were housed in a church which had once been a pagan shrine, found themselves supplanted in the titulature of their resting place by the second-century bishop Irenaeus, who had been laid to rest beside them (Coville 1928, 445–64). The growth in the popularity of local (dead) bishops as recipients of cult can be ascribed partly to local patriotism and partly to the growing prominence of living bishops in the life of the city.

This explosion of building and cultic activity at Lyon was part of a general trend, but there were, as at Vienne, special reasons for bishops to show an interest in building up the status of their city as a Christian centre. Under the Early Empire the secular Lugdunum had been the capital of the Three Gauls, meeting-place of the provincial council and centre of the imperial cult. In the aftermath of the Severan destruction in 197 and the economic difficulties of the third century, the prosperity of Lyon declined steeply, while the division of Lugdunensis into two provinces and later into four left Lyon only a small province to dominate, as seat of both governor and metropolitan bishop. Underlying the assertion of the importance of Lyon in church politics would have been a consciousness of leadership in the past which encouraged bishops to aim for primacy in the future, although that aim was not to be achieved in full until the ninth century.

In other cities, however, bishops were motivated less by the past than by the need to exploit existing Christian resources to enhance the position of their cities in relation to the rest. At Tours, the local resource was St Martin, whose cult had been somewhat neglected by his immediate successor, Brictius. Bishop Perpetuus (c. 458–88) more than compensated for this with the building of a new church to St Martin, an edifice of great splendour, which was described by Gregory of Tours (*Hist. Franc.* 2.14). It was 160 ft long, 60 ft wide and, to the vaulting, 45 ft high. It had fifty-two windows, with thirty-two in the sanctuary and twenty in the nave, 120 columns and eight doors. Within it was adorned with inscriptions composed by the best available Gallic literary talents, Sidonius and Paulinus of

Périgueux. Around the basilica on three sides was an enclosure or *atrium*, which, like the church itself, afforded sanctuary and also, by Gregory's time, housed other buildings, including the bishop's *salutatorium*, the treasury, a baptistery, a convent, a little cell belonging to a priest called Winnocus and an *oratorium* (Pietri 1983, 390–405). The size of Perpetuus'‚church may be compared usefully with the cathedral church of Clermont built within the city walls a few years earlier by Bishop Namatius (*Hist. Franc.* 2.16): the Clermont church, we are told, was 150 ft long (Perpetuus passed this by 10 ft), 60 ft wide and 50 ft high and was designed in the shape of a cross with 70 columns (there were 120 at Tours), 42 windows (52 at Tours), and, as at Tours, 8 doors. While we cannot assume that Perpetuus was deliberately trying to build a bigger church than had Namatius (there may have been other standards of comparison unknown to us now), it is worth noting that the dimensions of both churches are comparable with the basilica to St Ferreolus at Vienne, although there is no known link between them.

Between the third and fifth centuries, then, the appearance of cities in Gaul was changed in two fundamental respects. One was the creation of central defensible areas enclosed by walls, although areas outside the walls probably continued to be inhabited. The second was an apparent cessation of most monumental building, with the single and conspicuous exception of churches. This does not mean that the clergy, who were tied to the urban centre by the rules of the church, became the sole inhabitants of cities; at the very least they would have required support from the produce of traders and craftsmen, stonemasons and mosaic workers, weavers of vestments and makers of oil lamps, as testified by the recent discoveries at Vienne of a glass-worker's shop and a potter's workplace, the latter in the by-then-disused parascaenium of the Odeon (Pelletier 1988, 36, 47–8). But the fact that the only new buildings of any size to meet the eye in a fifth-century city were churches indicated a change in the nature of cities which was not simply a matter of topography. Church buildings represented the power of the Christian establishment, but they were also there to be used. The change was in not only the outer world of the buildings of the city but the inner world of the citizen.

Bishop, city and liturgy

The bishop was obliged to reside in the urban centre, where church-building was concentrated and where the main liturgical festivals took place. Attendance at these had to be maximized and episcopal efforts to ensure a large turn-out drew country dwellers back to the centre and provided an important counterweight to what Sidonius saw as the general aristocratic tendency to reside in villas in the countryside. Clearly piety on rural estates could not be overtly discouraged, but centrifugal tendencies on the part of lay landowners had to be resisted. Sidonius was keen to get his own friends off their estates and into church and was able to make a special plea for the Rogations, a penitential rite copied from Mamertus of Vienne, for which, he claimed, his congregation displayed an unprecedented degree of attention and enthusiasm (*Ep.* 5.14). He also applied the same rule to the clergy, castigating two acquaintances among the Vienne clergy for spending more time on their 'suburban' estates than in 'cultivating' the Church (*Ep.* 7.15). The remoteness of some lay aristocrats from their bishop may explain why, when a fire and other disasters broke out at Vienne, the common people, who lived in the city anyway, stayed and supported their bishop while their betters initially ran away (Sidonius, *Ep.* 7.1.6). In seeking to 'centralize' liturgical activity, bishops were of course acting in the interests of their own power; but they were also a reminder and a continuation of the tradition of a town-based administration derived from the Early Empire.[1]

In attracting the less prosperous to their festivals, bishops had a double advantage. One was that Christian processions were, in the absence of games, the best form of entertainment available. The other was the economic rôle of the Church. Bishops held the wealth of the Church 'in trust' for the 'poor of Christ' and were (in theory) obliged to redistribute it to the needy. That obligation ensured that the bishop could enjoy all the benefits of being a permanent patron of the city poor. Moreover, much of the wealth of the city was by then concentrated in the bishop's hands and his

---

[1]   This did not preclude some church-building in the countryside. A series of bishops of Tours built churches in villages (*Hist. Franc.* 10.31). Brictius built five, Eustochius four, and Perpetuus five, plus the church of St Laurence at Montlouis.

power to provide immediate relief at a time of disaster added an extra dimension to his authority at times of insecurity, invasion or natural disasters. When crops were burned in the Rhône valley in the early 470s, Patiens of Lyon released sufficient grain from his personal granaries to feed the population, not just of Lyon, but of many *civitates* in the Rhône valley (Sidonius, *Ep*. 6.12.5; Whittaker 1983, 177). The scale of that intervention may have been exceptional, but the economic power of the church provided the only available 'safety-net' for the city poor in times of dearth or crisis.

Thus within the setting of a city's internal politics, its identity and its history, bishops used their economic power and personal authority to formulate a city's Christian identity. In so doing, they progressively transformed the concepts and exercise of patronage (Ste Croix 1954; Rousseau 1976), that most Roman of activities, replacing traditional forms of civic munificence with Christian services to the city. This in turn caused the concept of 'Roman', which in the fifth century was still tied to the secular Empire, to evolve towards a closer and finally exclusive association with Roman Christianity. The ebbing of Roman control entailed not only the departure of governors and the administrative presence of Rome but the loss of other institutions associated with Rome, such as public games financed by the emperor. Early in the fifth century, as a response to crisis, which may have been exceptional, the nobles of Trier had appealed to the emperor to provide games for the city after one of its periodic sacks by barbarians. Salvian reported this request (*On the Government of God* 6.85) to illustrate the moral degeneracy of the Treveran aristocrats, but it has been suggested that they may have in fact have had a more respectable motive, that of proving to the emperor and to themselves that they were still 'Roman' (Ward-Perkins 1984, 106). But Christian views of Roman-ness could not, of course, include that form of munificence; and the Church, along with patrons among the laity, did not rely on imperial largesse for the performance of its services to the city.

The most public, and most effective, expression of a city's Christian identity lay in the Christian festivals of the liturgical year, ritual processions and acts of worship which focused on the sacred shrines and provided opportunities for virtuoso displays of episcopal rhetoric and other talents on a regular basis. Not much is known in detail about the Gallic Christian year; liturgical calendars were probably based on the celebrations of each individual city and were without universal application. But the liturgical year was designedly as crowded as possible. A list of vigils at Tours in the time of Perpetuus is supplied by Gregory, more than a century later (*Hist. Franc.* 10.31). There seem to have been sixteen vigils in all and the list included Christmas, Epiphany, Easter and Whitsun, celebrations of Peter and Paul, one extraneous local saint, Symphorian of Autun, episcopal cult for the probable first bishop, Litorius, and for Martin's successor, Brictius, and a considerable amount of celebration of St Martin himself. Not all the saints thus honoured had basilicas of their own to house the vigils, and the basilica of St Martin was used as a host for other recipients of cult, notably Symphorian, Brictius and Martin's spiritual guide, Hilary of Poitiers. Other known recipients of cult at Tours are not present on Gregory's list because they did not have official vigils, including Gervasius and Protadius, brought to Tours by St Martin from Italy and given a basilica by Perpetuus' predecessor, Eustochius (*Hist. Franc.* 10.31.5; *Glor. mart.* 46), and St Laurence, who received a basilica from Perpetuus himself. Nor were festivals centred only on basilicas: St Martin's cult was celebrated also at his monastery at Marmoutiers on the far bank of the Loire and the river barrier and absence of a permanent bridge seem to have proved no deterrent to regular processions to the site, perhaps across a temporary bridge of boats (Pietri 1983, 421–9). This close, and necessary, association of ritual procession and holy site is not, of course, unique to Gaul, but it is essential to the understanding of the relationship of Christianity to the city. Churches were not simply splendid new features of the local landscape, a public demonstration of ecclesiastical wealth, but were living centres of regular public worship, which concentrated on and invoked the presence and power of local saints. We do not know directly why ordinary members of bishops' congregations became Christian, but the incessant annual repetition of public honours to the city's heavenly patrons could not have failed to have had a psychological effect.

But repetition, while being reassuring, can also become tedious. Hence arose the need for innovation, and for the spectacularly staged special occasion. Public miracles, for example an exorcism by Germanus of Auxerre (418–48) (Constantius of Lyon, *Vit. Germ.* 28) or the extinguishing of a fire in the city by Mamertus of Vienne, who reportedly quelled the flames merely by walking towards them (Sidonius, *Ep.* 7.1.4), both broke the monotony and allowed for extra demonstrations of religious power and authority. Thus Mamertus exploited his miracle to underline the moral of the fire disaster, with attacks on sin and the advocacy of tears to prevent fires and faith to avert earthquakes. Earthquakes and fires were not predictable occurrences but they added to a doom-laden atmosphere in which episcopal exhortations to prayer and repentance could find a ready hearing. When Sidonius turned to express his appreciation of the effect of the Rogations, imitated from Mamertus' example, he admitted that he had had problems before. The few who turned up at services (he says) were unenthusiastic and sleepy, wandered out for meals and confined their prayers to conflicting petitions about the weather (*Ep.* 5.14.2). The Rogations, however, had brought about a striking improvement, which no doubt owed something to the looming threat of the Goths.

As we have seen, the physical structures which transformed the appearance of cities also provided the focus for the activities of the living church. But the Christianizing of attitudes was not only turned inwards. No picture of what made a city Christian in Gaul would be complete without a brief look at the diplomatic activity of the bishop abroad. Here too, just as cities were redefining themselves in Christian terms, so outside their boundaries, bishops took on the rôle of secular negotiators and thus contributed to the redefining of the wider world as 'Christendom'. As is well known, the time-honoured function of advocacy of non-religious interests of cities fell increasingly into bishops' hands. Most famous of episcopal diplomats was Germanus of Auxerre, who engaged in both secular and religious missions. As papal legate to Britain, he demolished the local Pelagians in debate (Constantius of Lyon, *Vit. Germ.* 14) and, through prayers and a well-timed battle-cry, the Saxons in battle (*Vit. Germ.* 17–18). As ambassador for the citizens of Auxerre he was to be found at different times at Arles before the prefect (*Vit. Germ.* 23–4) and, on his last mission, at Ravenna before the emperor's ministers (*Vit. Germ.* 38–40). Germanus is remembered now mainly through his *Life* by Constantius of Lyon, written some thirty years after his death, which portrayed him as the idealization of a type (Van Dam 1985, 147–8). Later traditions showing bishops as mediators between Roman and barbarian powers include accounts of Orientius of Auch as a go-between on behalf of the Goths (*Vit. Orient.* 3: *Acta Sanctorum* 1 May, p. 61) and a journey of Aravatius of Tongres (Gregory of Tours, *Hist. Franc.* 2.5) to Rome to beg for help against the Huns. These are paralleled by the contemporary evidence of the Spanish bishop Hydatius' embassy to Aëtius in 431 (Hydatius, *Chron.* 96) to complain about the Suevi, and the missions of Epiphanius of Pavia and, later, four south Gallic bishops in 474–5, which resulted in a treaty between Rome and the Goths. Most telling, however, is Sidonius' casual assumption that diplomatic activity was the norm and that previous experience of it was a good qualification for a potential bishop: Simplicius of Bourges had already had dealings on his city's behalf with 'skin-clad kings and purple-robed emperors' (Sidonius, *Ep.* 7.9.19).

A further element in the Christianization of cities and their ties with the other cities and provinces was the procuring of relics by bishops from their friends (Van Dam 1985, 165–72), usually by fair means, although, as we have seen in the case of Mamertus of Vienne and the head of St Julian noted above, this was not invariably so. At the point of the arrival of the relics in their new home, the profits gained from the private world of episcopal friendship were realized in public festival and celebration. If *adventus* of emperors, like their financing of local games, had become a thing of the past, the public arrival of a new relic, which brought with it the presence of a new patron saint, could be just as dramatic and more locally appealing – emperors always went away, while the relics stayed for good. When relics of two saints from Italy, Agricola and Vitalis, arrived from Bologna at Clermont, the Bishop, Namatius, led a procession out to the fifth milestone beyond the city to welcome the two saints, who promptly showed their power by a rain miracle (they remained miraculously dry during a downpour). The procession then returned to Clermont, where a new church to house the saints was dedicated in front of the assembled citizens (Gregory of Tours, *Glor. mart.* 43–4). It is fortunate for us that Gregory of Tours was well informed about traditions in some other cities as well as his own, as fifth-century accounts of the *adventus* of saints are rare, the exception being the *De Laude Sanctorum* (*In Praise of the Saints*) which describes the arrival of a parcel of relics at Rouen early in the fifth century (*PL* 20.448). But there can be no doubt that *adventus*-type ceremonies would have taken place every time a new saint arrived. Thus cities would both celebrate the advent of yet another protector and affirm their links with that part of the wider world from which the relic had come.

Trade in relics and liturgical innovation are not features confined to Gaul. Local ecclesiastical aristocracies used them to boost their own power and that of the church, certainly in Africa and probably in less well-documented provinces such as Spain, where similar conditions applied. But Gaul is an area where the interaction of the ebb of Roman power and influence with the growth in power of local 'Roman' churches can be clearly seen. When bishops felt the need to set their city's Christianity in a wider context, it was not that of the Roman Empire in any secular sense but of what would become 'Christendom'. For example, pairs of local saints could be assimilated to the Apostles Peter and Paul, with the suggestion that the local pair 'founded' the Christian city just as Peter and Paul 'founded' Christian Rome: two comparatively obscure martyrs at Lyon received this treatment in an anonymous fifth-century homily (Eusebius Gallicanus, *Hom.* 55.4). If it was a matter of comparing local martyrs with international saints, naturally the local prevailed: 'it is a great thing', wrote the anonymous author of the homily at Lyon, 'to pay our vows in public celebrations of saints whom all share; but we should regard as a still more glorious festival our rejoicing at the virtues of our own citizens. And thus we offer cult to the martyrs born here and honour to our special patrons' (ibid., 55.1). Even the Holy Innocents and Bethlehem could not compete with the Lyon martyrs of 177, notably Pothinus, 'our blessed father . . . bishop of this church' and 'my' Blandina, the local girl: 'you, [Bethlehem] perhaps excel in numbers [of martyrs], but I [Lyon] in their merits: yours were killed, but they were not confessors of the faith' (ibid., 11.3).

Conclusion

The Christianity of Gallic cities was assisted by the failure and gradual demise of the Roman political order in the fifth century, which made local populations more dependent on the city unit and its leaders, and concentrated economic and social, as well as religious, power in the hands of Christian bishops. Long-standing rivalries between cities found a new outlet in the competitive struggle for status in the church provincial hierarchy, the building of new churches and more impressive collections of holy relics, which in turn prompted extensive cultic activity. Bishops' initiatives on their own account and in co-operation with others helped in the creation of the idea of a Christian world populated by other Christians, martyrs and relics independent of the secular Roman state and no longer directly reliant on the continuation of the Western Empire. In 456, fourteen years before his own consecration, Sidonius Apollinaris had referred to secular Rome as the 'shadow of Empire'; it was largely due to the upper classes' translation of traditional obligations of leadership in the cities of Gaul into Christian terms that 'Rome' survived in the Christian Church.

Bibliography

Audin, A. (1956), *Essai sur la topographie de Lyon* (Lyon).

Blanchet, A. (1907), *Les enceintes romaines de la Gaule* (Paris).

Boussard, J. (1948), 'Étude sur la ville de Tours du Ier au IVe siècle', *Revue des Études Anciennes* 50, 313–29.

Chastagnol, A. (1973), 'Le repli sur Arles des services administratifs gaulois en l'an 407 de notre ère', *Revue Historique* 244, 305–14.

Coville, A. (1928), *Recherches sur l'histoire de Lyon du Vme siècle au IXme siècle (450–800)* (Paris).

Descombes, F. (1978), 'La topographie chrétienne de Vienne des origines à la fin du VIIe siècle', *Les Martyrs de Lyon (177)*, Colloques internationaux du CNRS 575 (Paris).

Février, P.A. (1977), 'Towns in the Western Mediterranean', in M.W. Barley (ed.), *European Towns, Their Archaeology and Early History* (London), 315–42.

Gauthier, N. (1980), *L'évangélisation des pays de la Moselle. La province romaine de Première Belgique entre Antiquité et Moyen Âge (IIIe–VIIIe siècles)* (Paris).

Griffe, E. (1966), *La Gaule chrétienne à l'époque romaine*, 2nd edn (Paris).

Harries, J. (1978), 'Church and State in the *Notitia Galliarum*', *Journal of Roman Studies* 68, 26–43.

Le Blant, E. (1856), *Inscriptions chrétiennes de la Gaule* i (Paris).

Palanque, J. (1949), 'Les premiers évêques d'Aix-en-Provence', *Analecta Bollandiana* 67, 377–83.

Palanque, J. (1951), 'Les évêchés Provençaux à l'époque romaine', *Provence Historique* 1/3, 105–43.

Pelletier, A. (1974), *Vienne gallo-romaine au Bas-Empire 275–469 après J.C.* (Lyon).

Pelletier, A. (1982), *Vienne antique* (Roanne).

Pelletier, A. (1988), 'Découvertes archéologiques et historiques à Vienne (France) de 1972 à 1987', *Latomus* 47, 34–52.

Pietri, L. (1974), 'Les tituli de la basilique Saint Martin édifiée à Tours par l'évêque Perpetuus (3e quart du Ve siècle)', *Mélanges d'histoire ancienne offerts à W. Seston*, 419–31.

Pietri, L. (1983), *La ville de Tours du IVe au VIe siècle: naissance d'une cité chrétienne*, Collection de l'École Française de Rome (Rome).

Remy, B. (1970), 'Les limites de la cité des Allobroges', *Cahiers d'histoire* 15/3, 195–213.

Reynaud, J.-F. (1973), 'Les fouilles de sauvetages de l'église Saint-Just et du group épiscopal de Lyon (églises Saint-Etienne et Sainte Croix)', *Comptes Rendues de l'Academie des Inscriptions*, 346–64.

Reynaud, J.-F. (1976), 'Fouilles récentes de l'ancienne église St-Laurent de Choulans à Lyon', *Comptes Rendues de l'Academie des Inscriptions*, 460–87.

Reynaud, J.-F. (1978), 'Saint-Ferréol, une des plus anciennes églises viennoises', *Archeologia* 122, 44–51.

Rousseau, P. (1976), 'In search of Sidonius the Bishop', *Historia* 25, 356–77.

Ste Croix, G.E.M. de (1954), '*Suffragium*: from vote to patronage', *British Journal of Sociology* 5, 33–48.

Van Dam, R. (1985), *Leadership and Community in Late Antique Gaul* (California).

Ward-Perkins, B. (1984), *From Classical Antiquity to the Middle Ages: Urban Public Building in Northern and Central Italy, AD 300–850* (Oxford).

Whittaker, C.R. (1983), 'Late Roman trade and traders', in P.

Garnsey, K. Hopkins and C.R. Whittaker (eds), *Trade in the Ancient Economy* (London), 163–80.

Wightman, E.M. (1970), *Roman Trier and the Treveri* (London).

Wightman, E.M. (1977), The towns of Gaul with special reference to the north-east', in M.W. Barley (ed.), *European Towns, Their Archaeology and Early History*, (London), 303–14.

4

The use and abuse of urbanism in the Danubian provinces during the Later Roman Empire

Andrew Poulter

Along the length of the Danubian frontier from Noricum to the Black Sea, the public and private monuments of Roman cities reflect increasing prosperity for the majority under the Antonines and, for some, little short of extravagant indulgence under the Severi. In their adoption of Roman forms of civic organization and their display of material wealth, cities in the hinterland of the Danube were remarkable for their rapid development during the second century AD. Three factors, in particular, encouraged urban development. The first was imperial interest. During each successive stage in the consolidation of the Danubian frontier, territory in the hinterland was released from military control and the responsibility for local administration and taxation was handed over to newly created cities. Whatever the higher motivation may have been behind the foundation of cities, there were obvious advantages for Rome: conferring municipal status transferred financial and administrative obligations to civilian communities at no cost to the imperial treasury. It is no coincidence that the periods of rapid urban development in the Claudian, Flavian and then Trajanic periods were also times during which the army advanced towards its permanent second-century bases on the right bank of the Danube. The process was further encouraged by Hadrianic reforms which granted municipal rank to existing settlements and official status to the growing extramural settle-

ments (*canabae*), many of which also acquired urban rank under
the Severi (Mócsy 1974, 218–21; Poulter 1983, 78–85). Secondly,
once established, the cities, *municipia* as well as *coloniae*,
attracted veterans from the legionary and auxiliary garrisons,
swelling the number of citizens with money to invest and the
status to assume curial office.[1] If imperial interest and the steady
influx of new citizens promoted the rapid development of the
Balkan cities, the new villa estates established within their territories must have profited from the proximity of a military market for
agricultural and industrial goods, providing landowners with the
wealth which financed the Antonine and Severan building pro-
grammes in the cities.[2]

   Until recently, archaeology has contributed little to our understanding of urbanism in the Later Roman Empire. Our perspective has been determined by ancient sources. Drawing upon the
literary and particularly legal evidence for Late Roman urbanism,
A.H.M. Jones concluded that the classical city survived in the
East as late as the reign of Justinian and, in the West, probably
even later (Jones 1964, 759–61). For Jones, the hallmark of the
classical city was the maintenance of local autonomy in the form
of curial administration and it was the very tenacity with which
cities clung to their civic institutions which demonstrated the
essential continuity between the cities of classical Greece and the
poleis of Justinian (Jones 1940, 251–8; 1964, 724; 1971, xii–xiii).
This conclusion has been supported by recent interpretations of
the archaeological evidence: although it is universally accepted
that the cities of the Balkans suffered destruction and economic
decline during the Gothic invasions of the third century, it has also

---

[1]   Even Black Sea cities seem to have acquired a new infusion of veteran
settlers from at least the Flavian period (Vulpe and Barnea 1968, 63–5).
Some cities in the eastern Balkans also acquired substantial numbers of
civilian immigrants, particularly artisans and craftsmen, from Asia Minor
(Poulter 1983, 94).
[2]   That villas were engaged in supplying the frontier garrisons is easier to
presume than to prove. However, cf. Italian traders on villa estates around
Lake Balaton (Mócsy, 1974, 124–5). The products of local pottery kilns
found an immediate market in the city of Nicopolis on the Lower Danube,
but this high-quality tableware also reached the Danubian frontier and the
valley of the Olt in Dacia Inferior (Poulter 1983, 89–90; Soultov 1983,
126).

been held as axiomatic that the Diocletianic reforms of army and administration revitalized cities throughout the Balkan provinces (Alföldy 1974, 198 and 205; Mócsy 1974, 297; Velkov 1977, 77–80). For the sixth century, a Justinianic revival of towns has been claimed, although admittedly, less widely accepted.[1] However, our literary sources are biased towards the Eastern Empire and, for the fourth century, as Jones admitted, there must have been marked differences between those cities where the curial class was able to raise imperial revenue and cover the cost of local public expenditure without resorting to burdensome levies from decurions in the form of liturgies, and those cities which could not (Jones 1964, 737). Where the curial class was subject to excessive taxation, it may be presumed that the decline of urban government would have rapidly followed.

Over the last two decades, research has yielded a considerable amount of new archaeological and epigraphic information which, if disparate and variable in quality, still offers a welcome supplement to the literary evidence. In the following discussion, particular attention will be paid to two principal characteristics of urban life, held by Jones to be pre-eminent and clearly present in the cities of the Early Empire: local autonomy and the vitality of urban communities, as expressed in the maintenance of urban institutions and the provision of public buildings. I shall examine first the character of cities in the hinterland of the Danube in the fourth century and then the evidence for sixth-century urbanism in the eastern Balkans. It will be argued that not only do Byzantine cities bear little resemblance to cities of the Early Empire, but that cities of the fourth century, from the Tetrarchy onwards, were very different in character from those of the first to third centuries and that their condition was markedly inferior to that of those cities of the Greek East which appear to have experienced difficulties but not terminal decline.

The hinterland of the Danube frontier comprised a broad band

---

[1] For the view that urbanism in the Balkans during the sixth century still preserved the essential character of the classical city see Velkov 1977, 77–82. However, it is now widely held that fundamental changes occurred during the fifth century and that the sixth-century city was very different from its classical predecesssor (e.g. Claude 1969, 156–7; Popescu 1975, 173–82; Dagron 1984, 1–19).

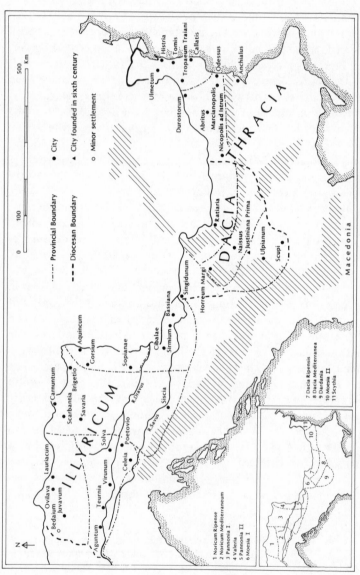

The Danubian Provinces during the Later Roman Empire

Provincial Boundary
Diocesan Boundary

● City
▲ City founded in sixth century
○ Minor settlement

0   100   500 km

N

Histria
Tomis
Tropaeum Traiani
Callatis
Ulmetum
Odessus
Anchialus
Durostorum
Abritus
Marcianopolis
Nicopolis ad Istrum

D A C I A
T H R A C I A

Ratiaria
Naissus
Justiniana Prima
Ulpianum
Scupi

Singidunum
Horreum Margi

Macedonia

Bassiana
Cibalae
Sirmium
Siscia

Aquincum
Gorsium
Sopianae

Carnuntum
Scarbantia Brigetio
Savaria
Solva
Poetovio
Celeia
Teurnia Virunum
Aguntum

Lauriacum
Ovilava
Bedaium
Juvavum

R. Dravus
R. Savus

I L L Y R I C U M

1 Noricum Ripense
2 Noricum Mediterraneum
3 Pannonia I
4 Valeria
5 Pannonia II
6 Moesia I

7 Dacia Ripense
8 Dacia Mediterranea
9 Dardania
10 Moesia II
11 Scythia

of territory, extending from Noricum Ripense in the north-west corner of the diocese of Illyricum through the diocese of Dacia to the province of Scythia at the north-east extremity of Thrace. The cities to be discussed are those which happen to provide appropriate evidence. Individually, these cities may be atypical, and the evidence, invariably incomplete, may not be truly representative of the city from which it derives. Archaeological dating for the fourth century is a particular problem: here 'Tetrarchic' is used to indicate a date in the late third or early fourth rather than towards the middle of the fourth century. Closer precision, in the current state of archaeological research, is rarely, if ever possible. There are further problems inherent in a general study. Cities vary considerably from region to region. For example, the Greek colonies on the Black Sea coast have little in common with the small *municipia* of Moesia or the large *municipia* of Noricum. Accordingly, for the fourth century, the cities will be discussed by region and further divided into groups where they appear to show general similarities. For the sixth century, since the number of sites discussed is much smaller, the evidence from each is described individually.

The fourth-century city

The cities of Noricum

During the second half of the third century, the cities of Noricum suffered a general economic decline which, no less than destruction levels, must have been caused, at least in part, by the Alamannic invasions (Alföldy 1974, 186). Under the Tetrarchy, the province was subdivided into Noricum Ripense and Noricum Mediterraneum, but the presumption that administrative and military reform promoted a revival of cities (ibid., 198) is less easy to substantiate. Repair and maintenance were carried out, if intermittently, but no city seems to have engaged in its own large-scale programme of reconstruction. Solva failed to acquire any new buildings of quality in the fourth century (Hudeczek 1977, 466-7). Iuvavum and Celeia show no signs of prosperity. All that can be said of Aguntum is that it was still occupied. At Virunum, the provincial capital of Noricum Mediterraneum, there was some reconstruction of public buildings: the baths were substantially restored, probably under the Tetrarchy (Alföldy 1974, 181), and a Diocletianic building inscription of 290 (*C.* 4826) attests some activity, although this may as easily have been the erection of buildings for the *officium* of the *praeses* as a civilian undertaking. A fragmentary dedication from Lauriacum (285/93), discovered in the vicinity of the legionary *principia*, is more likely to have been connected with the fortress than the city (Alföldy 1964/5, 207–18). Unlike the other Balkan provinces, there seems to have been no general provision of fortifications for the Norican cities: Ovilava and Celeia had fortifications, but those at Aguntum were never completed (Alzinger 1977, 398–9), and neither Virunum nor Lauriacum seem ever to have had city walls. It may be that the cities of Noricum were less exposed to the threat of incursions from beyond the frontier. Nevertheless, insecurity and occasional raids certainly did affect Noricum during the fourth century, and the lack of provision for urban defence remains curious.[1] Notable, also, is the paucity of evidence for Christianity. Celeia, Virunum, Teurnia, Aguntum and Lauriacum were all bishoprics and some Christian tombstones prove that Christian communities existed, although the only urban churches so far discovered are a small single-aisled basilica at Aguntum (Alföldy 1974, 210) and another, equally modest structure, at Lauriacum (Vetters 1977, 374–5).

The only certain epigraphic reference to municipal organization in Noricum during the fourth century is the modest dedication to Divus Jovius Maximianus erected in 311 by the *ordo* of Solva (*ILS* 661; another simple dedication by the *ordo*, *C.* 5327, may also be fourth century in date). The city's latest official inscription was set up in honour of the Emperor Constantine, but this was commissioned by the *praeses* (*C.* 5326). In Celeia, the *Norici Mediterranei* erected a dedication to Constantius and Constantine Caesars (323–37, *ILS* 723) and another to Constantius (*C.* 5208).

---

[1] The presence of the field army was required to repel an invasion, perhaps only of local importance, in *c.* 310 (*ILS* 664). A mid-fourth century destruction level at Lauriacum may represent destruction during another barbarian attack (Vetters 1977, 371). The construction of fortifications at Ybbs in the Inn Valley in 370 suggests that barbarian attacks were becoming a problem (Alföldy 1974, 203–4).

Possibly these were representatives of the provincial council which may have met here on occasion rather than in the capital of Noricum Mediterraneum, perhaps when the provincial governor was temporarily away from Virunum: the *praeses*, Martinianus, visited Celeia and erected a dedication to Constans (337–50, *C.* 5209). No mention is made, however, in any of these inscriptions of the *ordo*, last recorded on a dedication to the Emperor Carus (*C.* 5205).

Where there is evidence for building, this was invariably carried out on the orders of members of the imperial establishment. In 311, the *praeses* rebuilt a temple at Virunum which had been derelict for fifty years (*ILS* 4197). Probably in the same year, a temple was rebuilt at Bedaium (Seebruck) by a comitatensian unit, temporarily attached to the local ducal command (*ILS* 664). Another *dux*, Aurelius Iustinianus, repaired a *mithraeum* in Poetovio (*C.* 4039). At Ovilava, military brick stamps suggest that the *praeses* of Noricum Ripense authorized reconstruction at imperial expense (Alföldy 1974, 206): his *officium* was in the town, and so this building may be connected with his residence and administrative headquarters. Soldiers appear prominently in the epigraphic record. A *speculator* of *legio I Noricorum* set up a dedication to Mithras at Virunum (*C.* 4803): he may well have been detached for duties in the *officium* of the *praeses*. The same circumstance may account for the presence of Flavius Januarius at Ovilava (*C.* 13529). Before the end of the fourth century, Solva was garrisoned by a *cuneus equitum scutariorum* and a unit of *equites Mauri* (*Not. Dig. Oc.* 33.24, 31). Serving or retired soldiers were able to afford funerary monuments, as at Teurnia, where a white marble inscription records the burial of a young comitatensian soldier (*C.* 4742). Civilians are rarely mentioned on inscriptions, although one Christian inscription commemorates Herodiana, wife of Titus, at Virunum (*C.* 4921).

Central Illyricum

Four cities in central Illyricum were notably more populous and more important than the rest. The Late Roman walls of Savaria enclosed an area greater than the original 42 ha street grid of the early Roman *colonia*,[1] and Christian gravestones from the city, some of pretention (*RIU* 1.76–86), corroborate the evidence of hagiographical sources in indicating that the city was an important centre of early Christianity (Mócsy 1974, 332–3), a circumstance perhaps encouraged by the cosmopolitan character of its population, which included immigrants or traders from the East (*RIU* 1.78). After reconstruction at the end of the third century, Sirmium, at almost 100 ha, ranked as one of the largest cities in the Balkans. Sopianae (Pécs) possessed large cemeteries with lavishly decorated family tombs and chapels (Mócsy 1974, 332–3). Less is known about Siscia (Sisak) but it, too, would seem to have expanded in size in the fourth century. Who these new inhabitants were is less easy to ascertain, although none were – or claimed to have been – members of the curial class. Instead, soldiers and imperial administrators were well represented.[2]

The presence of well-to-do members of the imperial bureaucracy in these cities is easily explained. All four were chosen as centres of imperial administration. The *praesides* and the *officia* of Pannonia I, Pannonia II, Valeria and Savia were assigned to Savaria, Sirmium, Sopianae and Siscia respectively.[3] Sirmium had an arms factory (*Not. Dig. Oc.* 9.18) as well as a state weaving establishment (*Not. Dig. Oc.* 11.47). Siscia accommodated the provincial treasury and an imperial mint (*Not. Dig. Oc.* 11.24, 39). The cities were also regularly used during the frequent imperial visits to the Danubian frontier.[4]

---

[1]   The street grid covered an area of *c.* 700 × 600 m (Mócsy 1974, 78). The Late Roman walls have been recently discovered (Póczy 1977, 38, and 1980, 265).
[2]   For soldiers see below (pp. 108–9). For administrators see *ILJug* 271, from Sirmium, the tombstone of a *clavicularius ex officio praesidis*, and Fulep 1984, 278–9, reporting burials at Sopianae probably of members of the imperial administration.
[3]   The *praesides* were not, however, of equal rank and their status changed during the course of the fourth century (Mócsy 1974, 273).
[4]   Constans certainly stayed at Savaria in 339 (*CTh* 10.10.6). For other imperial visits cf. Tóth 1973, 130. For a full account of imperial visits to Sirmium, cf. *Sirmium* I, 22–166. Julian stayed in the *regia* at Sirmium (Ammianus Marcellinus 21.10), presumably the same residence as that used by Valentinian and referred to as the *palatium* (Ammianus Marcellinus 30.5).

It is not surprising, therefore, that buildings excavated within these cities appear to have served imperial needs, either as accommodation for the praesidial staff, or as imperial residences. In 375, Valentinian reluctantly stayed in Savaria: the city was in a sorry state of repair, although its imperial baths still functioned (Ammianus Marcellinus 30.5.15–16). Presumably, these were part of a *palatium*. A suitable candidate for the *aula* of this palace has been excavated: a basilical building (16 × 47.4 m) with apsidal end, its walls decorated with marble, its floors with mosaics. This building formed part of a large complex which included a bath suite and private accommodation. It took up at least two *insulae* in the centre of the ancient city, close to the presumed site of the forum (Tóth 1973).

Sopianae was radically reconstructed in the late third or early fourth century. After a century of apparent neglect, following the Marcomannic Wars, wattle and daub buildings were demolished and replaced by buildings on a new alignment (Fulep 1984, 33). The largest complex so far investigated comprised a central courtyard surrounded on three sides by wings of a large building (ibid., 34). It might be claimed that this was part of a new forum were it not for the fact that it included an extensive suite of baths. Such an impressive complex, which had a residential function, would provide suitable accommodation for the *praeses*. Finds of military tile-stamps of fourth-century date (ibid., 1984, 266) also suggest that official building was being carried out in the city.

The centre of Sirmium was completely rebuilt in the Tetrarchic period. The whereabouts of the imperial palace is not known, although it must have been close to the hippodrome, a monumental structure, erected in the very centre of the city, immediately south of the main west–east street (Popović and Ochsenschlager 1976). The imperial residence may have been immediately to the south where parts of another imposing complex have been uncovered (*Sirmium* VII, 10). South-west of the hippodrome, against the inside of the fortifications, large store-buildings were erected in the fourth century, and other *horrea* lay north-west of the hippodrome, south of another suite of baths, perhaps those constructed by Licinius during his stay in Sirmium in 306–14 (*Sirmium* VIII, 29–102). The city was particularly well equipped with bathing establishments. Yet another bath complex was constructed north of the southern store-buildings (*Sirmium* VII,

75–8). The presence of substantial store-buildings in the southern half of the city, close to the site of the *palatium* and the hippodrome, suggests that they may have been for imperial rather than civic use.

An unusually informative inscription from Savaria records the construction of *horrea* by Constans' Praetorian Prefect, Vulcacius Rufinus: supplies were provided for the granaries to make good a deficiency and then, since the granaries were of insufficient capacity, new ones had to be built, thereby securing, in perpetuity, the grain supply (*res annonaria*) (*IDR* 1.48 = *ILS* 727, AD 347–9). Rufinus proudly proclaimed his achievement, which he may have personally supervised (he was given special responsibility for Illyricum between 347 and 352: *PLRE* 1.782–3). The primary responsibility vested in a praetorian prefect was to ensure the supply of the *limitanei* and the imperial army on campaign (Jones 1964, 626–7). Only a few years later, in 354, this same praetorian prefect incurred the anger of Constantius II when he signally failed to expedite the transport of supplies from Aquitania to the field army, waiting impatiently on the Rhine: it was left to the luckless Rufinus to explain the delay to the Emperor's hungry troops (Amm. Marcell. 14.10.4). It is possible that Rufinus' concern for the *annona* in Savaria was precipitated by the need to provide supplies for Constans' visit to Illyricum in 349. However, it is likely that the building of new *horrea* was connected with a regular commitment, either to house provisions for the *officium* of the *praeses* or for a military garrison.

This brings us to another imperial interest in towns: their use as military bases. By the 380s, Balkan cities were used as permanent bases for limitanean units (Hoffmann 1969, 517–19). Sirmium housed infantry and cavalry (*Not. Dig. Oc.* 32.49, 54), as well as a naval flotilla (*Not. Dig. Oc.* 32.50), and Siscia too had a military garrison and a detachment of the Danube fleet (*Not. Dig. Oc.* 32.56–7). It could be that these units were only assigned to the towns in the late fourth century, conceivably even after the catastrophe of 378. However, there are reasonable grounds for dating the use of towns as military bases as early as the first half of the fourth century. Tombstones from Sopianae suggest the presence of a garrison (Fulep 1984, nos 42, 47, 59, pp. 262–4). Sirmium housed two legions and a unit of *sagittarii* under Constantius (Amm. Marcell. 21.11.2). A *numerus Ioviorum* was quartered in the city and may have been a regular garrison (*ILS* 9205).[1] In the centre of Sirmium, opposite the hippodrome, there were small, semi-detached 'shops' (*Sirmium* III, 21): their regular planning and proximity to the imperial quarter rather suggests that they were not shops at all but barracks. In the case of Savaria, the city probably had a garrison as early as 335/6, when the father of St Martin of Tours appears to have been serving there.[2] There are also a number of comitatensian units, listed in the *Notitia Dignitatum*, which have names which connect them with Balkan cities and may plausibly be explained by supposing that they had been stationed in these cities, probably as limitanean units, during the fourth century.[3] Among these were the *lanciarii Savarienses* (*Not. Dig. Oc.* 5.9, 7.82), possibly to be identified with the unit in which St Martin's father served (Hoffmann 1970, 86 n. 135). Amongst the fourth-century gravestones from Savaria, one records the death of a centurion who, since he died while still on active service, may well have been based in the city (*RIU* 1.84). Thus it seems likely that the use of major cities as bases for limitanean garrisons dates back at least to the middle of the fourth century and probably earlier still. Nor will these have been the only troops in these cities: all four commanded important lines of communication across Pannonia, and so, from the Tetrarchic period on, they must regularly have accommodated units of the field army passing through the Balkans.

[1] A soldier in this unit is commemorated on a funerary inscription from Sirmium set up by his wife. Presumably, the soldier had been based there, although the text records that he died at Aquileia. It has been suggested that this unit can be identified with the *Iovii Iuniores* and that the man died when campaigning in Italy with Theodosius the Great (Hoffmann 1969, 108–9). However, a late fourth-century date for tombstones in the Balkans would be most unusual and a date before *c.* 350 seems more likely.

[2] Sulpicius Severus' information that St Martin was born in Savaria, and that his father was a soldier and *tribunus* (*Vita Martini* 2.1–2) is likely to be accurate (Stancliffe 1983, 7 and 343). The date of Martin's birth is less certain, although 335/6 is more likely than the alternative dating to *c.* 316 (ibid. 122–33).

[3] These units could have been withdrawn for service with the field army as early as the reign of Constantius II or as late as the reign of Theodosius (Hoffmann 1969, 73–4, 225–6, 409–10). For another group of units based in the interior, including one at Ulpianum, see p. 114 below.

The cities of the interior which were not major centres of imperial administration seem to form a middle group, none ranking in importance with the provincial capitals but still sufficiently important to acquire impressive new fortifications and to yield evidence of some reconstruction during the fourth century.

The well-preserved, Late Roman walls of Scarbantia (Sopron) enclosed an elliptical area of 9 ha around the centre of the Early Roman city. As with the provincial capitals, a Tetrarchic date for their construction seems probable (Póczy 1977, 32–6). Within the city, the forum remained an open area throughout the fourth century, but the function of the surrounding buildings changed: the Capitoline temple was no longer maintained, and the rooms on the west side of the forum were used as grain stores. Some well-built stone houses were provided with hypocaust heating and painted wallplaster. One large building occupied two full *insulae*, obliterating the road which had originally separated them (ibid., 38–40). Finds provide no direct evidence for its purpose, although its size and central location suggest comparison with the palace complex at Savaria. Although Scarbantia has produced no fewer inscriptions of the Early Empire than other Pannonian cities, the only Late Roman example is a dedication to Diocletian and Maximian erected by a *beneficiarius consularis* (*RIU* 1.178). Like Savaria, Scarbantia occupied an important road junction in the hinterland of the frontier and, by the late fourth century, it housed a limitanean garrison (*Not. Dig. Oc.* 34.30).

Gorsium (Tác) has been extensively excavated. Here, there was certainly considerable building activity during the late third or early fourth century which involved a radical replanning of the city's roads and buildings. Gorsium may have been renamed Herculia under the Tetrarchy,[1] and the new layout demonstrates that the city was of importance in the Late Roman period and that it benefited from imperial interest. Like the provincial capital, Sopianae, Gorsium occupied a strategic location at the centre of a road system which linked the interior with the frontier. Whereas Sopianae lay at the southern extremity of

[1] Whether Tác is the site of Late Roman Herculia is still a matter of controversy: in favour see J. Fitz, *Alba Regia* 21 (1984), 279–81; against, see E. Tóth, *Arch. Ért.* 109/1 (1982), 55–72.

Valeria, Gorsium was a convenient regional centre for the northern part of the province.

Occupying a prominent site in the centre of Gorsium, immediately east of the forum, the temple complex dedicated to the imperial cult and probably used by the *concilium provinciae Pannoniae Inferioris* was still in use during the third century (Mócsy 1974, 175). However, by the fourth, it was abandoned and the site only partly re-used for later buildings (Fitz 1976, 47–9). The forum complex was abandoned, the site levelled and a new *cardo* built across it, leaving the remaining space open and used only for ovens (Fitz 1982, 204–6). Late Roman fortifications, surrounding the centre of the city, have recently been identified, along with a north gate, flanked by rectangular, projecting towers (Fitz 1986, 109–61). It seems certain that the new *cardo* was laid out at the same time as the city was fortified: the new road provided direct access from the north gate to the *decumanus maximus*, which it joined immediately south of the demolished forum complex. Even if the forum was still in use in the late third century, it can hardly have survived the replanning of the city and the construction of its fortifications. There is no sign elsewhere in the centre of Gorsium of a new forum which might have replaced that now buried beneath the *cardo*.

Immediately north of the *decumanus maximus*, west of the new road a large building (65 × 49 m) replaced earlier Roman structures, destroyed in the third century. With its cross-hall fronted by a colonnade, its central courtyard, a bath suite and a range of rooms on the north side which included a reception chamber with apsidal end, the complex closely resembles the palace at Savaria. Although it remains doubtful whether the building was ever used as the praesidial residence for Valeria, since the *officium* is attested at Sopianae, it seems entirely reasonable to agree with the excavator that this building did serve an official and probably imperial function (Fitz 1976, 23–9). It may have been the official residence of the *dux*.[1] A sizeable structure (72.4 × 14 m) was also erected on the opposing, south side of the *decumanus maximus*, but this one was subdivided into two-roomed units, each 6 × 6 m square, with the northern

---

[1] For a *dux* choosing to reside in a town rather than a fort see p. 115 below on Tomis.

entrances fronted by a colonnade. It is possible that these were
shops (so Fitz 1976, 53-7 and 1978, 238-9). However, the
northern colonnade follows the symmetry of the colonnade in
front of the official residence on the other side of the street, which
suggests that they were contemporary. Moreover, the block of
rooms was clearly planned and constructed as a single complex.
Most buildings which served as shops in Late Roman towns are
irregular constructions, each built separately by individual
owners. Finds provide no clue as to the function of this building,
although they do confirm that it was in use during the fourth
century. It seems most likely that the complex formed part of the
same building programme as the official residence: possible uses
are as store-rooms or barracks for a limitane garrison.

Elsewhere in the town, away from the centre, there were some
town houses (Fitz 1976, 57-61), but large areas, especially around
the official residence and over the abandoned temple site, were left
vacant for much of the fourth century. It seems probable that, as
at the provincial capitals, the large new buildings at Gorsium were
constructed in the Tetrarchic period, and the radical nature of the
replanning of the site suggests that they were part of a systematic
reorganization of the interior of the city following the erection of
the fortifications. It is particularly significant that the new activity
in Gorsium suggests imperial involvement, since it does not seem
to have coincided with any new investment of wealth in civic
buildings. Indeed, the forum itself would seem no longer to have
been required.

Little is known about most of the minor towns in the Pannonian provinces during Late Antiquity. Cibalae was of importance
to judge from its size of *c.* 56 ha and the Late Roman walls of
Bassiana enclosed *c.* 19.5 ha.[1] This city certainly had an imperial
function: it contained a state weaving factory (*gynaecium*) (*Not.
Dig. Oc.* 11.46).

Unlike the cities in the interior, those on the Danube bank seem
to have been unable to maintain the prosperity they evidently

[1] For Bassiana see *Antiquity* 10 (1936), 475-7 and plate VI. The aerial
photograph clearly shows the forum complex in the centre of the Late
Roman fortifications, but, since the building's plan is only evidenced by the
robbing of the walls, it is uncertain whether the building survived into the
Late Roman period.

enjoyed in the second and early third centuries. Aquincum appears to have been in decline, although wealth was still invested in the villa estates in the surrounding countryside (Mócsy 1974, 310). At Carnuntum, the *municipium* was still inhabited, and the city acquired its own fortifications, but no new public buildings were erected in the fourth century, and those which continued to function were not fully maintained. Nor were private houses kept in a good state of repair (Stiglitz *et al.* 1977, 593–613). The only attested building activity is the repair of a *mithraeum* in 308 – and that was carried out by the Emperors Diocletian and Maximian and their Caesars during the meeting at Carnuntum (*ILS* 659). The city was deserted and in ruins by the late fourth century (Amm. Marcell. 30.5.2).

Only at Singidunum is there some indication of Late Roman building (Mócsy 1974, 312). Like Brigetio, Singidunum had been elevated to the status of *colonia* during the third century (*C.* 4335), and civic organization was still functioning in 272 (*IMS* 46) despite the Gothic invasions. However, the last official monument known to have been put up by the *ordo* was a simple altar dedicated to Diocletian and Maximian in 287 (*IMS* 20). No inscription mentions civic administration at Aquincum and, at Carnuntum, the last official inscription set up by the decurions dates to 305/7 (*C.* 3522).

At no site on the middle Danube have inscriptions or the excavation of Late Roman cemeteries indicated the presence of wealthy inhabitants comparable with the evidence from the provincial capitals.

Of the small *municipia* founded in Moesia Superior during the late second and early third centuries, none are commemorated by more than a handful of inscriptions. Although they would all seem to have had the usual range of civic magistracies, none probably grew to any size or achieved more than moderate prosperity before the third-century Gothic invasions (Mócsy 1974, 223–5). None have produced fourth-century civic inscriptions. Only at Naissus (Niš), birthplace of Constantine, are there are a number of Late Roman funerary inscriptions and some rich burials in the Late Roman cemetery. Even so, this city was no more than a couple of hectares in size (Mócsy 1974, 31). Nevertheless, many of these towns occupied important locations on roads linking the Danubian *limes* with Macedonia and western Illyricum with the

eastern provinces. This no doubt explains their military importance, shown by the presence of armaments factories at Naissus
and Horreum Margi (*Not. Dig. Or.* 11.37, 39). Amongst the
pseudocomitatensian forces of eastern Illyricum listed in the
Notitia Dignitatum, several had earlier been based in the interior,
as we have seen (p. 109). Most occupied strategic bases on the Via
Egnatia, the main Balkan road linking west Illyricum with the
eastern provinces, although one, the Scupenses, was presumably
based in Scupi (*Not. Dig. Or.* 9.43) and another, the Ulpianenses,
in the city of Ulpianum (*Not. Dig. Or.* 9.44). As in the case of
Savaria, it is not improbable that these urban garrisons were
already established before the middle of the fourth century.

The Lower Danube

In the Thracian diocese, as in central Illyricum, the cities of the
interior seem to have been better able to survive the third century
than those on the Danube, while the cities on the Black Sea coast
appear to have maintained an unusually high degree of civic pride
in public building and private wealth.

At Histria, the Tetrarchic fortifications protected only *c.* 7 ha,
an even smaller area than the still modest 30 ha included within
the Early Roman defences (Condurachi *et al.* 1954, 67–92). New
buildings included an area of workshops on the south side of the
city and a new set of baths, smaller than the large complex now
abandoned and outside the city walls. Inscriptions are few but
include at least one retired soldier who chose to settle in the town
(*IGL* 110).

Odessus was also chosen as a suitable place for retirement by a
veteran from a *vexillatio II Scutariorum* (*SGLI* 130). The city's
own monumental baths no longer functioned in the fourth
century, but, as at Histria, were replaced by a more modest suite,
closer to the harbour (Toncheva 1968, 232–3; Mirchev 1970, 473).
The city's port probably still attracted traders and a copy of
Diocletian's Price Edict was certainly on display (*AE* 1978, 714).
Apart from simple graves, its cemeteries included burial
chambers, hollowed out of the natural limestone (Mirchev 1951b).

On an inscription from Callatis, the *boulē* and *dēmos*,

Diocletian and Maximian are honoured by two priests of the city (*IGL* 85).

Fourth-century Tomis was in a class of its own. Within the city, extensive levelling was followed by new buildings, including a series of terraced warehouses fronting the port with a lavishly decorated assembly room, its floor adorned with a polychrome mosaic covering more than 2,000 m^2 (Bucovală 1977), probably a donation from a wealthy trader. Another large building, this time a warehouse for linen merchants, was paid for by Ermippos, son of Atas, and provided as a gift for the citizens of Tomis.[1] Traders from the eastern provinces regularly visited the city. Some never left. A wine merchant from Alexandria (*IGL* 28) died there, as did a certain Torpilla from Epiphaneia in Cilicia, probably the wife of a trader (*IGL* 24). The Late Roman cemeteries at Tomis include extensive underground chamber burials, some decorated with wall-paintings (Bardenache 1968; Barbu 1971). Tomis also performed an imperial function as provincial capital. The *praeses* of Scythia, his staff and their families lived in the city (*IGL* 5). The *dux* of Scythia may well also have preferred Tomis to more spartan conditions on the Danubian frontier: Aurelius Firminianus set up a dedication to Magna Mater (*IGL* 2), and was also responsible for the construction of an official gate (*porta praesidiaria*) in Tomis, built on the instructions of Maximian and Diocletian (*IGL* 3).

On the Danubian frontier, no inscription attests urban administration during the fourth century. Durostorum is last mentioned by an inscription commemorating Aurelian's victory over Zenobia and the Carpi (*C.* 12456), but nothing is known about the Late Roman city except that at least one inhabitant could afford a richly painted brick mausoleum (Danov and Ivanov 1980, 105–6). The total disappearance of inscriptions which mention cities or decurions is especially remarkable since imperial dedications

---

[1] This large, rectangular building (110 × 40 m) has been interpreted as a bath–house (Bucovală 1977, 30–3), although there is no evidence that it served such a function: see the description by Popescu, *Dacia* n.s. 10 (1966), 391–2. The Greek dedicatory inscription, inscribed on the lintel over the entrance, which still survives *in situ*, describes the building as a *lentiarion*, which here surely refers to its function as a store or possibly market for linen merchants. Cf. the *lentiaris*, probably a linen merchant in Serdica, attested on *IGBulg* 4.1922.

and military funerary inscriptions are still not uncommon finds from the Danubian forts.

In the interior, inscriptions are much fewer in the Late Roman period, but excavations have provided new information. Marcianopolis was probably the residence of the *praeses* of Moesia II. Both Diocletian and Constantine visited the city. During the Gothic Wars, Valens used the city as his headquarters. When the Goths revolted, Lupicinus, *comes per Thracias*, was in the city with soldiers (Amm. Marcell. 31.5.4–8). Whether the *praetorium* in which he entertained Fritigern was a permanent headquarters or residence of the *praeses* is uncertain, but a military presence in Marcianopolis can be presumed from the time of the Tetrarchy. The city had a *fabrica* (*Not. Dig. Or.* 11.34), and this arms factory was already in use and under military supervision by the early fourth century (Mihailov 1965). It therefore comes as no surprise that the city has provided the best evidence for a wealthy population who owned town houses, well provisioned with high-quality figure mosaics (Mirchev 1951a; Minchev and Georgiev 1979).

Elsewhere, living standards were notably inferior. The last inscription to record the *boulē* and *dēmos* of Nicopolis ad Istrum dates to 270/1 (*IGBulg* 2.645). The only fourth-century building known to have been erected mentions an official, probably the governor of Moesia II, but not the city or its civilian administration (*IGBulg* 2.656). Abritus probably received municipal status under the Severi (Poulter 1983/4, 111). It was destroyed during the third century, and later a fortification of 10 ha was constructed over the levelled remains of the early town. The fortifications resemble closely those provided for the Tetrarchic fort of Yatrus on the Danube. Within the fourth-century city, excavation has been limited, although discoveries include a substantial *horreum* close to the west gate and a peristyle building in the centre, notably similar in plan to the *principia* at Yatrus and also showing striking resemblances to the palace complexes of Pannonia (ibid., 119–22).

Of all the fourth-century cities of the region, Tropaeum Traiani has been the most extensively excavated. The city was refounded and its walls rebuilt in 315/17 on imperial instructions (*IGL* 170). The last official inscription to mention the city is a small, crude altar, dedicated to Hera and probably of early fourth-century date

(*IGL* 171). The primitive inscription suggests a decline in civic standards, as does the fact that the language used for this official inscription was not Latin, as in earlier dedications set up by the *municipium*, but Greek. The fourth-century town walls enclosed 10.5 ha. Inside, buildings were constructed of mud-brick with stone foundations, bonded with earth. There is nothing comparable here to the elegant houses at Marcianopolis. The only concession to civic pride took the form of porticos along the main west–east road: the two colonnades were continuous and did not lead to a forum for which there seems to have been no provision. The so-called *basilica forensis* in the centre of the town, the only stone building so far dated to the early fourth century (50 × 18 m), was not a municipal building but a *horreum* (Poulter 1983/4, 117–19). The granary was erected in the very centre of the city, precisely the location one would expect a forum to have occupied.

Marcianopolis must have regularly housed detachments of the field army as well as military personnel in control of the *fabrica* and probably the bodyguard of the *dux*, and there is some reason to suppose that military garrisons were maintained in some of the other cities of the lower Danube in the late third or early fourth century. A comitatensian *vexillatio* of *equites Dalmatorum* was based at Anchialus on the Black Sea coast under the Tetrarchy (*ILS* 2792; Hoffmann 1969, 257–8). The wife of a *biarchus* who served in the *schola palatina* of Licinius erected a funerary monument to her husband at Ulmetum (*IGL* 206). The soldier died in the battle of Chrysopolis in 324. Presumably he had been based in this strategic road-centre in the hinterland of the Scythian frontier.[1]

The character of the fourth-century city

That the cities of the region underwent profound changes between the second and fourth century seems certain. Quantifying and, in particular, interpreting the nature of those changes is more difficult: more research needs to be done both on the cities

---

[1] In the second century Ulmetum had been a large and prosperous *vicus* with a mixed population of Bessi and Roman citizens (*IDR* 5.62–9). Like Abritus, it probably acquired municipal status during the third century.

themselves and their territories. Nevertheless, it would seem reasonable both to attempt to draw some general conclusions and to suggest a number of tentative explanations.

Broadly, the cities can be divided into four categories. Those on the river bank would seem to have suffered most: from Lauriacum to Troesmis, there is scant evidence for any urban revival in the fourth century. In the interior, while other cities declined those which became imperial capitals were provided with new buildings, and their cemeteries indicate that some of these cities were inhabited by wealthy individuals. The remaining group, the cities on the Black Sea coast, were in a class of their own: they provide the clearest impression of modest prosperity.

Even this preliminary conclusion requires closer scrutiny: it may conceal more than it explains, since such a generalization in terms of wealth, whether private or public, is not, in itself, a satisfactory index of urbanism. Whereas it is certain that the generation of wealth and its investment in cities was provided by the curial class in the second and early third centuries, this cannot be presumed to have been so in the fourth: direct evidence, in the form of inscriptions or the construction of buildings demonstrably for the use of the civilian population or the civic authorites, is lacking. But it is striking that, where inscriptions do record building, the work was carried out by *praesides* (Virunum), *duces* (Ovilava, Poetovio, Tomis), by emperors themselves (Carnuntum, Tropaeum Traiani), or, in the case of the *horrea* at Savaria, by a Praetorian Prefect.

The only exception is Tomis, which, although it profited from imperial building under the Tetrarchy, seems to have had citizens of sufficient wealth and civic pride to erect public buildings at their own expense. Like other cities on the Black Sea coast, Tomis retained its conspicuous prosperity thanks to its trading contacts with Asia Minor and the eastern Mediterranean. Consequently, it is not surprising that the public buildings provided by private citizens were storehouses and assembly rooms for traders close to the port.

Where epigraphic proof is not available, the character of new buildings within cities (apart from those on the Black Sea coast) suggests that they were constructed by imperial directive. The store-buildings in Sirmium were almost certainly for imperial use, and so, probably, were the granaries in Tropaeum Traiani and

Abritus. Imperial palaces occupied large portions of the cities of Savaria, Sirmium and probably Sopianae. Others must have existed in Marcianopolis, Tomis and Virunum. Even smaller cities, such as Gorsium and Abritus, acquired administrative buildings which would seem more appropriate as imperial residences than civic offices. Where individuals are named on inscriptions, they are regularly soldiers or members of the praesidial administration. Although it may be correct to argue that there was a shift in wealth from the older cities to the new centres of imperial bureaucracy (Mócsy 1974, 308), it remains doubtful whether the citizens of these towns derived any profit from their new status.

The clearest indication of imperial concern for cities is the erection of fortifications during the first quarter of the fourth century. At Tomis and Tropaeum Traiani, walls were built on imperial instructions. In the case of Tropaeum Traiani and Abritus, the style of fortifications is so similar to the Tetrarchic fortifications of the Danubian frontier that it is likely that military engineers were involved in their planning and probably also their execution (Poulter 1983/4). A similar military involvement and imperial directive seems equally likely for Scarbantia and Bassiana in Pannonia (Póczy 1977, 38). There were good reasons for ensuring that cities, especially those occupying strategic road centres, were well defended: apart from protecting imperial residences and *horrea* for the supply of the army, cities provided accommodation for praesidial and ducal *officia*. The latter functions were already established under the Tetrarchy, and it is likely that Marcianopolis was not exceptional in already housing an imperial armaments factory by the early fourth century. As the fortifications were themselves Tetrarchic, it seems reasonable to conclude that they were provided with the primary objective of securing the new centres of imperial administration. The converse may also apply. Failure by the cities of Noricum to acquire urban fortifications may reflect their lesser importance both as military and political centres.

Military garrisons appear to have been common in cities. Barracks are probable at Sirmium and Gorsium. The presence of limitanean garrisons can be detected at Savaria before the middle of the fourth century, at Anchialus under the Tetrarchy and at Ulmetum under Licinius. Far from being a new burden which cities acquired late in the fourth century, it seems likely that urban detachments were already garrisoning cities under the Tetrarchy. The financial cost to the cities involved in housing such forces could only have been exacerbated by the visits of emperors and units of the field army.

The size of the largest cities should not be taken to imply a large urban population. In Savaria and Sopianae, substantial portions of the city's area were occupied by imperial buildings. Although Sirmium (100 ha) counts as one of the largest cities, almost all the buildings excavated in the southern half of the city were reserved for imperial use. Where cities appear to have had fewer imperial functions, the fortified area is correspondingly smaller: Scarbantia (9 ha) and Tropaeum Traiani (10.5 ha) seem to be closer to the norm for cities which did not act as provincial capitals.

Internal planning no longer seems to follow classical tradition. Nowhere is there any sign that new municipal buildings were constructed in the fourth century, nor does any inscription attest the repair of existing buildings. At Scarbantia, the buildings alongside the forum seem to have been used for storage. In this case, it is not possible to determine when the civic centre ceased to function, but, in the Tetrarchic reconstruction of Gorsium and the Constantinian replanning of Tropaeum Traiani, no provision seems to have been made for a forum and basilica. This suggests either that these buildings were no longer considered appropriate or that the citizens themselves no longer had the financial resources to build them. Although there are demonstrably fewer inscriptions, public and private, datable to the fourth century, it is surely significant that soldiers and members of the imperial bureaucracy are well represented, whereas only two *principales* can be identified, one from south of Singidunum (*IMS* 153), the other at Halmyris, south of Histria on the Black Sea coast (*IGL* 167). Both inscriptions demonstrate no direct connection with either city: they were set up in the countryside, probably on or close to private estates.

If there was a marked decline in urban vitality, both in the willingness of wealthy citizens to take curial office and in their ability to provide the resources for civic building, it is not possible to link this directly with the economic collapse of the third century. Urban administration was still functioning at Solva, Aquincum, Callatis, Tomis and Tropaeum Traiani under the

Tetrarchy. At Singidunum, Durostorum and Nicopolis, urban government existed as late as the reign of Aurelian and probably, therefore, survived under the Tetrarchy. However, these latest records of municipal organization are all confined to the erection of crude altars, and not a single inscription identifies municipal magistrates or the corporate body of a *municipium* or *polis* later than the Tetrarchy, not even during the reign of Constantine or his sons when the restoration of frontier security ought to have favoured a revival in economic prosperity and an investment in cities. Attempts were made to maintain civic institutions as late as the end of the fourth century. Decurions, though difficult to obtain, were still being forced into accepting their duties even after the Gothic Wars. Recruits for the *curia* were difficult to find for Moesia II in 383 (*CTh* 12.1.96). Further laws of 386 (*CTh* 1.32.5) and 392 (*CTh* 12.1.124) suggest that the problem had not been solved but, equally, indicate that some decurions continued to exercise authority and accept the burdens of office. There is no reason to suggest a conflict in the evidence. Curial administration survived – if only just – at least until the very end of the fourth century. However, cities would seem not to have returned to their former prosperity in the Late Roman period and, where prosperous inhabitants can be identified, except in the cities of the Black Sea coast, their status and wealth appear to derive from their professions as soldiers or members of the imperial administration. Moreover, the abandonment of civic fora and the total disappearance of epigraphic evidence for urban administration under the Tetrarchy is surely significant.

The underlying causes of the decline of cities and, in particular, of urban administration may be sought in the changes in the countryside and on the frontier during the third century. Repeated invasions and economic collapse certainly disrupted the villa economy in the Balkans. Since the wealth of most towns must have derived from the exploitation of their agricultural territories during the Early Empire, the drop in cities' prosperity during the third century is readily understandable. In the fourth century, although rich villas existed, they are fewer and larger than during the second century. Where their distribution can be studied, it seems that, whereas medium-sized villas cluster around the Early Roman towns, the distribution of Late Roman villas bears little relationship to the urban centres (Poulter 1983, 92–3 and 97–100, for the Lower Danube). Thus it would seem possible that one major factor contributing to the cities' decline was the disappearance of the medium-sized villa estates which had provided the majority of decurions. A second and related cause may well have been the decline in the status and wealth of the frontier garrisons. The withdrawal of the best legionary and auxiliary forces to serve in the field army must have reduced the importance of the frontier as a significant market for surplus goods produced in its hinterland: this may, in particular, explain the rapid and complete collapse of cities on the frontier itself. The cities on the Black Sea coast constitute the only exception to the general picture of decline or of prosperity linked closely to the presence of imperial administration. These continued to maintain their trading links with the East and were thus not dependent upon the exploitation of their small agricultural territories.

However, even on the Black Sea coast, despite their modest economic revival in the fourth century, there is still precious little evidence that the Greek colonies maintained their traditional forms of self-government and civic buildings. Here, as elsewhere along the Danube, evidence for urban administration disappears under the Tetrarchy. It would therefore be tempting to seek another explanation which might account for the decline in urban government in the early fourth century. It has been observed that cities played an important rôle as centres of imperial administration and probably acted as military bases, temporary and permanent, as well as providing accommodation for imperial use and praesidial government. The burdens upon the curial class in the Danubian provinces must have been proportionately greater than in the more prosperous provinces away from the frontier. Could it be that the abrupt disappearance of civic inscriptions reflects a crisis in the confidence of the curial class? If the Diocletianic reforms imposed too high a burden upon the *curiales*, still struggling to overcome the effects of military and economic chaos in the frontier zone, then this could account for the downturn in their fortunes and, consequently, those of their cities. Building still continued and was presumably paid for by the citizens (Jones 1964, 758). However, the new buildings were erected by order of the military or civilian command and there is no indication that there existed any surplus of wealth which was used in civic projects. Over and above the additional calls upon civic revenues to provide for military and praesidial obligations, provincial governors were themselves not averse to pocketing civic revenues (ibid. 749). The incentive to compete for civic office must have been of little real significance when there were fewer *curiales* able to take office and when a city was *de facto* – though not *de iure* – subject to the exactions of the local military commander or the *officia* of *praesides*.

Although the underlying economic problems, which weakened the ability of cities to function effectively, may well have arisen in the third century, it is possible that the abrupt disappearance of civic inscriptions reflects an equally abrupt decline in the ability and willingness of the remaining curial class to shoulder the full weight of the liturgies imposed by the very Tetrarchic reforms in government which have been so often credited with actually stimulating an urban revival.

The Byzantine city of the sixth century

The fate of cities in the fifth century would repay treatment in its own right, although it would be a study which, given the paucity of material evidence, would prove frustratingly difficult. However, the general picture is clear and worth reviewing. In Noricum, with the collapse of imperial control of the frontier, reflected in the cessation of coinage and hence military pay *c.* 400, the unfortified cities seem to have been gradually abandoned and the civilian population took refuge in hilltop 'Fliehburgen' which have provided the best evidence for organized communal life, although the major buildings were not civic fora or town houses but churches. Only the hilltop city of Teurnia seems to have survived as late as *c.* 500 (Alföldy 1974, 213–20). In Pannonia, there is some indication that urban fortifications continued to protect the indigenous population well into the fifth century, and, although there is little sign that the cities of northern and central Illyricum functioned beyond the first quarter of the fifth century, the cities of southern Illyricum, including Sirmium, ceded to the Eastern Empire in 437, maintained their existence and ecclesiastical administration down to the middle of the fifth century and beyond (Mócsy 1974, 347–53). On the Lower Danube, no city seems to have been destroyed during the Gothic Wars at the end of the fourth century, and occupation continued until the middle of the fifth, when cities were sacked during the Hunnic invasions.[1] The fate of cities in the second half of the fifth century remains obscure, although a revival in occupation, coin circulation and building is evidenced by the end of the fifth century and the reign of Anastasius. Refuge settlements on hill tops are a feature of the countryside in the fifth century and, as in Noricum, churches are the most substantial of the internal buildings (Poulter 1983, 97–100). With the collapse of imperial authority, there is some reason to suspect that it was the Church which played a major rôle in maintaining the morale of the surviving urban communities. In the life of Saint Severinus in Noricum and the activities of bishops on the Lower Danube, there is some indication that cities maintained a precarious existence at least until *c.* 450 (Alföldy 1974, 220–4). However, it is only with the reassertion of Byzantine control over the southern Balkans that urban life was briefly revived on the Lower Danube. Whether the sixth-century cities on the Lower Danube resembled their predecessors is the subject of this final section.

The city excavated at Tsarichin Grad has been convincingly identified as Justiniana Prima (Kondić and Popović 1977, 367–71). This new city was founded by Justinian close to his birthplace and designated as the seat of provincial and religious administration for northern Illyricum (Procopius, *Buildings* 4.1.17–27; Justinian, *Nov.* 11). It may be fairly assumed that it was designed to conform, as closely as circumstances allowed, to the contemporary ideal of a city, and that this intention was reflected in the city's layout, buildings and amenities.

The most striking first impression of Tsarichin Grad is its strongly defensive position, the second is just how small an area its primary fortifications protected – barely 5 ha. Of this, one-fifth was taken up by the episcopal basilica and stores or accommodation for the bishop and his staff, occupying a separate enclosure and a dominating position on top of the hill, overlooking the rest of the town to the south-east (Kondić and Popović 1977, 310–18).

---

[1] See A.G. Poulter, *Moesia Inferior and the Lower Danube* (unpublished Ph.D. thesis, University of London), 461–73. The 1989 excavations have shown that Nicopolis was destroyed sometime after *c.* 430, and so probably when the Huns sacked the neighbouring city of Marcianopolis *c.* 447.

The centre of the city was a circular piazza, located at the intersection of the two main roads leading from the south and east gates. This was no forum: although surrounded by a colonnade, it measured only 22 m in diameter and was never a focus for commercial activity or civic administration. To the north-east lay a church. Private buildings flanked the steep road descending to the south. To the west, a road led up to the episcopal enclosure. Only to the east, along the short road which led to the east gate, were there small, two-roomed buildings, interpreted as shops (Bavant 1984, 275-8).

The excavation bears out Procopius' description of the city's amenities, according to which it boasted churches, fountains, an aqueduct, baths, paved streets, private buildings and colonnades. Significantly, although Procopius refers to administrative buildings, he does not mention civic administration, and no buildings have been found which appear to have served such a function. The only large complex which could be interpreted as an administrative building was connected to a separate residence and lay close to the city's south gate. This large, two-storeyed building provided direct access to the curtain-wall and the western gate tower: an interpretation as a military structure with a residence for a military commander, responsible for the defence of the city, seems reasonable. Basilicas line the main south street, but only a few buildings could qualify as civilian houses and some of these presumably accommodated the clergy serving the city's churches. Nor is there much evidence for industrial activity, although agricultural implements are well represented in the finds (Kondić and Popović 1977, 379 and plates 29-31).

Either side of the main axial road which traversed the city from north to south, excavation has been largely confined to adjacent buildings, but there is little chance that the periphery of the city contained a significant urban population: the ground slopes so steeply down to the defences that there is scarcely any suitable space for building. The city was later extended with the addition of a second fortification, enclosing 2.25 ha to the south of the original walls. This would not seem to have been constructed to protect civilian settlement: churches take up a large proportion of the enclosure (Bavant 1984, 281-2).

The population of Justiniana Prima was small, perhaps a few hundred, probably less. This would seem at variance with Procopius' description of the city as populous, indeed the largest city in the region. However, the surrounding countryside appears to have been densely populated in the sixth century, and, if this extramural settlement is included in the total, then the population dependent upon the city may well have been considerably larger than the evidence of limited intramural occupation would suggest (ibid. 284–5).

Sixth-century Tropaeum Traiani was still contained within its fourth-century defences, which enclosed 10.5 ha. Excavations along the main west–east road have uncovered four large, sixth-century Christian basilicas and, at the intersection of the road with the main north–south street, the fourth-century *horreum* had been converted into an aisled market. One large house has been excavated close to the east gate and, north of the main road, shops with workshops or living accommodation (Barnea *et al.* 1979, 82–3 and 97–102). None of the outlying *insulae* have been examined, but there would seem to have been no great density of building in the centre of the city after the clearance of houses which had spread amongst the porticos lining the main street during the fifth century (ibid. 88). The impression is one of an open-plan city with a relatively small population although, as at Justiniana Prima, indications of settlement outside the fortifications suggest that there may have been a large extramural population (ibid., 64 and 71). The prominent location given to churches is notable; so, too, is the absence of civic buildings or fora. The main street, lined with porticos, is a modest concession to urban planning, apparently not matched by the maintenance of public baths or substantial houses as at Tsarichin Grad.

The British excavations at Nicopolis ad Istrum in northern Bulgaria have identified the site of the sixth-century city, an enclosure of 5.7 ha (Poulter 1988). The city's walls, protected by some twenty towers, each projecting *c.* 15 m, reused the south side of the abandoned Roman city and followed the crest of the plateau on its own well-protected south side, overlooking the river Rositsa. The site seems to have been abandoned in the early seventh century and only sporadically occupied later. As a result, the distribution of buildings across the site, evidenced in the geophysical survey, provides a remarkably complete picture of sixth-century town planning – or the lack of it.

The contrast with the Roman city is particularly instructive.

Unlike its predecessor, Byzantine Nicopolis had no carefully paved limestone streets, nor does the distribution of buildings suggest any concern for a regular layout. A range of buildings extended east from the main west gate across the centre of the site, and large buildings or complexes of buildings occupied the south-west quarter of the enclosure. Workshops have been excavated, apparently isolated in the centre of the city. The main Christian basilica, erected on the highest point of the site on the east side of the plateau, appears not to have been surrounded by other buildings. The geophysical survey also suggests that a second basilica, excavated on the south-eastern side of the enclosure, was the only building on this part of the site. Remarkably, there is no sign in the resistivity survey of any buildings in the north-east quarter of the city and in the central western area. That these areas were never used for building is now supported by the results of a magnetometer survey, which largely failed to locate any structures in these parts of the site.[1] Possibly these areas were used for quartering livestock or provided temporary accommodation for the field army. Again, neither excavation nor the geophysical survey has produced any evidence for municipal buildings or a substantial population within the fortifications, although mud-brick houses covered the ruins of the abandoned Roman city to the north.

Unlike the interior, the Byzantine cities on the Black Sea coast still displayed signs of prosperity and economic activity. Traders from the East visited Tomis (*IGL* 23, 44), Callatis (*IGL* 92-3) and Odessus (*SGLI* 96-7, 100-2, 111, 117). In Odessus, the preparation of hides, presumably for export, seems to have been an important local industry (*SGLI* 99-100, 102-4, 126). If raw materials were being exported, one important import must have been wine: a trader from Alexandria was engaged in supplying

---

[1] Since the final phase of occupation ended in destruction, even flimsy structures which the resistivity survey failed to detect would show up as strong magnetic anomalies. On the Lower Danube during the sixth century, mud-brick was generally used for domestic housing, and burnt mud-brick was certainly located by the magnetometer survey, although only where it overlay rough stone foundations, already identified by the resistivity survey. Both geophysical surveys were conducted by Dr P. Strange, Dept of Electrical and Electronic Engineering, University of Nottingham.

Tomis (*IGL* 28). Illustrative of the commercial links between the Black Sea coast, Asia Minor and the eastern Mediterranean is the distribution of Late Roman fine ware which reached the Black Sea cities (Minchev 1983, 194–6), but failed to penetrate far inland to the cities of the interior, either because there was insufficient demand or because their inhabitants lacked the income to afford imported luxuries. The fortifications of Tomis were rebuilt in the sixth century (*IGL* 7; Pârvan 1914, 422–3 and 437). The work was paid for by individuals, presumably citizens of substance (*IGL* 9), and one section was completed by the 'makelarioi', probably an association of merchants (*IGL* 8). The city was even enlarged by the construction of a new city wall, although this new quarter was reserved for Christian basilicas, not residential accommodation or municipal buildings. All the major cities acquired new churches in the sixth century, many of which, such as those at Callatis, received lavish decoration (Barnea 1958, 331–49). Ecclesiastics feature in the inscriptions of Tomis (*IGL* 32, 45, 48), Callatis (*IGL* 91) and Odessus (*SGLI* 107). Urban garrisons may be presumed for most of the cities, as at Tomis (*IGL* 30, 41) and probably at Odessus (*SGLI* 89, 91–2), where the *magister militum per Illyricum* had his headquarters (*SGLI* 87–8).

Of all the coastal cities in northern Thrace, Histria provides the most completely excavated plan. Although, during the sixth century, the city retained in use its fourth-century fortifications enclosing *c.* 7 ha, small mud-brick houses occupied much of the plateau outside the city, extending over a further 25 ha (Ştefan 1976, 48–50). The city's fortifications were restored during the reign of Anastasius (*IGL* 112–13). Rebuilding involved a reconstruction of the main gate and probably also the construction of a modest piazza (22 × 7 m), immediately inside the entrance. This open space, the only candidate for a sixth-century forum, did not, however, serve any obvious political or economic function: it rather acted as a forecourt to the Christian basilica built immediately to the east (Sion and Suceveanu 1974, 11–13; Condurachi *et al.* 1954, 85–6 and 99–106). Occupation continued as late as the sixth century in the 'industrial quarter', in the form of small workshops, and also on the eastern side of the city, in the 'temple sector', although buildings were poorly constructed of mud-brick and stone with no indication of systematic planning (Condurachi *et al.* 1954, 293–324). The baths, possible shops and markets between the main square and the 'economic quarter' no longer functioned in the sixth century (Ştefan 1976, 46–51). Still, some pretension and wealth is demonstrated by the construction of at least six large town houses, grouped together on the eastern side of the city. Built with stone and mortared walls, each had an internal courtyard, in one case adorned with a peristyle equipped with well-executed white marble capitals, while one of the houses had its own chapel and bath suite (Condurachi 1971, 173–89). Histria was the most northerly coastal city in Thrace and has produced understandably less evidence of prosperity than its neighbours further away from the frontier. Even so, Histria possessed at least a few modestly wealthy inhabitants and, though it was hardly populous, if the extramural population is included, the city must have had several hundred inhabitants. However, civic administrative buildings are absent, and the city did not maintain the standard of amenities which it had possessed in the Early Empire.

All the cities which have been discussed in this section possessed impressive fortifications, their strength enhanced, as at Justiniana Prima and Nicopolis, by natural defences. However, none has provided any evidence for a planned urban grid of streets or regular *insulae* for housing. In the case of the two new creations of Nicopolis and Justiniana Prima, this fundamental aspect of urban planning was certainly never applied. Some basic amenities were provided in the form of an aqueduct and baths at Justiniana Prima, but this city seems to have been exceptional. The greatest expenditure appears to have been invested in the construction and decoration of churches, which occupied the most important sites in the centre of the cities and along the principal roads. A limited number of wealthy families built houses either along the main streets or, most evidently at Histria, in a separate quarter on the periphery of the city. They presumably played their part in the administration of their communities, but seem not to have been anxious to proclaim their status: only one *principalis* is indirectly attested, a certain Marcus, from Tomis (*IGL* 36). Further south, the power of this class may have been stronger: *potentiores* were buying up land owned by the Church (Justinian, *Nov.* 65, AD 538). The dichotomy between the Church and the class of *potentiores* was probably complicated by the military. The influence of military commanders and the part played by urban garrisons in the life of the cities remains a matter of conjecture, but their presence and comparative wealth, expressed in the occasional erection of inscriptions, suggests that they may well have formed an important element in the urban community.

There were differences between the cities. The cities of the interior demonstrably lack the signs of economic activity, such as imports of North African fine wares, which are found on the Black Sea coast, where trade and industry linked the cities more closely with Asia Minor and the eastern Mediterranean. Inland, wealth remained firmly dependent upon the production of an agricultural surplus, which must have been particularly difficult at a time when the frontier garrisons regularly failed to guarantee security.[1] The creation of the *quaestura exercitus* by Justinian in 536 (Justinian, *Nov.* 41) joined the provinces of Scythia and Moesia II with Caria, the Cyclades and Cyprus. This otherwise curious union was probably precipitated by the inability of the Danubian provinces to provide sufficient supplies to feed the army and the need to facilitate the importation of foodstuffs: the promulgation of the law is explicitly concerned with the regular supply of the *annona*.

Nowhere is there any suggestion that there existed civic autonomy in the form of municipal administration. No inscription, public or private, refers to civic organization; no city has produced any building which could have accommodated a council meeting; and there seems to have been no provision for a civic centre worthy of description as a forum. The church, restricted group of *potentiores* and perhaps the military establishment occupied the cities. Only small numbers of less wealthy artisans and shopkeepers lived within the fortifications, and none of these are likely to have played an active rôle in government, except perhaps on the Black Sea coast, where a commercial class achieved wealth and conceivably some political importance. Although the intramural population was small, all the excavated sites suggest that cities were encircled by extensive extramural settlements. It is difficult not to conclude that the majority of the population attached to cities was actually excluded from these

---

[1] For a catalogue of major invasions and local incursions of Slavs, Avars and Bulgars throughout the sixth century, which must have been especially serious for those cities located close to the Danubian frontier, see Lemerle 1954, 265–508.

fortified enclosures, which, far from protecting an urban settlement, functioned simply as centres for ecclesiastical and military administration.

This change cannot be dated as late as the reign of Justinian. Despite the claims of Procopius (*Buildings* 4.5–11), no city has provided any evidence for Justinianic reconstruction.[1] The rebuilding of Histria and the reconstruction of forts on the Danubian frontier of Scythia can be dated to the reign of Anastasius.[2] At this time, the city of Ratiaria was rebuilt and the well-cut gate inscription optimistically expressed faith in the future: *Anastasiana Ratiaria semper floreat* (Velkov 1984, 92–4). The foundations of the Byzantine *polis* in which *potentiores* and the Church dominated the organization of the city were clearly laid by the very beginning of the sixth century. Its origins must go back still further and not necessarily only as far as the political and military upheavals of the fifth century.

Conclusion

Much work still needs to be done on cities in the Danubian provinces in the Late Roman period. Moreover, it is difficult to assess the importance of such changes as did occur without a clear understanding of urbanism in the region in earlier periods of Roman rule. The cities of the Antonine and Severan periods

[1] Apart from Justiniana Prima, there is no convincing evidence for building activity during the reign of Justinian from any city nearer to the Lower Danube than Mesambria, south of the Haemus mountains, where, curiously, building tile was being imported from Constantinople (Ognenova-Marinova 1969, 109–20). The only support for Procopius' catalogue of restored and newly built sites in the eastern Balkans comes in the text of an inscription from Bylis on the Albanian Adriatic coast which claims that this city's fortifications were rebuilt in emulation of the achievements of Justinian who built *phrouria* in Mysia, Scythia, Illyricum and Thrace: *Monumentet* 1 (1987), 63–72.

[2] In addition to the Anastasian building inscription (*IGL* 112), some of the Anastasian tile-stamps came from the fortification wall, close to the main gate (*IGL* 113). On the Danubian frontier of Scythia, Dinogetia (Gărvan) was rebuilt under Anastasius (*IGL* 246). A possible exception is a building inscription from Tomis which may commemorate the erection of a Justinianic church (*IGL* 87).

succeeded because they were able to maintain the support of a wealthy curial class: there is no indication here that towns themselves possessed an important function as commercial or industrial centres except on the Black Sea coast, where cities demonstrated notable resilience, maintaining a remarkable degree of prosperity until the late sixth century. Elsewhere, cities suffered from the economic and military disasters of the third century. The reforms of the Tetrarchy may well have precipitated the rapid decline of the curial class, and, although a curial class continued to exist, there is little sign that it continued to invest or even had any interest in preserving the local autonomy which cities had enjoyed during the Early Empire.

By the fifth century, the Church seems to have emerged as the most important factor in maintaining some form of local government. Whereas the cities of Noricum and central Illyricum did not survive the collapse of imperial authority in the first half of the fifth century, cities appear again in the late fifth century with the revival of Byzantine power on the Lower Danube. However, the *poleis* of the sixth century bear little or no resemblance to the cities of the fourth, let alone the second century. They were essentially centres of imperial and ecclesiastical administration, and the civilian population appears to have been dependent upon, but largely excluded from, these Byzantine citadels. Autonomy for an urban population appears not to have been even considered. The curial class would probably have agreed, as early as the Tetrarchy, that imperial involvement in the cities amounted to an abuse of their former rights of local autonomy. By the sixth century, it is doubtful if the urban population remembered or even understood the concept of urban self-government which had proved so attractive to the cities of the Early Empire.

Bibliography

Alföldy , G. (1964/5), 'Ein Diokletianinschrift aus Lauriacum', *Jahreshefte des Österreichischen Archäologischen Instituts* 47, 207–18.
Alföldy, G. (1974), *Noricum* (London).
Alzinger, W. (1977), 'Das Municipium Claudium Aguntum', *ANRW* ii.6.300–413.

Barbu, V. (1971), 'Din necropolele Tomisului', *Studii și Cercetări de Istorie Veche* 22/1, 47–68.

Bardenache, G. (1968), 'Un documento tardo di sincretismo pagano', *Studii Clasice* 10, 177–83.

Barnea, I. (1958), 'Roman-Byzantine basilicae discovered in the Dobrogea between 1948–58', *Dacia* n.s. 2, 331–49.

Barnea, I., Barnea, A., Cătăniciu, I.B., Mărgineanu-Cărstoiu, M. and Papuc, Gh. (1979), *Tropaeum Traiani*, i. *Cetatea*, Bibliotecă de Arheologie XXXV (Bucharest).

Bavant, B. (1984), 'La ville dans le nord de l'Illyricum', in *Villes*, 245–88.

Bucovală, M. (1977), *Marele edificiu roman cu mozaic de la Tomis* (Constanța).

Claude, D. (1969), *Die byzantinische Stadt im 6. Jahrhundert* (Munich).

Condurachi, E. (1971), 'Problema unor basilici creştine de la Histria şi Callatis', *Pontica, Studii şi Materiale de Istorie, Arheologie şi Muzeolografie* (Constanța) 4, 173–89.

Condurachi, E. *et al.* (1954), *Histria: Monografia Archaeologica* i (Bucharest).

Dagron, G. (1984), 'Les villes dans l'Illyricum protobyzantin', in *Villes*, 1–19.

Danov, H. and Ivanov, T. (1980), *Antique Tombs in Bulgaria* (Sofia).

Fitz, J. (1976), *Gorsium* (Székésfehérvár).

Fitz, J. (1978), 'Forschungen in Gorsium im Jahre 1975', *Alba Regia (Annales Musei Stephani Regis,* Székesfehérvár) 16, 236–40.

Fitz, J. (1982), 'Forschungen in Gorsium im Jahre 1979', *Alba Regia* 20, 201–58.

Fitz, J. (1986), 'Forschungen in Gorsium im Jahre 1981/2', *Alba Regia* 24, 109–61.

Fulep, F. (1984), *Sopianae* (Budapest).

Hoffmann, D. (1969), *Das spätrömische Bewegungsheer und die Notitia Dignitatum*, vol. 1 (Dusseldorf).

Hoffmann, D. (1970), *Das spätrömische Bewegungsheer und die Notitia Dignitatum*, vol. 2 (Dusseldorf).

Hudeczek, E. (1977), 'Flavia Solva', *ANRW* ii.6.414–71.

Jones, A. H. M. (1940), *The Greek City from Alexander to Justinian* (Oxford).

Jones, A. H. M. (1964), *The Later Roman Empire 284–602* (Oxford).

Jones, A. H. M. (1971), *The Cities of the Eastern Roman Empire*, 2nd edn (Oxford).

Kondić, V. and Popović, V. (1977), *Tsarichin Grad* (Belgrade).

Lemerle, P. (1954), 'Invasions et migrations dans les Balkans depuis la fin de l'époque romaine jusqu'au VIIe siècle', *Revue Historique* 211, 265–308.

Mihailov, G. (1965), 'Epigraphika', *Izvestiya na Narodniya Muzei Bourgas* 2, 150–3.

Minchev, A. (1983), 'The Late Roman fine ware imports to the western Black Sea coast', in Poulter (ed.), ii.194–201.

Minchev, A. and Georgiev, P. (1979), 'Razkopki v Marcianopolis prez 1975 g.', *INMV* 15, 101–11.

Mirchev, M. (1951a), 'Podova mozaika v Reka Devniya', *INMV* 8, 119–21.

Mirchev, M. (1951b), 'Kusno-rimiskiyat nekropol na Odessos', *INMV* 8, 91–6.

Mirchev, M. (1970), 'Rimski Termi v Varna', *Actes du premier congrès international des études sud-est européennes* (Sofia), 455–77.

Mócsy, A. (1974), *Pannonia and Upper Moesia* (London).

Ognenova-Marinova, L. (1969), 'Les briques à estampilles de Nessèbre', in T. Ivanov (ed.), *Nessèbre* i (Sofia), 109–20.

Pârvan, V. (1914), 'Zidul cetaţii Tomis', *Analele Academiei Română Memoriile Secţiunii Istorice* (Bucharest) ser. 2, 37, 415–44.

Póczy, K. (1977), *Scarbantia* (Kecskemét).

Póczy, K. (1980), 'Pannonian cities', in A. Lengyel and G.T.B. Radan (eds), *The Archaeology of Roman Pannonia* (Budapest), 239–74.

Popescu, E. (1975), 'Zur Geschichte der Stadt in Kleinskythien in der Spätantike: ein epigraphischer Beitrag', *Dacia* n.s. 19, 173–82.

Popović, V. and Ochsenschlager, E.L. (1976), 'Der spätkaiserzeitliche Hippodrom in Sirmium', *Germania* 54, 156–81.

Poulter, A.G. (ed.) 1983, *Ancient Bulgaria: Papers Presented to the International Symposium on the Ancient History and Archaeology of Bulgaria, University of Nottingham, 1981*, 2 vols (Nottingham). Includes, at ii.74–118, Poulter, 'Town and country in Moesia Inferior'.

Poulter, A.G. (1983/4), 'Roman towns and the problem of Late Roman urbanism: the case of the Lower Danube', *Hephaistos* 5/6, 109–32.

Poulter, A.G. (1988), 'Nicopolis ad Istrum, Bulgaria. An interim report on the excavations 1985–7', *The Antiquaries Journal* 68/1, 69–89.

Sion, A. and Suceveanu, A. (1974), 'Contribuţii stratigrafice la urbanistica Histriei Romane (seclolele II–VI e.n.)', *Monumenti Istorice şi de Artă, Revista Muzeelor şi Monumentelor* (Bucharest) 43/1, 5–15.

Soultov, B. (1983), 'The typology and chronology of provincial Roman pottery from Lower Moesia', in Poulter (ed.), ii.119–28.

Stancliffe, C. (1983), *St Martin and his Hagiographer* (Oxford).

Ştefan, S. (1976), 'Cercetări aerofotografice privind topografia urbana a Histriei. iii: Epoca Romana tîrzie (sec. IV–VII e.n.)', *Monumente Istorice şi de Artă, Revista Muzeelor şi Monumentelor*, 43–51.

Stiglitz, H., Kandler, M. and Jobst, W. (1977), 'Carnuntum', *ANRW* ii.6.583–730.

Toncheva, G. (1968), 'Odessos i Marcianopolis v svete novuih arheologicheskih issledvanii', *Sovetskaya Arheologiya* 1, 230–5.

Tóth, E. (1973), 'Late Antique imperial palace in Savaria', *Acta Archaeologica Academiae Scientiarum Hungaricae* 25, 117–37.

Velkov, V. (1977), *Cities in Thrace and Dacia in Late Antiquity* (Amsterdam).

Velkov, V. (1984), 'Buzpomenatelen nadpis za imperator Anastasii (491–518) ot Ratsiariya', *Arheologiya* (Sofia) 26.2/3, 92–4.

Vetters, H. (1977), 'Lauriacum', *ANRW* ii.6.355–79.

Vulpe, A. and Barnea, I. (1968), *Din Istoria Dobrogei*, iii: *Romanii la Dunarea de Jos* (Bucharest).

5

The end of the city in Roman Britain

Richard Reece

The range of urban units

From the point of view of the Roman administrator around the year AD 220 Roman Britain contained the same units of urban administration as most of the other provinces of the Empire. The provinces of Britain were divided up into *civitates*, administrative areas of a size similar to the mediaeval county, or larger, with a town to act as administrative headquarters. These towns are often known as the '*civitas* capitals' and authority almost certainly had a hand in their genesis because they were planned from the first on the grid-iron pattern which was totally foreign to Britain. London grew, probably by trade, but did not have a *civitas* around it. At some stage it rose in status, perhaps to a *colonia*, then to a provincial capital, and finally to be metropolis of the Late Roman group of British Provinces or Diocese. Colchester, Gloucester and Lincoln had military origins but when the army moved on northwards and westwards out of the lowland zone they were fashioned into *coloniae*, colonies for veteran soldiers. At York a *colonia* was founded beside the legionary fortress. These, to a visiting imperial official, were the towns of Roman Britain. There is the strong possibility that a few new *civitas* capitals were later created, and therefore some *civitates* were subdivided, but this remains uncertain (Frere 1987, 188–98).

The archaeologist has added to this sequence the category of small town. A good example is Hibaldstow which provides a substantial amount of information for a recent study of one category of small town, the roadside settlement (Smith 1987). I think it would be fair to say that the official visiting Roman Britain would not have recognized these straggling, lightly populated, unplanned settlements, with few, if any, examples of public buildings, as towns. I would endorse this opinion, for there is no evidence that they fulfil my basic criterion for urban function, a population greater than that which can feed itself off the surrounding land. Until this criterion is fulfilled it seems better to talk of the agricultural village of varying size.

The decline of the towns

There is no written evidence, so far as I know, that any urban settlement in Roman Britain was demoted in the third, fourth, or even the fifth century. It could well be argued that whenever Roman administration ceased in Britain towns lost their Roman status, but that point is not capable of development. If we want to talk about the changing fortunes of towns in Roman Britain we are forced to use archaeological evidence. This immediately separates out discussion of Britain from discussion of most of the other provinces of the Empire because their stories depend mainly on historical sources. The two different types of source have very different methods and lead to conclusions of different emphasis so that it is highly unwise to make comparisons between the two cases. Britain is poor in written sources, but has perhaps the best-developed archaeological sources. Inscriptions, being written sources, obviously belong to history and not to archaeology, which is the attempt to make sense of the uninscribed rubbish left by the past. This causes many procedural problems which have been argued out at length among archaeologists (Reece 1988), but which seem to be of little interest to ancient historians.

This leaves us with a method for discussing the rise and fall of towns in Britain which seems very simple – a discussion of the nature and density of occupation on the agreed town sites of Britain – but which is in fact very difficult. The survey work of such occupation has not been done, and there is no generally agreed criterion for 'urban density of occupation'. Since we are concerned with the later period, perhaps from the third century onwards, it would be permissible to take the archaeological state of towns early in the third century as a datum from which to

measure later success or failure. This would not be my preferred
method, since it bypasses the question of whether these nodes on
the communication system were ever really towns in anything but
the pointless and superficial sense of status, but as I have treated
the subject at length elsewhere (Reece 1988) I will leave it alone
here.

Most commentators would agree that the early third century is
the high point of town life in Britain. It is the point by which the
civic buildings are mostly constructed and functioning, town
houses have been re-built in stone and furnished with paintings
and mosaics, defences, whether of banks or walls or both, have
been constructed, and the province seems to be functioning well
(Frere 1987, 229–56). Detailed study of a *civitas* capital such as
Silchester (Boon 1974) might raise doubts as to whether anything
less than this peak of occupation would satisfy our visiting Roman
administrator as to urban status. Even at its height, such a town
would seem a sleepy garden suburb compared with the bustle of a
truly Mediterranean city.

Standard commentaries (e.g. Salway 1981, 371ff) may allow
that some problems occurred in town life in the late third century,
but hold that they were repaired by the emperors' interest in
Britain early in the fourth century, and that thereafter town life
flourished until it fell victim to the troubles of the fifth century. I
doubt this because there are so many cases where towns show gaps
in occupation in the fourth century which were not there earlier.
Some of these points were collected in an earlier paper (Reece
1980), but a comprehensive survey has never been done. The
clearest example of such problems occurs at London (Merrifield
1983, 172ff) where substantial areas, especially in the western half
of the city, show very little occupation indeed. A list of other
details, such as the failure to re-build the basilica at Wroxeter
after a fire (Atkinson 1942, 123–6), or the failure of Wheeler at
Verulamium to find much in the way of fourth- or fifth-century
activity (Wheeler 1936, 28–32), is always countered by the findings
of Barker at Wroxeter (Barker 1979) and Frere at Verulamium
(Frere 1983, 212–28), both of which seem to support occupation
into the fifth century.

An exchange such as this misses one of my main points, for it is
not a matter of opposing areas which do not continue into the
fourth century with areas that do. Each time that an area is agreed

to be unoccupied in the later period, the argument against the complete survival of town life advances. If we supposed that the areas dug by Atkinson and Barker, by Wheeler and Frere, were equal, and even if we assumed that the Barker and Frere areas were totally filled with occupied buildings, on the lines of the time around AD 220, then this would suggest a 50 per cent loss in town life between 220 and the fourth century. Of course the picture is not so clear cut as this, but I think it is true to say that if all the problems were taken into account then a 50 per cent reduction in town life would be a minimum figure. At this point we have to ask whether the genteel and spacious settlement of *c*. 220 can afford a loss of 50 per cent occupation, and still count as a town. I think not; others disagree.

There is one other point which needs to be taken into account, and that is the actual material found, the animal bone refuse, the pottery and the coins, all of which were discarded as rubbish. A thriving building, or street, or town keeps itself free of rubbish; rubbish tends to build up where households, or neighbourhoods, or urban units are failing in organization. A drain needs to be kept free in order to work; a roadside ditch needs to be empty to take storm water, a building needs to have a relatively well-swept floor if it is to be of maximum use. Yet some of the best deposits of Late Roman material are to be found in just such spots. It has to be mentioned, in passing, that there is less problem in dating coin and pottery deposits to the end of the fourth century than to almost any other period in Roman Britain. The coins cannot be dated to any other period because, for example, they have not been issued before the House of Valentinian (364–78) or the House of Theodosius (378–402), and there is no evidence at present that they continue in use beyond about 410. In the same way, pottery shows several forms which are unknown early in the fourth century, but which also fail to appear consistently in deposits later than the very beginning of the fifth century. Deposits containing such pottery and coins have to be dated after about 350 and probably before 410. Good deposits, which show disuse and disorganization, occur in a roadside ditch at Lincoln (Darling 1977), in a yard or building at Cirencester (McWhirr 1986), and in the theatre at Verulamium (Kenyon 1934).

If the areas of Roman towns which were either unoccupied in the later fourth century, or where deposits of material suggested breakdown in the later fourth century, were subtracted from the urban whole, then I suggest that the remaining occupation, seen as a unit on a 'clean', that is a green-field, site would be seen as a substantial village. This is a matter of density of occupation and diversity of occupations and not a statement about abstractions such as legal status. I have little doubt that administration continued to be effected in the fourth century, as before, from these administrative villages, and I am therefore not at all surprised that they achieve sometimes new, and sometimes newly furbished, defences in the fourth century. These defences also appear at some of the 'small towns', which I consider large villages, and there is not as yet any clear indication that such defences can be taken to confer urban status on whatever is inside them. Indeed one such defended area, Gatcombe, south-west of Bristol, is variously referred to as a villa (Branigan 1977) and a 'small town' (Cunliffe 1967).

Towns and deromanization

The discussion of what actually happened can be clearly seen to have moved away from fact, whether the orthodox view or the alternative view is followed. The fact is the finding of a certain piece of pottery or a certain coin in a certain position. Description of this as occupation or desertion is a matter of interpretation and of choice; there is no clear right or wrong about it. The archaeological material might support the idea that the first two centuries showed Britain moving towards the Mediterranean version of the town, and, in the later third and fourth centuries, moving away. My view of the fourth century, in which the density of occupation in towns declined, but in villages remained the same or increased, leads to a map of Britain in which most of the settlements are of roughly the same size and local importance, with the old *civitas* capitals having a wider significance to the Imperial bureaucracy. I see this as a part of the change from a Romanizing Britain in the second century to a deromanizing Britain in the fourth and fifth centuries. I do not see a dividing line formed by the end of formal administration from the Roman Empire sometime about AD 406 because such legalistic quibbles have no interest for me as an archaeologist. I see a gradual change from a near acceptance of towns in 220 to their complete irrelevance in 450.

The fact that the material suggests this view is in itself sufficient justification for holding it: there is no need to seek to explain how such changes might have taken place; but in fact I find the subject interesting and am quite happy to pursue the interpretative line further. Some people seem addicted to the idea that prosperity is uniquely tied to the flourishing of towns. I do not hold this article of belief. All the material evidence suggests a more widespread prosperity in the fourth century in Britain without an increase in urban life, and almost certainly with at least a reduction in the intensity of urban life. Coins are much more widely distributed than before, and are proportionately more common in rural, non-town, sites (Reece 1987, ch. 5). Mosaics, expensive decorations which show a considerable economic surplus accruing to their owner, are more common in the fourth century and are predominantly in the countryside (Smith 1969). Money which had been sent out of the province in the second century to bring in supplies of fine pottery from Gaul, such as Samian and colour-coated wares, in the fourth century remained in Britain to purchase much larger amounts of New Forest (Fulford 1975) and Oxfordshire (Young 1977) pottery which were distributed over a much wider range of sites. These potteries were sited in the countryside, presumably to be in touch with their major markets, while their predecessors in Colchester and near London were sited near second-century towns to take advantage of those earlier concentrations of population.

But the view from the town is the Romanizing view, and there is nothing strange in the idea that Britain was never totally Romanized so that the towns sat, as administrative superstructures, on a native basis. If the military and economic events of the third century loosened the administrative direction of the provinces then there is nothing odd in seeing the local nexus of markets assert itself. This local nexus can never have been suppressed by the *civitas* capitals because they are spaced much too widely over the country to act as cattle and vegetable markets. What emerges in the fourth century is the British system of village markets which had no need for higher centres. The *civitas* capitals are completely acceptable within this framework, and they fulfil this rôle of village market, but the only thing which marks them off from other settlements, their administrative rôle, can never have sustained urban life without the active will of the local inhabitants. The peace of the second century allowed the bureaucracy to promote, by example and exhortation, the civic way of life. Later years did not allow this luxury; without it, and without much of their revenue (Jones 1964, 732ff) the survival of town life depended on the will of the people. I suggest that the material remains available show that this will was not present in Britain.

Towns and Christianity

But this is not the end of the change we are considering. However far town life sank, for instance in Gaul, there still remained a detectable nucleus, and this was often associated with the Christian church. In Britain either there was little Christianity, or the church was not basically urban. Charles Thomas has assembled the basic evidence (Thomas 1981) which suggests that there clearly was continuing Christianity, but even he cannot find continuing bishoprics. The simplest answer is to accept the decline in towns and suppose that when a form of Christianity stronger than the Constantinian faith of expedience grew up (Lane Fox 1986, 667 ff), towns and urban bishops were irrelevant. The British case therefore diverges from the continental case because we do not have the urban Christian channel of continuity.

Discontinuity

Even to the most orthodox commentator the change from an urban framework in Britain, to rural, has to grow out of the Late Roman way of life. It is impossible, at present, to prolong life in towns with Roman material until the Saxon material arrives (Brooks 1988; Reece 1989). This can only mean that the Saxons are not responsible for the decline in town life. The change began before the end of the fourth century, and continued into the fifth century. It seems to happen a little in advance of the disappearance of Roman traits in the material culture which can be described as deromanization. If the blood-and-thunder explanation of Saxon attack is no longer available, it is difficult to see this change as anything more than fashion. This, to some people, will be a failure of explanation, for fashions may be regarded as inconsequential obsessions. This seems quite reasonable, so long as the predilection for the town, the use of pottery, the use of coinage, the preference for four-square mortared stone buildings over wood, are all regarded as part of this change in fashion.

Conclusion

Britain in the first century BC flirted with Roman ways, and this may have made it easier for an expanding Empire to ensure a conquest (Groenman-van Waateringe 1979). By the fourth century, Mediterranean influence in north-west Europe was on the wane and, after a short period of self-absorption, the interests of Britons turned to the nearby continent. The Roman Empire had been a passing fancy in the real development of Britain, and towns were one of the sorts of bead that the natives first considered and then rejected.

Bibliography

Atkinson, D. (1942), *Report on Excavations at Wroxeter*, Birmingham Archaeological Society (Oxford).

Barker, P.A. (1979), 'The latest occupation on the site of the Baths Basilica at Wroxeter', in P.J. Casey (ed.), *The End of Roman Britain*, BAR 71 (Oxford), 175–81.

Boon, G.C. (1974), *Silchester, the Roman Town of Calleva* (London).

Branigan, K. (1977), *Gatcombe Roman Villa*, BAR 44 (Oxford).

Brooks, D. (1988), 'The case for continuity in fifth century Canterbury re-examined', *Oxford Journal of Archaeology* 7/1, 99–114.

Cunliffe, B.W. (1967), 'Excavations at Gatcombe, Somerset', *Proceedings of the University of Bristol Spelaeological Society*, 2/2, 126–60.

Darling, M.J. (1977), 'A group of Late Roman pottery from Lincoln', *The Archaeology of Lincoln* xvi/1 (London).

Frere, S.S. (1983), *Verulamium Excavations* ii (London).

Frere, S.S. (1987), *Britannia*, 3rd edn (London).

Fulford, M. (1975), *New Forest Roman Pottery*, BAR 17 (London).

Groenman-van Waateringe, W. (1979), 'Urbanization and the north-west frontier of the Roman Empire', in W.S. Hanson and L.J.F. Keppie (eds), *Roman Frontier Studies 1979*, BAR 71 (Oxford), 1037-44.

Jones, A.H.M. (1964), *The Later Roman Empire* (Oxford).

Kenyon, K. (1934), 'The Roman theatre at Verulamium', *Archaeologia* 84, 213-61.

Lane Fox, R. (1986), *Pagans and Christians* (London).

McWhirr, A. (1986), *Houses in Roman Cirencester*, Cirencester Excavations III (Cirencester).

Merrifield, R. (1983), *London, City of the Romans* (London).

Reece, R. (1980), 'Town and country: the end of Roman Britain', *World Archaeology* 12/1, 77-92.

Reece, R. (1987), *Coinage in Roman Britain* (London).

Reece, R. (1988), *My Roman Britain* (Cirencester).

Reece, R. (1989), 'Models of continuity', *Oxford Journal of Archaeology* 8/2, 231-6.

Salway, P. (1981), *Roman Britain* (Oxford).

Smith, D.J. (1969), 'The mosaic pavements', in A.L.F. Rivet (ed.), *The Roman Villa in Britain* (London).

Smith, R.F. (1987), *Roadside Settlements in Lowland Roman Britain*, BAR 157 (Oxford).

Thomas, C. (1981), *Christianity in Roman Britain* (London).

Wheeler, R.E.M. (1936), *Verulamium, a Belgic and Two Roman Cities*, Society of Antiquaries (London).

Young, C.J. (1977), *Oxfordshire Roman Pottery*, BAR 43 (Oxford).

6

'The cities are not populated as once they were'[*]

Philip Dixon

For the student of Late Roman and post-Roman Britain the fate of the Roman towns is a recurrent theme. In this paper I propose to examine the final stages of one range of towns, normally now called '*civitas* capitals', since discussions of the end of Roman towns have normally concentrated on these sites. In what follows 'town', unless otherwise modified, refers to these settlements. Even Reece, to judge from the citation of examples in his paper (1980), is principally considering the regional centres, the *civitas* capitals, and not the so-called 'small towns', some of which are indeed larger in area than the smallest of the *civitates* (for an excellent modern summary of the types and their development see Millett 1990, 65–126 and 145–51). Gildas, too, has these sites in mind (*Ruin of Britain* 3.2), and controversy is concerned with the eclipse of these once important 'public towns', rather than with the much more obscure fate of the small towns, for which one may now consult Burnham and Wacher (1990). I shall be arguing that our interpretations of the Late Roman *civitates* misrepresent their nature when they are discussed in economic terms; that to consider them as social units reconciles the controversy between Reece's position and more traditionalist notions of the town and

[*] The present account is a revised version of a paper originally presented to a Day School in Birmingham in 1987, and subsequently circulated (Dixon 1988) as delivered.

allows us a clearer picture of the transition between the Roman province and the English successor kingdoms.

The view that the Anglo-Saxon conquerors of Roman Britain shunned the old Roman towns, through fear, or simply through inexperience with them, is surprisingly widespread. It may have its roots in poetry. In the middle Saxon period, perhaps about AD 700, an English poet pictured a ruined town:

> Snapped rooftrees, towers tottering
> The work of the Giants, the stonesmiths
> Moulders. Rime scours gatetowers, rime on mortar,
> Shattered are shower shields, roofs ruined.
> Age underate them.

The Ruin

Modern scholars have normally agreed with this picture of decay: 'here and there squatters may still have inhabited the ruins' (Frere 1974, 422; similarly Wacher 1974, 416). The Roman town was brought to an end, and if a new English town was built on the same spot 'it was largely an accident of geography' (Wacher 1978, 267). Attempts to provide an alternative view, and demonstrate continuity, have proved indecisive. Martin Biddle (1977), for example, after a lengthy discussion, concluded that what remained was 'a thread of continuity, however non-urban in character'. The town, that is to say, survived, but not as a town.

Without explicit documentary references, scholars have turned to the evidence of archaeology. But in the case of towns, this evidence is particularly ambiguous. Many of the Roman sites underlie modern cities, and the opportunities for all but the smallest investigations are few. The excavator is too often confronted with a partial slice through a single *insula*; we must be extremely cautious about projecting the results of this small-scale work on to a picture of a town as a whole. Even those few towns not now encumbered by modern occupation are not as simple for the archaeologist to understand as they might appear, for towns are huge areas; in Britain their range is from a few tens of acres for a small town, to over three hundred for the walled area of Londinium. The cost of large-scale work is prohibitive: the excavator of Wroxeter has estimated that the investigation of a third of the Roman town of Wroxeter would take about 1.25

million man weeks (Barker 1986, 64). On current prices, then, the excavation of the whole town would cost about £100 million. It is, therefore, no surprise to find how little in reality we know about the nature, and the fate, of Roman towns.

Wroxeter, a now deserted site near Shrewsbury, at present provides the clearest evidence for substantial survival of life within a town. Barker's excavations on part of the baths *insula* have demonstrated that the basilica was replaced by a very large rectangular timber building, beside a complex of smaller structures which may have incorporated a covered street, similar to a shopping mall. Dating evidence is unclear, but it is suspected that these buildings were finally dismantled, and this part of the town abandoned, during the sixth century (Barker 1986, 172–3).

Other sites have produced interpretations with different emphases. At Cirencester it is suggested that activity within the town ceased or diminished, and that the amphitheatre outside the town walls to the west became a defence (Wacher 1964, 17). Arles in Provence provides us with a settlement in which the amphitheatre remained the population centre of a shrunken town, and eventually contained three small castles, a couple of hundred houses and a church, and continued in this extraordinary mediaeval squalor until the clearance of the Roman site in the nineteenth century. The occupation of Cirencester, however, seems to have been a much more short-lived affair, and its date and nature have recently been questioned by Reece (1989, 110). Resolution of the matter must await the publication of the work.

Excavations in the Roman town of Exeter have found sub-Roman burials by the forum. They suggest that an early church is to be sought in this area, such as that recently discovered at St Paul-in-the-Bail, in a focal position in the forum at Lincoln (Gilmour 1979; Allen *et al.* 1984, 386–9). Burials, perhaps of the early fifth century, have been found in Canterbury (Bennett 1980, 406–8). These sites show us continued activity within the Roman walled areas; but when this activity is to create a cemetery in or near the forum it marks an overwhelming change in attitudes to planning and burial in the Roman town, and none is yet proof of the survival of town life. Clearer signs of this can be seen at Verulamium, where fourth- and early fifth-century buildings were cut through by a water-pipe, with the implication of organized co-operative works within the town which in 429 may have been the location for the debate between the provincials and St Germanus of Auxerre (Frere 1983, 21, 24 and 214–26; Thompson 1984).

In order to explain the paucity of the evidence for building and life in towns after the beginning of the fifth century, most commentators have invoked the occurrence of a catastrophe. What sort of disaster it was, however, is not clear. Gildas seems to be telling us of destruction by fire and invasion, battering rams, walls laid low to their foundations, fragments of corpses (*Ruin of Britain* 24.3–4). That the towns were brought to ruin in this fashion is now largely discounted, not least because excavation has found little trace of this sort of discontinuity. Even the notorious house of slaughter at Caistor-by-Norwich, long claimed as the best evidence of Anglo-Saxon aggression (e.g. Hawkes and Dunning 1961, 25; Myres and Green 1973), is now in doubt: the bodies in the Roman building seem to have been part of a long-subsequent cemetery (Darling 1987).

Wacher has provided an alternative explanation (1974, 414ff; 1978, 266–7): he suggested that the towns were fatally weakened by a plague, referred to by Gildas, which Wacher considers would have been brought by traders to the cities, and would have had its greatest impact on the townspeople, leading to the desertion of the town, and not on their Anglo-Saxon enemies in the countryside, who thus became dominant. The evidence for this *famosa pestis* was examined by Todd (1977). His conclusion that the fifth century was not a period of plague, and may, indeed, have been unusually free of pestilence, is now generally accepted. It seems unlikely, then, that a fifth-century epidemic caused the disappearance of Roman towns in Britain.

Economic catastrophe, a fate more perhaps in keeping with the mood of our own times, is the model chosen by Arnold (1984, ch. 2, especially pp. 38–48): towns were dense urban centres in which coins ceased, the economy collapsed into barter, industries failed, famine followed, and the townspeople fled into the countryside. The size of the population in question has been variously estimated, and may perhaps have been as many as 200,000 people (Jones 1979; Millett 1990, 181–3). Some of this picture may be got from a reading of the account of Gildas, but it is very awkward for this interpretation that within the countryside of Roman Britain there are still no traces of a movement of people into the rural hinterland, whose most prominent features, the rural villas, seem to have come to an end at about the same period as the towns themselves (Esmonde Cleary 1989, 158; Millett 1990, 223; compare Dixon 1985, 22–3). Gildas himself speaks of towns in his own day, probably about AD 540, in a brief observation: 'The cities of our land are not populated even now as once they were; right to the present they are deserted, in ruins and unkempt' (*ne nunc quidem ut antea civitates patriae inhabitantur; sed desertae dirutaeque hactenus squalent*) (*Ruin of Britain* 26.2, trans. Winterbottom 1973, 28). The statement is ambiguous (does it imply a reduced level of occupation or total abandonment?), and contributes little to our understanding of sub-Roman British towns, particularly in view of Gildas' habit of quotation and citation of parallels from Holy Writ, in which the destruction of cities by fire, plague, and wickedness forms a rhetorical trope. It is worth noting that in the Danubian provinces of the Empire both coins and mass production failed, but towns remained (see chapter 4 in this volume).

Towns in Roman Britain

What do we know about the nature of Roman towns themselves? A surprising amount comes from the examination of only a few well-known and spectacular sites, such as Pompeii, with its densely and regularly planned streets, or Ostia, with its multi-storeyed tenement blocks. Life in these towns was like Roman urban life as depicted by writers such as Juvenal, Martial and Seneca – noisy, cramped and bustling. For Roman Britain these provide us with a model, as Alan Sorrell's famous and popular reconstructions of Silchester, Verulamium and London make clear: the walled area is filled with rows of small houses and shops around the mansions of grandees, with the major public buildings standing in the middle of a sea of urbanism (see, for example, Sorrell 1981, 54, 60, 70 and 79; for a word-picture on the same lines, see Arnold 1984, 21–2).

A different view was put forward by Reece (1980). He identified the Roman town in Britain as a 'tender Mediterranean plant in foreign soil', which failed to take root; he saw the collapse of towns as a phenomenon largely of the fourth century, when farmhouses took their place inside towns, not as *rus in urbe* but as the headquarters of great estates, which he characterizes as 'Verulamium Estates Ltd'. Reece's paper excited opposition even before its publication (Reece 1980, 90–1), and has since encountered hostility from traditionalists, who point to the vigour of towns in the fourth century, as measured by new public works, and new and yet grander private houses (for a summary of the dispute see Reece 1989, 112–13; see also chapter 5 in this volume). To concentrate on the fourth century, however, may be to focus on too late a period, and to speak simply of Romano-British towns as a group may be to class together sites of more than one category, each with different histories.

At least some of these towns seem to have shrunk almost from the very moment of their foundation. The well-known aerial photographs of Caistor-by-Norwich imply a town layout left unfinished (Myres and Green 1973, map 1; Wacher 1974, 229–30), and recent work in London suggests the abandonment of part of the city area as early as the second century (Dyson and Schofield 1981, 41–3). This early shrinkage of the occupied area is an oddity, and another is that few of these towns have revealed signs of small buildings. Caerwent, it is true, has produced some back-to-back housing, but this was a *civitas* capital in an industrial area, close to the army, and not typical of the class (Wacher 1974, 386–8). London has revealed a fine block of small shops and strip housing (Esmonde Cleary 1989, 82), though the intensely mercantile phase of occupation here may belong to the first and second centuries. In contrast to the population density of a mediaeval town, however, the *civitates* are remarkably free from the repetitive lines of one- or two-unit houses needed to accommodate an urban proletariat of the sort envisaged by the catastrophe theory of the end of towns. Such houses can be identified in the early Middle Ages, for example in the Six Dials excavations of the Anglo-Saxon new town at Hamwic/Southampton (Holdsworth 1984, 334–6), and about half of the area of a high mediaeval town would normally consist of small artisan houses, occupied by about nine-tenths of the population. Work in the *civitates*, in contrast, has produced townscapes containing only a few of these small houses and shops: they mostly consist of massive public buildings and rows of large houses, such as we can see at Cirencester, Gloucester and Verulamium. These are towns filled with stately courtyard homes and what Wacher, in a phrase which emphasizes a traditional view of the function of a town as an economic and densely residential unit, called 'comparatively useless public monuments' (1974, 219–20). Not all these buildings were finished. At Silchester Fulford has suggested that the great basilica in the forum was left incomplete, and perhaps unroofed (Fulford 1985, 59ff). The scene reminds one of Pliny's experience in Bithynia, where aqueducts cracked, and an unneeded amphitheatre was falling down, all because rivalry between cities was pushing the leaders of the townships to works greater than they could afford (Pliny, *Letters* 10.37, 39). All this was taking place in Asia Minor, an area in which urbanization was a centuries-old habit; in Britain, where a town was a Roman novelty, even more over-optimistic plans might be expected.

A clue to the process of town formation in Roman Britain may be found in the development of Stonea, in the southern Fens. This failed settlement was never a town, and its location within an area likely to be an Imperial estate highlights a probable difference between it and other centres, but the site provides us with a clear model of Roman aims and methods, emphasized by its location on marginal lands, unencumbered by later buildings. An Iron Age enclosure nearby suggests a pre-Roman focus of occupation; Stonea itself was first and most importantly an administrative centre, with a massive tower-like public building, begun perhaps under Hadrian. A little later a grid of streets was laid out around the tower, and a few houses were built, leaving much of the grid empty. After less than a century of desultory occupation the administration block was demolished, and the land was given over to farming (Potter and Jackson 1982). The explanation of this seems to be that the site failed to attract a population: once the town as an administrative centre was set up, the transference of local residents from its *territorium* could be slow, and the success of the enterprise might well depend on attracting members of the élite to the new site.

Some continental towns

The classes of people resident in towns thus require further study. The excavations at Nicopolis ad Istrum have revealed an intriguing picture. The town was abandoned in the unrest of the mid-third century. In the fourth century it was restored, with rows of large courtyard houses filling up the town area. The total occupation at this point need have been no more than twenty-five or thirty important families, together with their households. In a separately walled *castellum*, built during the subsequent decline of the town, stood a Late Roman basilical church, and perhaps a palace complex, with little in the way of town planning, and no obvious array of houses (see pp. 126–7). This combination, church and palace in a shrinking Roman town, is identified at the core of sub-Roman Paris, however complex the history of its suburbs (Duby 1980, 412–13). At Tours, similarly, the late town was a small area within the walls of Roman Caesarodunum, housing the bishop's church and house, and a palace for the Frankish court.

Other continental towns give us useful pointers both to the nature of the late town, and the way in which changes took place. At Mainz (Weidemann 1968; Böhner 1977, 190–3) the Roman fortress was deserted, and the civilian settlement outside its walls was occupied. A Frankish manor ('Hof') provided the focus of secular power in the area, but this lay outside the new town until the thirteenth century. This was a town with quite certain continuity of occupation, but the arrangement of its early mediaeval parishes and of their churches shows the breakdown of an earlier symmetry into an irregular pattern. We should note with interest that this identical process, when seen in England (for example, at Canterbury or Winchester), has been held to demonstrate not a simple change but a hiatus in occupation (Tatton-Brown 1984, 5). At Kreuznach in Austria, a town ravaged in 270 and 367, a fort was built on part of the *vicus*. The fort area was royal demesne land after the end of the Empire, and a new Frankish manor was built there (Böhner 1977, 190). At Bonn the fortress became a Frankish royal holding, and long remained state property under the name Bonnburg. Outside the walls the inhabitants lived in the shadow of a Late Roman church which had been built in the extramural cemetery (ibid., 196–8). A similar picture is clear at Alzey, which 'became part of the royal domain since it had previously been Roman state property' (ibid., 188–9). Three manors were built outside the royal holding in the Roman fort. The manors became the focus of the town, and the fort was finally dismantled to provide building stone.

The evidence from the continental Empire, then, suggests that urban shrinkage could occur even in sites whose continuity is certain beyond the fifth and sixth centuries. There are, indeed, probably more signs of this on the continent than in Roman Britain: walled areas, especially those of forts, became royal demesne in the successor kingdoms; civilian settlements may have as their foci, by population drift, the cemetery churches and monasteries built outside the Roman walls, and similar foci may be provided by a secular power, the extra-urban sites of Germanic nobles.

The transition from Roman to sub-Roman towns

In England, patterns of the same sort may be traced, in which a church and a palace lay within the Roman walls, and other occupation lay in the suburbs. At York, for example, the earliest stages of the growth of the mediaeval town were long obscure. Excavations below the Minster, however, uncovered the massive hall of the basilica at the centre of the legionary fortress, and revealed that this very large building had been kept in repair, with some modifications to its rooms and to the corridors, until the whole structure was destroyed by fire. Pottery from this final phase has been identified as of the immediately pre-Viking period (Ramm 1971; D. Phillips, pers. comm.). If these interpretations are substantiated when the site is published, the most likely occupants of the basilica are the Anglian kings of the house of Edwin. Their church, well known from Bede (*Hist. Eccles.* 2.14, 20), is yet to be found, but may have lain to the north of the present Minster within the fortress. Current work in the urban centre to the south of the river suggests that Late and sub-Roman activity continued here. The Anglian town itself, as the recent work at the Redfern glass factory has now revealed, lay to the east, outside the Roman walled area. In the case of London, the early church of St Paul stood within the Roman town at Ludgate Hill; an occupation of the governor's palace within the walls, similar to that of the *regia* at Cologne, is suspected, but not proved; by the seventh century, at least, a hall of the King of Kent is recorded (Biddle and Hudson 1973; Vince 1990, 54). The site of the fort, at Cripplegate, was recognized in the late Saxon period as a fortress, and called Aldermanbury, the 'fortification of the

Alderman', and may have been a separate focus. All this was within the Roman walled area. The Anglo-Saxon trading town lay along the Strand to Aldwich ('Oldtown'), outside the Roman walls (Vince 1990, 16–17). Winchester similarly seems to provide us with an example of the combination of church-beside-palace in a Roman centre: here the cathedral was built in *c.* 648 towards the centre of the Roman town, south of the *via principalis*. No contemporary palace is at present known, but the royal palace of the later Saxon period is thought from documentary evidence to have lain a little to the north of the cathedral, beside 'palace gate' at the centre of the new town, and this may be the location of the early Saxon palace. Excavations to the east of the Roman town inside and outside the walls are suggesting abandonment within the walls, and early occupation along the road outside the gate (Biddle 1973 and 1974).

A clue to this 'thread of continuity' (Biddle 1977, 103) is provided by the way the Anglo-Saxons named their Roman *civitates*. Only London and York were singled out as trading centres ('wic'), and are found as Lundenwic and Eoforwic in the middle Saxon period (Smith 1937, 275–9; Vince 1990, 25). In both cases the trading centre itself is likely to be the settlement outside the walls of the Roman town. Three of the former Roman towns have names of rather different origin – Chelmsford is purely English, the ford of Ceolmaer, St Albans is named by association with its martyr, and Lincoln by contraction from its Roman name. The rest of the *civitates*, no fewer than seventeen of the twenty-two major Roman towns, were given names which single them out as defensive sites – three by a name plus '-byrig', and fourteen by a name plus '-ceastre' (Carver 1987, 48). These major towns struck the Anglo-Saxons, then, as fortresses. Whose fortresses they were we cannot directly say, but it would be a mistake to assume without argument that they were the fortresses of a surviving urban population.

On the continent, as we have seen, the Roman walled area of several towns became royal demesne, and we have hints of the same process in the coastal fortresses of sub-Roman Britain. When religious communities arrived in the newly converted English kingdoms, monasteries were established for them by the kings in Saxon-shore forts at Reculver, Bradwell, probably at Burgh Castle, and perhaps at Porchester. By this gift the monks were probably not being given defences for their protection: at Bradwell, at any rate, even on an exposed coast where pirate raids might be feared, the early church was built across the Roman gate, and the wall was robbed out for building materials. This land was thus almost certainly given to the monks not because it was a fortress, but because, being a fortress, it was royal land, and so was available for disposal by the newly converted monarch. We see exactly this pattern in the siting of the cathedral at Utrecht (Haslinghuis and Peeters 1965). After St Augustine's mission, bishops' seats were established inside the Roman towns of Canterbury, Winchester, York, London and Rochester. Was this, as seems widely assumed, simply because Augustine's instructions from Pope Gregory told him to concentrate on the towns (for this view see Hill 1977, 300), even though he found the towns 'a virtually empty shell' (Tatton-Brown 1984, 14)? Since the Roman Mission spent nearly two years based across the Channel while reconnoitring the land, this surely seems a strange decision. In a later period almost all these towns contained royal palaces, and the choice of *civitates* as bishops' seats was presumably a recognition that secular power already resided in the royal house inside the Roman walled area.

Our model of the Late Roman and sub-Roman town may thus involve a few substantial land holders, the rich men of whom fourth-century Ausonius is an example, who had a town house and a country house not too far away so that he could move from one to the other without trouble (Ausonius, *De Herediolo* 29–32). These townspeople required substantial houses, and their civic pride and entertainment entailed the construction of 'comparatively useless public monuments' and more or less grandiose public works. Their households needed a range of services provided by a comparatively small number of shops, and a limited range of artisans and craftsmen – cobblers, carpenters, jewellers, and the like. The mass-producing industries and the wholesale marketing lay in the countryside, linked more with the small towns and the villa economy than with that of the public towns themselves. These latter towns were dominant administrative and cultural centres, not centres of population, and, above all, not centres of an urban proletariat. This need not have been the aim in their foundation: Stonea shows us how even the plans of Hadrian could run awry, and the wide urban areas of the initial foundation demonstrate the failure of provincial towns to live up to the Mediterranean scheme.

The 'black earth' which overlies so many Roman buildings in Britain has caused considerable perplexity (for a summary see Arnold 1984, 30–1). Its source is still debated: Frere considered it windblown rubbish (1966, 93; similarly Blockley 1980); analysis suggests a soil of cultivation (MacPhail 1981; Yule 1990). Current work in York is identifying in the black earth weeds similar to those outside the town on the banks of the Ouse. This does not, however, mean that the countryside had invaded the town, and the consequent perception of this black earth as a symptom of urban decay, collapse and decline (Arnold 1984, 31; Esmonde Cleary 1989, 146–8) is misconceived. If, as seems increasingly likely, the black earth should prove to be imported and dumped topsoil, its presence on so many sites implies a major programme of public works. A Late Roman town in Britain thus may well have consisted of grand houses set in newly landscaped parks and gardens.

This model of the public towns does not, therefore, require a termination by a pandemic catastrophe by sword or plague, or, indeed, any collapse of urban life through overwhelming and rapid economic crisis. It turns on the question of the ownership of the walled areas. The owners, and certainly the controllers, of these fortified zones were the *decuriones*, with perhaps a latent claim of overlordship by the emperor. During and after the rebellion of 407, the natural successors to these owners were the usurpers of Zosimus (6.5) and Procopius (*Vandal Wars* 1.2.28), presumably members of the Romanized upper classes who assumed power within their own regions, as the Romanized habits of the group suggest (Constantius, *Life of St Germanus*; Gildas, *Ruin of Britain* 25.3). How they contrived their lives will presumably have varied from place to place. Some at least will have needed a palace, perhaps, like the large wooden building at Wroxeter, or the *principia* at York, within a town. Since, on this interpretation, they owned the town, whether anyone else lived inside the walls would then be a matter of the choice of the individual oligarchs or monarchs. The transition to post-Roman English town will thus have been not a sudden collapse, but a steady and progressive change, entirely in keeping with Gildas' brief remark, and the survival of any town would depend on the well-being of a few dozen families – a very different matter from the catastrophes implicit in any view of the Late Roman town as a significant centre of urban population.

On this interpretation a very clear distinction must be drawn between the provincial Roman *civitas* capital, and the early mediaeval town established in the eighth century and later, frequently on new sites, or on or near the small Roman towns. These new centres of the developing Anglo-Saxon kingdoms had, it seems, a dense and largely proletarian population. The sub-Roman public town, in contrast, became scarcely more than a palace and church within a defended *enceinte*, perhaps with a satellite commercial centre beside it. It continued in this form until the pressure of new invaders both in England and on the continent – Khazars, Magyars or Vikings – persuaded the rulers of the need to re-establish the suburban trading centres inside the Roman walls, and Lundenwic became Lundenburh.

Bibliography

Allen, J., Henderson, C. and Higham, R. (1984), 'Saxon Exeter', in Haslam (ed.), 385–414.

Arnold, C.J. (1984), *Roman Britain to Saxon England* (London).

Barker, P. (1979), 'The latest occupation of the site of the Baths Basilica at Wroxeter', in Casey (ed.), 175–81.

Barker, P. (1986), *Understanding Archaeological Excavation* (London).

Barker, P. (forthcoming), *Excavation on the Site of the Baths Basilica at Wroxeter* (London).

Barley, M.W. (ed.) (1977), *European Towns* (London).

Bennett, P. (1980), '68–69a Stour Street', *Archaeologia Cantiana* 96, 406–10.

Biddle, M. (1973), 'Winchester, the development of an early capital', in H. Jankühn, W. Schlesinger and H. Steuer (eds), *Vor- und Frühformen der europäischen Stadt im Mittelalter* (Göttingen), i.229–61.

Biddle, M. (1974), 'The archaeology of Winchester', *Scientific American* 130/5, 33–43.

Biddle, M. (1977), 'Towns', in D.M. Wilson (ed.), *The Archaeology of Anglo-Saxon England* (Cambridge), 99–150.

Biddle, M. and Hudson, D. (1973), *The Future of London's Past* (London).

Blockley, K. (1980), 'The Marlowe car park excavations', *Archaeologia Cantiana* 96, 402–5.

Böhner, K. (1977), 'Urban and rural settlement in the Frankish kingdom', in Barley (ed.), 185–202.

Burnham, B. and Wacher, J. (1990), *The Small Towns of Roman Britain* (London).

Carver, M. (1987), *Underneath English Towns* (London).

Casey, P.J. (ed.) (1979), *The End of Roman Britain*, BAR 71 (Oxford).

Darling M.J. (1987), 'The Caistor-by-Norwich "massacre" reconsidered', *Britannia* 18, 263–72.

Dixon, P.W. (1985), 'Catastrophe and fallacy: the end of Roman Britain', *Landscape History* 6, 21–5.

Dixon, P.W. (1988), 'Life after Wroxeter', in A. Burl (ed.), *From Roman Town to Norman Castle: Essays in Honour of Philip Barker* (Birmingham), 30–9.

Duby, G. (ed.) (1980), *Histoire de la France urbaine* i, *La ville antique des origines au IXe siècle* (Paris).

Dyson, T. and Schofield, J. (1981), 'Excavations in the City of London: second interim report, 1974–8', *Transactions of the London and Middlesex Archaeological Soc.* 32, 24–81.

Esmonde Cleary, A.S. (1989), *The Ending of Roman Britain* (London).

Frere, S.S. (1966), 'The end of Roman Britain', in J. Wacher (ed.), *The Civitas Capitals of Roman Britain* (Leicester), 87–100.

Frere, S.S. (1974), *Britannia*, 2nd edn (London).

Frere, S.S. (1983), *Verulamium Excavations* ii (London).

Fulford, M.G. (1985), 'Excavations on the sites of the amphitheatre and forum-basilica at Silchester, Hampshire: an interim report', *Antiquaries Journal* 65, 39–81.

Gilmour, B. (1979), 'The Anglo-Saxon Church at St Paul-in-the-Bail, Lincoln', *Medieval Archaeology* 23, 214–8.

Haslam, J. (ed.) (1984), *Anglo-Saxon Towns in Southern England* (Chichester).

Haslinghuis, E.J. and Peeters, C.J.A.C. (1985), *De Dom van Utrecht* ('s-Gravenhage).

Hawkes, S.C. and Dunning, G.C. (1961), 'Soldiers and settlers in Britain, fourth to fifth century', *Medieval Archaeology* 5, (1961), 1-70.

Hill, D. (1977), 'Continuity from Roman to Medieval: Britain', in Barley (ed.), 294-302.

Holdsworth, P. (1984), 'Saxon Southampton', in Haslam (ed.), 331-43.

Jones, M.E. (1979), 'Climate, nutrition and disease: an hypothesis of Romano-British population', in Casey (ed.), 175-81.

MacPhail, R. (1981), 'Soil and botanical studies of the Dark Earth', in M. Jones and G. Dimbleby (eds), *The Environment of Man: The Iron Age to the Anglo-Saxon Period*, BAR 87 (Oxford), 309-31.

Millett, M. (1990), *The Romanization of Britain* (Cambridge).

Myres, J.N.L. and Green, B. (1973), *The Anglo-Saxon Cemeteries of Caistor by Norwich and Markshall* (London).

Potter, T.W. and Jackson, R.P.J. (1982), 'The Roman site of Stonea, Cambridgeshire', *Antiquity* 56, 111-20.

Ramm, H.G. (1971), 'The end of Roman York', in R.M. Butler (ed.), *Soldier and Civilian in Roman Yorkshire* (Leicester), 179-99.

Reece, R. (1980), 'Town and country: the end of Roman Britain', *World Archaeology* 12/1, 77-92.

Reece, R. (1989), *My Roman Britain* (London).

Smith, A.H. (1937), *The Place-Names of the East Riding of Yorkshire and York*, English Place-Name Society xiv (Cambridge).

Sorrell, A. (1981), *Reconstructing the Past*, ed. M. Sorrell (London).

Tatton-Brown, T. (1984), 'The towns of Kent', in Haslam (ed.), 1-36.

Thompson, E.A. (1984), *Saint Germanus of Auxerre and the End of Roman Britain* (Woodbridge).

Todd, M. (1977), '*Famosa Pestis* and Britain in the fifth century', *Britannia* 8, 319-25.

Todd, M. (ed.) (1989), *Research on Roman Britain, 1960-89*, *Britannia* Monograph 11 (London).

Vince, A. (1984), 'The Aldwych: mid-Saxon London discovered', *Current Archaeology*, 310-12.

Vince, A. (1990), *Saxon London: an Archaeological*

Investigation (London).

Wacher, J. (1964), 'Cirencester, 1963: fourth interim report', *Antiquaries Journal* 44, 9–18.

Wacher, J. (1974), *The Towns of Roman Britain* (London).

Wacher, J. (1978), *Roman Britain* (London).

Weidemann, K. (1968), 'Die Topographie von Mainz in der Römerzeit und dem frühen Mittelalter', *Jahrbuch des Römisch-Germanischen Zentralmuseums Mainz* 15, 146–99.

Winterbottom, M. (ed.) (1973), *Gildas, The 'Ruin of Britain' and other Works* (Chichester).

Yule, B. (1990), 'The Dark Earth and late Roman London', *Antiquity* 64, 620–8.

7

Public buildings and urban change in northern Italy in the early mediaeval period

Cristina La Rocca

In many regions the fall of the Roman Empire in the West led to the complete disappearance of the cities. In northern Italy, by contrast, the cities proved remarkably tenacious. Most of the Roman cities of the region survived into mediaeval times, and their physical appearance provided notable evidence of continuity, for example in the walls and street plans. But, of course, much was changed. The great public buildings which had given the Roman cities their distinctive character survived, if at all, only as ruins, and, after a long decline, the Roman political institutions, council and magistrates, ceased to function.

A wide variety of evidence is now available for the history of the north Italian cities in the early mediaeval period: literary and documentary material and the results of the extensive archaeological activity of recent years. Not surprisingly, scholars have differed on the interpretation of all this information and in particular over the extent of the continuities between the ancient and the mediaeval cities. As so often, historians and archaeologists have sometimes adopted different perspectives. As the study of the documentary sources becomes ever more detailed and accurate, historians have tended to stress the persistence of the concept and function of the *civitas* and the continuity of the town both as the privileged seat of public authority and as the focal point of social and economic relationships in its area. Archaeologists, on the other hand, are inclined to emphasize the disparities between the material and the written evidence, and to insist on the rural character of the early mediaeval city. Moreover, this is only one aspect of the larger problem of the evaluation of the early mediaeval period in Italian history. Lombard Italy, long neglected, and scorned by historians like Pepe and the Croce school as a lapse into barbarism, has since World War II undergone a revival of interest, pioneered by Bognetti, who, however, somewhat exaggerated its break with the past. As is now widely recognized, the period deserves to be studied in its own right, rather than as a staging-post between the world of Rome and that of the mediaeval city-states.[1]

Structurally and materially the early mediaeval city was very different from the Roman one, but this very fact testifies to the development and continuing vitality of the city, linked to the needs and configuration of urban society. Continuity too should not be viewed as the simple persistence of the past, as by Mengozzi, who attempted to trace juridical and institutional aspects of the mediaeval city back to Roman precedents, as if the Lombard age had simply been an unhappy interlude without further consequences (Mengozzi 1914). It is instead important to

---

[1] Wickham 1981 provides an excellent introduction to the period for English readers. Bognetti's classic studies are collected in Bognetti 1966–8; for an assessment of his work see Tabacco 1970. General discussions of the cities include Bognetti 1959; Fasoli 1960; Fasoli *et al.* 1961; *Topografia urbana e vita cittadina nell'alto medioevo in Occidente* (Spoleto 1974), especially Février's contribution (Février 1974); Roncayolo 1978; Ward-Perkins 1983 and 1984; Bordone 1983, 1986 and 1987; *Archeologia urbana in Lombardia* (Modena, 1984); Sergi 1985; La Rocca 1986 and 1987; Brogiolo 1987; Wickham 1988. The survival of urbanism in Lombard Italy is minimized, following Bognetti, by Fumagalli 1983 and 1985, and Galetti 1982–3, 1983a, 1983b and 1985; cf. the insistence on the rural character of towns throughout early mediaeval Europe by Hodges 1982, and Hodges and Whitehouse 1983. Studies of individual cities include: Bologna (Fasoli 1960–3, Ortalli 1984, and Gelichi and Merlo 1987); Brescia (Panazza and Brogiolo 1988); Ferrara (Patitucci Uggeri 1974, and Visser Travagli and Ward-Perkins 1985); Lucca (Belli Barsali 1973); Milan, (Violante 1974, Andrews 1986, and Caporusso 1986); Novara (Motta 1987); Parma (La Ferla 1981); Pavia (Bullough 1966 and Hudson 1981 and 1987); Verona (Hudson 1985 and La Rocca 1988 and 1989).

determine whether, despite the substantial changes that came about during the early Middle Ages, the cities preserved their functional autonomy in relation to the surrounding territory, that is, whether the image of the city as a structure different from the rural world was maintained. In this perspective, the change in the physical appearance of the city goes hand in hand with the persistence of a desire to build. The modifications made to the Roman infrastructure thus turn out to be the fruit of conscious choices and not simply the passive and casual adaptation of what remained. The city survived because it could change in response to new needs (Violante 1974, 71–87).

In this paper I shall focus on one aspect of the early mediaeval Italian cities: public buildings and properties, and the attitudes to them both of the citizens themselves and of their rulers. Changes in rulers' attitudes towards the urban heritage reflect the kind of image of themselves those rulers wanted to convey to city dwellers. The attention given to public buildings was not determined just by personal liberality or the availability of resources. Rather, it was a tool to build a political platform of public consent. The persistence of such preoccupations signifies not only that the city materially continued to exist, but that within it lived the community of *cives*, who were conscious of their own special identity in respect to the *rustici*, and whose importance was fully recognized by those in power.

Cracco Ruggini has drawn attention to two different, but frequently overlapping, ancient conceptions of the city (Cracco Ruggini and Cracco 1977; Cracco Ruggini 1982). The first, pre-Christian in character, saw the city as the 'civilized' place *par excellence*, in contrast to the country, a wild region whose human inhabitants lived isolated and brutish lives. Against this coupling of *civitas* and *civilitas* can be set the Christian, or, more specifically, the monastic conception, according to which the reign of corruption is in the town and the country is the place of prayer, isolation and redemption. As Cracco Ruggini notes, in the fourth and fifth centuries the growing uncertainty of the times contributed to the inclusion of the city walls as an essential element in the definition of the city itself. The Roman *civitates* were transformed into closed *castra* raised above the surrounding territory, and so Ambrose's celebrated reference to 'the corpses of half-ruined cities' (*semirutarum urbium cadavera*: *Epist.* 39,

PL 16) does not describe the ruins of cities which had been effectively abandoned, so much as the changed physiognomy of urban centres that had nothing in common with the classical concept of *urbs*. Cracco Ruggini maintains that the assimilation of *civitas* and *castrum* continued until the tenth century, at which time a new, more strictly mediaeval concept of the city took shape. Therefore, she claims, since early mediaeval society did not succeed in formulating its own image of the city, it did not make it its driving force.

The evidence collected here shows rather that the relationship between *civitas* and political power was not uniform or straightforward during the early mediaeval period. It also demonstrates how the growth of church foundations within the city, which came about mostly during the Lombard period, contributed to the reconciliation of the monastic and classical conceptions of the city, a process which was completed in the Carolingian age with the creation of the figure of the city patron saint (Orselli 1985). At the same time it can be shown that cities never lost their urban identity as distinct from fortified centres, thanks both to the strongly evocative Roman architectural heritage and to the citizens, who regarded themselves as *cives* and so greatly contributed to the city's identity.

While present archaeological research tends to identify the sixth century as the moment of substantial change, it is clear that such a transformation was actually the result of a long process which began during the third century. It seems to have been then that the first public buildings were abandoned. In the third and fourth centuries, city aristocracies lost interest in donating public buildings to their native cities. As the ideological significance of such buildings faded, so too did their fame and political significance in a local context. The economic resources of the élites were used privately, in the construction of sumptuous residential villas or in the embellishment of ecclesiastical buildings.[1] In parallel to this, the tendency for the emperor to claim the role of defender of the cities was heightened, encouraging the construction of city walls. This initiative, which certainly sprang from defensive needs, had a

---

[1]   Ward–Perkins 1984, especially pp. 14–21. For the abandonment of public buildings at Milan see Krautheimer 1983, 107–48 and Cagiano de Azevedo 1986, 145–86. On the decline of Luni, an extreme case, see Ward–Perkins 1978.

profound effect on the concept of the city and its material appearance. The walls completely enclose the urban area and differentiate what lies within from what lies outside.

From the fourth century onwards the city came to be identified as an area surrounded by a circle of walls. The lack of these is in contrast seen as a sign of decline or at least as an anomaly. So, for example, to illustrate the advanced state of decadence into which Ostia was falling in the sixth century, Procopius stresses the fact that 'the once flowering city' was now unprotected by walls,[1] and Cassiodorus, describing the flourishing economy of Squillace, expresses surprise that the town is not fortified, and, as a result, is in doubt whether to call it a *civitas ruralis* or a *villa urbana* (*Variae* 12.15.5). By contrast, Jordanes, describing the village which Attila had fortified as his camp, remarks that, in view of the technical perfection of its wooden palisade, it was a village 'like a splendid city' (*vicum, inquam, ad instar civitatis amplissimae*: *Getica* 178).

It is chiefly the cities fortified in this period which have survived to the present day, almost as though imperial protection was directed only towards those urban centres which offered the greatest guarantees of stability and failure to construct defences was both a symptom of existing decline and the cause which accelerated a centre's abandonment.[2] Though defence works helped to define city limits and strengthen the city, attention paid to other large constructions gradually died away, partly because the sheer cost of restoration and maintenance placed an unbearable economic burden on local administration. Perhaps not enough attention has been paid to the fact that the decay of ancient buildings during the early mediaeval period was the continuation of a process that had begun about two centuries before the Lombard migration. Above all it should be remembered that the exuberant flowering of public buildings in northern Italy did not cover the whole Roman period, but merely the first two centuries of the Empire. This period of architectural initiative can therefore be seen as a splendid interlude, the product of the local élite's need for self-affirmation, and not as a constant characteristic of the Roman city.

In an age in which the figure of the emperor came in part to

[1] *Gothic Wars* 1.26.8. On Procopius' descriptions of fortifications see Ravegnani 1980 and 1983, 71–91.
[2] For a list of abandoned towns see Schmiedt 1974.

replace that of the city *patronus*, the Ostrogothic King Theodoric's building policy stands out.[1] The *Anonymus Valesianus* (70–1) dubs him 'lover of building and restorer of cities' (*amator fabricarum et restaurator civium*), and reports that at his capitals Ravenna, Pavia and Verona he built or repaired not only the city walls but also ancient public structures like porticoes, aqueducts, baths and amphitheatres. By such munificence Theodoric hoped to confer legitimacy on his rule. His desire to associate himself with the glorious Roman past even extended to construction methods. Thus he ordained that old materials should be restored to their former splendour and new sections should be carried out to such a standard that 'only the newness of the fabric distinguishes them from the work of the ancients' (Cassiodorus, *Variae* 7.5.5). The re-use of ancient stones, which Theodoric encouraged, should therefore be attributed not to economic difficulties or incapacity to work newly hewn stone, but rather to the continuing appeal of ancient tradition. When Theodoric authorizes the inhabitants of Catania to build the walls of their city with stones from the long-collapsed amphitheatre, the reason he gives is that the cities must not 'display just shameful ruins' and that the new walls must give new dignity to 'what can be of no benefit where it lies'.[2] Theodoric's building policy may have run counter to the trends of the times in its attempt to revive obsolete concepts and ideals, but it is, none the less, significant that his desire to legitimize his authority expressed itself in relationship to the city. It was the cities that Theodoric picked on as decisive in setting the seal on his legitimacy.

In this context, it is the Lombard invasion of 568 which constitutes the real break with the past. The ruling class underwent a radical transformation, with Lombard military chiefs taking the place of Latin bureaucrats. The new rulers adopted a quite different attitude from their predecessors to the public buildings of the cities, which they regarded not as a collective heritage but as royal property (Tabacco 1979; Delogu 1980;

[1]   On Theodoric see Burns 1984, 67 ff; Wolfram 1988. On his building policy see Frugoni 1983, 37–54; Lusuardi Siena 1984; Ward-Perkins 1984, 29–30.
[2]   Cassiodorus, *Variae* 3.49.3. Stone from the amphitheatre was also used to rebuild the city walls at Milan (Lusuardi Siena 1986, 211–12).

Racine 1986). Our source material on the period is partial and fragmentary, but a fruitful comparison may none the less be made between the archaeological data and our two main literary sources, with their opposing biases, Paul the Deacon's *History of the Lombards* and Gregory the Great's *Dialogi*.[1]

Paul tells us that, when Pavia surrendered to the Lombard King Alboin in 572, following a three-year siege, Alboin's horse fell as he entered the city, and all attempts to raise it failed. One of the Lombards then reminded the king of his threat to put the whole population to the sword and urged him to spare them 'because in this city there is a truly Christian people'. The King agreed, and the horse got up (Paul, *HL* 2.27). A Christian and urban population, it seems, required a radical change of behaviour from the King, a show of civility and good nature. It is with this episode that the cities make their début in Paul's *History*. Previously the world of the cities was foreign to the Lombards' experience, but now, with their entry into Italy, it becomes the background against which events are set and which gives them their shape and significance. Cities constituted the administrative and institutional hinge of Lombard rule: the Lombards chose the cities as their administrative headquarters and a city, Pavia, as their capital, and in making these choices they were not just following tradition, but were influenced by the presence in the urban environment of elements professionally and culturally suited for such a rôle. The cities also served as a sort of thermometer indicating attitudes in good times and bad. Thus disasters affecting cities, like floods and plagues, had a symbolic significance for those who, like Gregory the Great, disapproved of the turn events had taken. The surmounting of city walls by the neighbouring river, the Tiber at Rome, the Adige at Verona, the Serchio at Lucca, was a paradox pregnant with meaning: the river invaded the city, eliminating its defences and abolishing the boundary between city and countryside.[2]

However, the Lombards were not absorbed straightaway into

---

[1]   Paul's *History* is edited in *MGH, Scriptores rerum Langobardorum* 45–187. Discussions of the work include Bognetti 1966–8, iii.159–84; Sestan 1970; Morghen 1974; Alfonsi 1980; Bullough 1986. For Gregory's *Dialogi* see De Vogüé 1978; Boesch Gajano 1979.

[2]   Gregory, *Dial.* 3.19, following Paul, *HL* 4.104–5. On miracles and extraordinary events as political symbols see Boglioni 1974; Cracco Ruggini 1981; Boesch Gajano 1981.

the world of the cities. They remained apart from and mistrustful of the Romans and Byzantines they had conquered and their city-based world. Only a generation after the conquest do we find the first signs that this separation was breaking down, such as the appearance of Roman and Byzantine fashions in Lombard grave goods (Bierbrauer 1984) or the assumption of the Roman title Flavius by King Authari (584–90) and his successors (Paul, *HL* 3.16). The Lombards' misgivings about the city are reflected in Paul's account of the years after their arrival in Italy, in which the city becomes the scene of violent happenings, a sort of world 'turned upside down', in clear contrast to Roman *civilitas*. The baths, the traditional place for social intercourse, are the setting for the deaths of Helmichis and Rosamund, and it is in the *palatium*, the seat of public authority and justice, that Alboin himself is betrayed and killed (*HL* 2.28–9).

The initial Lombard settlements were not spread throughout the cities but concentrated in particular sites around the gates and ancient public buildings, for example the theatre at Fiesole and Verona, the amphitheatre at Lucca, the circus at Milan, and the *capitolium* at Bergamo. This pattern of settlement seems not to have been determined by military needs or designed for the control of the population, but rather to have arisen because it was in such places that space was available within the walls. Once in possession of state property, the Lombards seem to have initially settled where it was most convenient to do so, in or around public buildings or the *palatia*, in areas which, because they were in the public domain, were unencumbered by private buildings (Cagiano de Azevedo 1974, 312–24; Hudson 1987, 246–7; La Rocca 1988, 79–87; Settia 1988). Very likely, many public buildings changed their appearance now, some being adapted to residential use, while others, which now served no purpose, disappeared, their materials sometimes being used for new buildings. None the less it would be wrong to suppose that the abandonment of a public building automatically led to private occupation of the land, to an anarchic and indiscriminate use of city property (so Cagiano de Azevedo 1974, 321). The fact that much land devoid of building remained state property is amply demonstrated by later royal diplomas.[1]

---

[1] Schiaparelli (1903), nos 57.160–2, 71.83–5, 89.240–2. The first two documents date to 905, the third to 913.

The Lombards not only took up residence in state properties, but also introduced the practice of burial there, another mark of their separateness from the Romans. Thus Alboin was buried under the steps of the *palatium* at Verona, setting a precedent which was to be much followed in the early mediaeval period (Paul, *HL* 2.28; La Rocca 1988, 77–90 and 1989, 159–66).

During the seventh century, the Lombard kings increasingly extended their attention beyond the enclaves in which they had settled to the city as a whole, and a corresponding change came over their style of behaviour, reflected in Paul's character sketches of individual kings (Taviani 1980). He praises the first kings for their martial qualities. Thus Alboin is 'a man fitted for wars and vigorous in every respect'; his prestige among foreign peoples is due to his 'generosity, glory, success in war and valour', and he is contrasted with the eunuch Narses, whose successes in battle were due 'more to the prayers he poured forth to God than to arms' (Paul, *HL* 1.27, 2.5). By the next generation we find a marked shift towards classical *civilitas*. The qualities stressed now are kings' physical beauty and the nobility of their conduct. Thus Authari was 'blooming with youth, fair in stature, had flowing golden locks and a handsome face' (*HL* 3.30).[1] The shift to this new royal ideal coincides with a new institutional order, with the re-establishment of the monarchy after the interregnum of 574–84: now 'there was no violence, no plots; no one was despoiled or subjected to unjust requisitioning; robbery and brigandage ceased' (*HL* 3.16). From Rothari (*c.* 643) on, Lombard kings were buried not in public buildings in the Lombard enclaves but in churches, striking evidence of the *rapprochement* between the two cultures.[2]

The new munificence of Lombard kings found expression particularly in buildings, but, by contrast with Theodoric, the emphasis is not on the restoration of the old but on the founding

---

[1] Others in the Lombard élite might also be expected to conform to the new model. Thus Ratperga, wife of the duke Pemnon, a 'countrywoman' (*rusticana*), 'often begged her husband to divorce her and marry another wife who would be worthy of so great a duke' (Paul, *HL* 6.26).

[2] Lombard royal church burials: Rothari and his queen Gundiperga (Paul, *HL* 4.136), Grimoald (5.155), Pertarict (5.157), Cunipert (6.170), Aripert (6.176), Liutprand (6.187). See Ward-Perkins 1984, 79–80.

of new ecclesiastical buildings, both within cities and in their suburbs. The founding and building of churches by Lombard kings and those connected with them is regularly commemorated on funerary inscriptions (Orselli 1978 and 1981; Consolino 1987, 166–70). A good example is the epitaph of Theodote, once the mistress of King Cunipert, commemorating the building of the monastery of S. Maria at Pavia:

> *per te semper Virginis nitiscit pulchrum dilubrum.*
> *auferens vetusta instauras vilia cuncta . . .*
> *nec sunt in orbe tales praeter palatia regum.*

> Through you the fair shrine of the Virgin always shines.
> You remove the old and renew all that is base . . .
> Apart from kings' palaces, there is nothing comparable in the world.[1]

Here the present is regarded as superior to the past, and there is no sense of ancient glories to be recovered. This belief in the superiority of the present to the past may be linked with the nationalist and anti-Roman tendency detected in the reign of Liutprand (712–44) by Bognetti (1961, 445–7). Byzantine soldiers are depicted as cowardly and arrogant (Paul, *HL* 4.30), and Lombard traditions are reasserted, as with the election of the king, now conducted not in the circus at Milan, in imitation of the Byzantine imperial elections, but outside Pavia, in front of the church of S. Maria *ad perticas*, founded by the Lombard Queen Rodelind and a traditional Lombard place of burial (Paul, *HL* 5.34, 6.55). The inscription set up by Liutprand on the façade of the palace at Corte Olona declares that, instead of building baths with colonnades and statues, in imitation of classical buildings, as he originally planned, Liutprand, inspired by God, decided to build the church of St Anastasius (*MGH, Poetae Latini Medii Aevi* i, p. 106; Calderini 1975; Badini 1980). Liutprand employs the ancient device of erecting an inscription (the first by a Lombard king), but does so to celebrate the new. Similarly, in the poetic encomium of Milan (*Versum de Mediolano civitate*; Pighi 1960) composed in

---

[1]   *MGH, Poetae Latini Medii Aevi* iv.2. no. 140B (p. 725).

Liutprand's reign, all the emphasis is on the glories of the contemporary city (Orselli 1981, 783; cf. Fasoli 1972).

The Lombard kings' lead in church-building was followed by the city élites. However, the impulse behind this re-emergence of private patronage was not the old aspiration to civic prestige as a means of political advancement, but the hope that the management of these ecclesiastical foundations would provide a new source of family wealth and prestige. The majority of these foundations in the Lombard period were of female monasteries and so served to provide a social rôle for young women or widows, passing over to them the task of administering the handling of future donations (Bocchi 1980, 274–5; Ward-Perkins 1984, 82–3 and 236–49). From the second decade of the eighth century, the increase in private urban charters, proving the existence of a housing market within the city, confirms the fusion between Lombards and Romans and the new relationship between the government and the city.

In the eighth century some Roman structures were converted to new uses. At Verona, Pavia and Milan, mints were established in buildings in the forum (La Rocca 1988, 108). In 726 Liutprand ordered that underground prisons should be established in the cities.[1] In a number of cities these prisons were set up inside ancient monuments, in the *curia* at Verona (ibid.), in the amphitheatre at Lucca (Belli Barsali 1973, 466), in the theatre at Florence (Davidson 1956, 105), in the tower of a city gate at Verona (Schiaparelli 1903, no. 87.232–4, dating to 913), and at Pavia in the area probably occupied by the theatre (Schiaparelli 1924, Lothar no. 2.253–4, dating to 947).

The Lombard attitude to the classical architectural heritage was thus ruthlessly utilitarian. Buildings for which they still had a use were preserved and maintained. Others were abandoned and stripped, and often disappeared. They never claimed credit for restoring ancient buildings. When they used *spolia* in their building work, as with the capitals of the church of S. Eusebio at Pavia (Peroni 1974, 353–7), they did so simply because it was by then established building practice, and it did not occur to them to

---

[1] *Lombard Laws*, Liutprand 80. The Latin text of the *Lombard Laws* is edited in *MGH*, *Leges* iv (Hanover, 1868). For an English translation see Drew 1973.

celebrate this, as Theodoric did, as giving antiquities a new lease of life. However, the Lombard rulers did retain the old public buildings as state property, unlike their Carolingian successors. In the ninth and tenth centuries the privatization of state holdings in the cities proceeded apace (Settia 1984, 35–47), and as a result private buildings sprouted up inside ancient structures (e.g. at Milan; Lusuardi Siena 1986, 237–40).

One feature of cities by which the Lombards certainly set store was the walls. The fact that the majority of cities preserved their Late Roman city walls intact until the twelfth century suggests that the walls were kept in good repair in the Lombard period, and at Verona we happen to hear of a *vicarius civitatis* responsible for the upkeep of the walls (Fainelli 1940, no. 147.205–8). The possession of walls was indeed regarded as necessary for city status. Thus when Rothari conquered Liguria, we are told that he razed the walls of many cities and ordered them to be called villages.[1] However, even though a city had to have walls, one cannot claim that they alone were enough to earn a place the title of *civitas*, nor that *castrum* and *civitas* had come to be synonymous (so, for example, Montanari 1978). A distinction between the two can be seen in Paul the Deacon, for example in his list of the principal Italian centres prior to the Lombard migration (*HL* 2.18), and one can conclude that the presence and institutional rôle of the bishop and professionally qualified *cives* in the cities continued to keep the two terms clearly distinct. The *cives* are referred to in edicts by various Lombard kings from Rothari on, and both Liutprand (in 723) and Ratchis (in 746) sought to prevent disturbances directed against their *iudices* in the cities (*Lombard Laws*, Liutprand 35, Ratchis 10).

The Lombards, then, did take over from the classical past the tradition of munificent building activity, but they gave expression to it not by looking back and seeking to revive the glories of antiquity but by erecting new buildings of their own to which they gave the original and distinctive Lombard stamp. In this they differed sharply from their Carolingian successors, who did indeed seek by establishing links with the Roman past to give expression and legitimacy to their rule (Delogu 1968; Tabacco

---

[1]   Fredegar, *Chronica* (*MGH, Scriptores rerum Merovingicarum* ii), 4.71. Destructions of city walls: Paul, *HL* 3.18; 4.23, 45; 5.28.

1981; Szabo 1986). The contrast is pointed up by the early ninth-century *Versus de Verona*. Whereas, as we saw, the earlier poem in praise of Milan concentrates on the splendours of the contemporary city, this poem celebrating Verona waxes eloquent about the city's classical past and its surviving remains (Orselli 1981, 783; Ward-Perkins 1984, 226–7).

The change in the physical appearance of the cities of northern Italy between Late Antiquity and the Middle Ages reflects the constant and diversified use made of the urban structures over the intervening period. In early mediaeval times the cities in Italy were not preserved as though they were museums, but that does not justify us treating the period as one of decadence. It had its own vitality and made its own contribution to the cities' heritage. Nor was the idea of the city as an entity distinct from the countryside lost in this period. However much cultivated fields may have appeared inside the city, it remained capable of forming new cultural models and exporting them to the countryside (Bierbrauer 1988; Wickham 1988).

Bibliography

Alfonsi, A. (1980), 'Aspetti del pensiero storiografico di Paolo Diacono', in *La storiografia ecclesiastica nella tarda antichità* (Messina), 11–25.

Andrews, D.D. (1986), 'Milano altomedievale sotto Piazza del Duomo: gli scavi del 1982 e 1983' in *Atti del 10 congresso internazionale di studi sull'alto medioevo* (Spoleto), 355–64.

Badini, A. (1980), 'La concezione della regalità in Liutprando e le iscrizioni della chiesa di S. Anastasio a Corteolona', in *Atti del 6 congresso internazionale di studi sull'alto medioevo* (Spoleto), 283–97.

Belli Barsali, I. (1973), 'La topografia di Lucca nei secoli VIII–X', in *Atti del 5 congresso internationale di studi sull'alto medioevo* (Spoleto), 461–554.

Bierbrauer, V. (1984), 'Aspetti archeologici di goti, alamanni e longobardi', in *Magistra barbaritas: i barbari in Italia* (Milan), 445–508.

Bierbrauer, V. (1988), 'Situazione della ricerca sugli

insediamenti nell'Italia settentrionale in epoca tardo antica e nell'alto medioevo (V–VII secolo): fonti, metodo, prospettive', *Archeologia Medievale* 15, 508–15.

Bocchi, F. (1980), 'Monasteri, canoniche e strutture urbane in Italia', in *Istituzioni monastiche e istituzioni canonicali in Occidente (1123–1215)* (Milan), 265–315.

Boesch Gajano, S. (1979), 'Dislivelli culturali e mediazioni ecclesiastiche nei *Dialogi* di Gregorio Magno', *Quaderni Storici* 41, 398–415.

Boesch Gajano, S. (1981), 'Demoni e miracoli nei *Dialogi* di Gregorio Magno', in *Hagiographie, cultures et sociétés: IVe-XIIe siècles* (Paris), 263–81.

Boglioni, P. (1974), 'Miracle et merveilleux chez Grégoire le Grand: théorie et thème', in *Cahiers d'études médiévales* i, *Épopée, légendes et miracles* (Montreal and Paris), 115–67.

Bognetti, G.P. (1959), 'Problemi di metodo e oggetti di studio nella storia delle città italiane dell'alto medioevo', in *La città italiana nell'alto medioevo* (Spoleto), 59–87 (= Bognetti 1966-8, iv.223–50).

Bognetti, G.P. (1961), 'I capitoli 144 e 145 di Rotari e il rapporto tra Como e i *Magistri Commacini*', in *Scritti di storia dell'arte in onore di Mario Salmi* (Rome), 155–71 (= Bognetti 1966-8, iv.433–53).

Bognetti, G.P. (1966-8), *L'età longobarda*, 4 vols (Milan).

Bordone, R. (1983), 'Tema cittadino e "ritorno alla terra" nella storiografia comunale recente', *Quaderni Storici* 52, 255–77.

Bordone, R. (1986), 'Nascita e sviluppo delle autonomie cittadine', in *Il medioevo* ii, *Popoli e strutture politiche* (Turin), 427–59.

Bordone, R. (1987), *La società cittadina del Regno d'Italia* (Turin).

Brogiolo, G.P. (1987), 'A proposito dell'organizzazione urbana nell'alto medioevo', *Archeologia Medievale* 14, 27–46.

Bullough, D.A. (1966), 'Urban change in early medieval Italy: the example of Pavia', *Papers of the British School at Rome* 34, 82–130.

Bullough, D.A. (1986), 'Ethnic history and the Carolingians: an alternative reading of Paul the Deacon's *Historia Lango-bardorum*', in C. Holdsworth and T.P. Wiseman (eds), *The Inheritance of Historiography, 350–900* (Exeter), 85–105.

Burns, T.S. (1984), *A History of the Ostrogoths* (Bloomington).
Cagiano de Azevedo, M. (1974), 'Esistono un'architettura e una urbanistica longobarde?', in *La civiltà dei Longobardi in Europa* (Rome), 289–339 (= Cagiano de Azevedo 1986, 57–98).
Cagiano de Azevedo, M. (1986), *Casa, città e campagna nel tardo antico e nell'alto medioevo*, ed. C.D. Fonseca, D. Adamesteanu and F. D'Andria (Galatina).
Calderini, C. (1975), 'Il palazzo di Liutprando a Corteolona', *Contributi dell'Istituto di Archeologia dell'Università Cattolica* 5, 174–203.
Caporusso, D. (1986), 'Milano: nuovi scavi archeologici nel centro storico in occasione della costruzione della linea 3 della metropolitana milanese', in *Atti del 10 congresso internazionale sull'alto medioevo* (Spoleto), 379–83.
Consolino, F.E. (1987), 'La poesia epigrafica a Pavia longobarda nell'VIII secolo', in *Storia di Pavia* ii, *L'alto medioevo* (Pavia), 160–76.
Cracco Ruggini, L. (1981), 'Il miracolo nella cultura del tardo impero: concetto e funzione', in *Hagiographie, cultures et sociétés: IVe–XIIIe siècles* (Paris), 159–202.
Cracco Ruggini, L. (1982), 'La città nel mondo antico: realtà e idea', in G. Wirth (ed.), *Romanitas-Christianitas: Untersuchungen zur Geschichte und Literatur der römischen Kaiserzeit Johannes Straub zum 70 Geburtstag am 18. Oktober 1982 gewidmet* (Berlin), 61–81.
Cracco Ruggini, L. and Cracco, G. (1977), 'Changing fortunes of the Italian city from late antiquity to early middle ages', *Rivista di Filologia e di Istruzione Classica* 105, 448–75.
Davidson, R. (1956), *Storia di Firenze* i (Florence).
Delogu, P. (1968), 'Strutture politiche e ideologia nel regno di Ludovico II', *Bullettino dell'Istituto Storico Italiano per il Medioevo e Archivio Muratoriano* 80, 137–89.
Delogu, P. (1980), 'Il Regno Longobardo', in P. Delogu, A. Guillou and G. Ortalli, *Longobardi e Bizantini* (Turin), 3–216.
De Vogüé, A. (ed.) (1978), *Grégoire Le Grand, Dialogues* (Paris).
Drew, K.F. (1973), *The Lombard Laws* (Philadelphia).
Fainelli, V. (1940), *Codice Diplomatico Veronese* i (Venice).

Fasoli, G. (1960), 'Che cosa sappiamo delle città italiane nell'alto medioevo' in *Vierteljahrschrift für Sozial- und Wirtschaftsgeschichte* 48, 289–305 (= Fasoli 1974, 181–98).

Fasoli, G. (1960–3), 'Momenti di storia urbanistica bolognese nell'alto medioevo', *Atti e Memorie della Deputazione di Storia Patria per la Province di Romagna* 12–14, 313–43.

Fasoli, G. (1972), 'La coscienza civica nelle *Laudes civitatum*', in *La coscienza cittadina nei comuni italiani del Duecento* (Todi), 11–44 (= Fasoli 1974, 293–318).

Fasoli, G. (1974), *Scritti di storia medievale* (Bologna).

Fasoli, G., Manselli, R. and Tabacco, G. (1961), 'La struttura sociale delle città italiane dal V al XII secolo', in *Vorträge und Forschungen* 11, 291–320.

Février, P.A. (1974), 'Permanence et héritages de l'antiquité dans la topographie des villes de l'Occident durant le haut Moyen Âge', in *Topografia urbana e vita cittadina nell'alto medioevo in Occidente* (Spoleto), 41–138.

Frugoni, C. (1983), *Una lontana città: sentimenti e immagini del medioevo* (Turin), trans. as *A Distant City: Images of Urban Experience in the Medieval World* (Princeton, 1991).

Fumagalli, V. (1983), 'La geografia culturale delle terre emiliane e romagnole nell'alto medioevo', in *Le sedi della cultura nell'Emilia Romagna: l'alto medioevo* (Milan), 11–27.

Fumagalli, V. (1985), '*Langobardia* e *Romania*: l'occupazione del suolo nella Pentapoli altomedievale', in *Ricerche e studi sul 'Breviarium Ecclesiae Ravennatis' (Codice Bavaro)* (Rome), 95–107.

Galetti, P. (1982–3), 'Per una storia dell'abitazione rurale nell'altomedioevo: le dimensioni della casa nell'Italia Padana in base alle fonti documentarie', *Bullettino dell'Istituto Storico Italiano per il Medioevo e Archivio Muratoriano* 90, 147–76.

Galetti, P. (1983a), 'La casa contadina nell'Italia padana nei secoli VIII–X', *Quaderni Medievali* 16, 6–28.

Galetti, P. (1983b), 'Città e campagna nella Pentapoli: strutture materiali e tipologia dell'insediamento nei secoli VIII–X', in *Istituzioni e società nell'alto medioevo marchigiano* (Ancona), 617–45.

Galetti, P. (1985), 'Struttura materiale e funzioni negli insediamenti urbani e rurali della Pentapoli', in *Ricerche e studi sul 'Breviarium Ecclesiae Ravennatis'* (Rome), 109–24.

Gelichi, S. and Merlo, R. (1987), *Archeologia medievale a Bologna: gli scavi del convento di San Domenico* (Bologna).

Hodges, R. (1982), *Dark Age Economics: the Origins of Towns and Trade* (London).

Hodges, R. and Whitehouse, D. (1983), *Mohammed, Charlemagne and the Origins of Europe: Archaeology and the Pirenne Thesis* (London).

Hudson, P. (1981), *Archeologia urbana e programmazione della ricerca: l'esempio di Pavia* (Florence).

Hudson, P. (1985), 'La dinamica dell'insediamento urbano nell'area del Cortile del Tribunale di Verona', *Archeologia Medievale* 12, 281-302.

Hudson, P. (1987), 'Pavia: l'evoluzione urbanistica di una capitale altomedievale', in *Storia di Pavia* ii, *L'alto medioevo* (Pavia), 237-316.

Krautheimer, R. (1983), *Three Christian Capitals* (Berkeley, Los Angeles and London).

La Ferla, G. (1981), 'Parma nei secoli IX e X: *civitas* e *suburbium*', *Storia della Città* 18, 5-32.

La Rocca, C. (1986), 'Città altomedievali, storia e archeologia', *Studi Storici* 27, 725-35.

La Rocca, C. (1987), 'Archeologia urbana e archeologia in città', *Segusium* 24, 57-68.

La Rocca, C. (1988), ' "Dark Ages" a Verona: edilizia privata, aree aperte e strutture pubbliche in una città dell'Italia settentrionale', in *Paesaggi urbani dell'Italia padana nei secoli VII-XIV* (Bologna), 71-122.

La Rocca, C. (1989), 'Le sepolture altomedievali nel territorio di Verona', in *Materiali di età longobarda nel veronese* (Verona), 149-86.

Lusuardi Siena, S. (1984), 'Sulle tracce della presenza gota in Italia: il contributo delle fonti archeologiche', in *Magistra barbaritas: i barbari in Italia* (Milan), 509-58.

Lusuardi Siena, S. (1986), 'Milano: la città nei suoi edifici: alcuni problemi', in *Atti del 10 congresso internazionale di studi sull'alto medioevo* (Spoleto), 209-40.

Mengozzi, G. (1914), *La città italiana nell'alto medioevo* (Roma).

Montanari, M. (1978), 'Una città e un castello: Imola e San Cassiano nei secoli XI-XII', *Studi Romagnoli* 29, 495-526 (=

Montanari, M. (1988), *Contadini e città tra 'Langobardia' e 'Romania'* (Florence, 1988), 79–112).

Morghen, R. (1974), 'La civiltà dei Longobardi nell' *Historia Langobardorum* di Paolo Diacono', in *La civiltà dei Longobardi in Europa* (Rome), 9–23.

Motta, M. (1987), 'Novara medioevale: problemi di topografia urbana tra fonti scritte e documentazione archeologica', *Memorie dell'Istituto Lombardo* 38, 167–348.

Orselli, A.M. (1978), 'La città altomedievale e il suo santo patrono (ancora una volta) il *campione pavese*', *Rivista di Storia della Chiesa in Italia* 32, 1–59 (= Orselli 1985, 245–327).

Orselli, A.M. (1981), 'Il santo patrono cittadino fra tardo antico e alto medioevo', in *La cultura in Italia fra tardo antico e alto medioevo* (Rome), 771–84 (= Orselli 1985, 415–35).

Orselli, A.M. (1985), *L'immaginario religioso nella città medievale* (Ravenna).

Ortalli, J. (1984), 'La tecnica di costruzione delle strade di Bologna tra età romana e medioevo', *Archeologia Medievale* 11, 379–93.

Panazza, G. and Brogiolo, G.P. (1988), *Ricerche su Brescia altomedievale* i, *Gli studi fino al 1978: lo scavo di via Alberto Mario* (Brescia).

Patitucci Uggeri, S. (1974), 'Scavi nella Ferrara medievale: il *castrum* e la seconda cerchia', *Archeologia Medievale* 1, 130–47.

Peroni, A. (1974), 'Architettura e decorazione nell'età longobarda alla luce dei ritrovamenti lombardi', in *La civiltà dei Longobardi in Europa* (Rome), 347–59.

Pighi, G.B. (ed.) (1960), *Versus de Verona, Versum de Mediolano civitate* (Bologna).

Racine, P. (1986), 'Poteri medievali e percorsi fluviali nell'Italia padana', *Quaderni Storici* 61, 9–32.

Ravegnani, G. (1980), 'La difesa militare delle città in età giustinianea', *Storia della città* 14, 87–116.

Ravegnani, G. (1983), *Castelli e città fortificate nel VI secolo* (Ravenna).

Roncayolo, M. (1978), 'Città', in *Enciclopedia Einaudi* iii (Turin), 1–79.

Schiaparelli, L. (1903), *I diplomi di Berengario I* (Rome).

Schiaparelli, L. (1924), *I diplomi di Ugo e di Lotario e di Berengario II e di Adalberto* (Rome).

Schmiedt, G. (1974), 'Le città scomparse e città di nuova formazione in Italia in relazione al sistema di comunicazione', in *Topografia urbana e vita cittadina* (Spoleto), 505–607.

Sergi, G. (1985), 'La città come luoghi di continuità di nozioni pubbliche del potere: le aree delle marche di Ivrea e di Torino', in *Piemonte medievale: forme del potere e della società. Studi per Giovanni Tabacco* (Turin), 5–27.

Sestan, E. (1970), 'La storiografia dell'Italia longobarda: Paolo Diacono', in *La storiografia altomedievale* (Spoleto), 357–86.

Settia, A.A. (1984), *Castelli e villaggi nell'Italia padana* (Naples).

Settia, A.A. (1988), 'Vicenza di fronte ai Longobardi e ai Franchi', in *Storia di Vicenza* ii (Vicenza), 1–24.

Szabo, T. (1986), 'Strade e potere pubblico nell'Italia centro-settentrionale (secoli VI–XIV)', *Studi Storici* 27, 667–83.

Tabacco, G. (1970), 'Espedienti politici e persuasioni religiose nel medioevo di G.P. Bognetti', *Rivista di Storia della Chiesa in Italia* 24, 504–23.

Tabacco, G. (1979), *Egemonie sociali e strutture del potere nel medioevo italiano* (Turin), trans. as *The Struggle for Power in Medieval Italy* (Cambridge, 1989).

Tabacco, G. (1981), 'I processi di formazione dell'Europa carolingia', in *Nascita dell'Europa ed Europa carolingia: un'equazione da verificare* (Spoleto), 17–43.

Taviani, H. (1980), 'L'image du souverain lombard de Paul, Diacre à la chronique de Salerne (VIII–X siècle)', in *Atti del 6 congresso internazionale di studi sull'alto medioevo* (Spoleto), 679–93.

Violante, C. (1974), *La società milanese nell'età precomunale*, 2nd edn (Rome and Bari).

Visser Travagli, A.M. and Ward-Perkins, B. (1985), 'Scavi a Ferrara', *Restauro e città* 1, 48–54.

Ward-Perkins, B. (1978), 'Luni: the decline and abandonment of a Roman town', in H.M. Blake, T.W. Potter and D. Whitehouse (eds), *Papers in Italian Archaeology* i (London), 313–21.

Ward-Perkins, B. (1983), 'La città altomedievale', *Archeologia Medievale* 10, 111–24.

Ward-Perkins, B. (1984), *From Classical Antiquity to the*

Middle Ages: Urban Public Building in Northern and Central Italy (Oxford).

Wickham, C. (1981), *Early Medieval Italy* (London).

Wickham, C. (1988), 'La città altomedievale: una nota sul dibattito in corso', *Archeologia Medievale* 15, 649–51.

Wolfram, H. (1988), *History of the Goths* (Berkeley, Los Angeles and London).

∞ 8 ∞

Antioch: from Byzantium to Islam and back again

Hugh Kennedy

There are, fundamentally, two different ways of identifying and approaching a historical problem. The first is to find an interesting or even unique piece of evidence and use it to illuminate the surrounding landscape. Typical of such an approach is the evidence provided by the deserted villages of the limestone hills of northern Syria; because the archaeological evidence is so rich and varied, the late antique economy of this small area has become the subject of continuing interest and serious debate (Tchalenko 1953–8; Tate and Sodini 1980; Kennedy 1985a, 157–62; Liebeschuetz and Kennedy 1989). If this unique evidence had not existed, it is hardly likely that the rural economy of this area would have received more than the barest mention.

A different approach from this evidence-led method is to identify a problem which is clearly of importance and then to search for evidence to shed some light on it. The study of the city of Antioch from the late sixth to the early twelfth century belongs firmly in this category. It is worth making this point because some of the evidence I will present may well seem unduly speculative and even tendentious compared with the rich late antique data from, say, Gerasa/Jerash (Kraeling 1938) or Ephesus (Foss 1979), but the enquiry is worth pursuing because of the central importance of Antioch in northern Syria. It was probably the largest city in the area in late antiquity, and it was certainly the political and ecclesiastical capital. The fate of Antioch is therefore crucial to

our understanding of Syria immediately before the Islamic conquest and of how that conquest affected it. The evidence may seem
slight but the subject is not and we must make the best of the
limited resources available.

The history of Antioch in the sixth century is marked by
repeated conquests and earthquakes (for the details, see Downey
1961, 503–78). In the late imperial period it was one of the greatest
cities of the Roman East and the administrative centre of Syria. It
boasted a palace, a cathedral, theatres, baths, colonnaded streets
and affluent suburbs. From the second quarter of the sixth
century this began to change. The first disaster was natural, the
earthquakes of 526, but this was followed by the humiliating
Persian conquest of 540 and large-scale deportations of the
inhabitants. There were repeated earthquakes and plagues
throughout the second half of the sixth century and a second
Persian conquest, which led in this case to prolonged occupation
in 611. Byzantine rule was restored in 628, but had hardly time to
be re-established before the Muslims took the city in 641.
Thereafter it lost its importance as a centre of government,
becoming first a military post and then a quiet provincial
backwater until the dramatic Byzantine reconquest of 969. This
put the seal on the Byzantine advances of the tenth century and
meant that Antioch was once again the capital of a Byzantine
province of Syria (for the political and religious importance of the
city in this period, see Dagron 1976, 205–8) and remained so until
conquered by the Seljuk Turks in 1084. They in turn were ejected
by the soldiers of the First Crusade after a hard-fought siege in
1097–8, and Antioch became the capital of a Crusader princi-
pality. That urban life continued at all through these vicissitudes
was probably due to three factors: the natural fertility of the site,
the memory of its ancient greatness and its continuing rôle as the
seat of one of the Patriarchs of the Orthodox church. It is the
purpose of this investigation to discover the extent and nature of
this survival.

Until the middle of the sixth century, the material from Antioch
is comparatively full and has been investigated by Downey in his
classic monograph on the city (Downey 1961). From the second
half of the sixth century, however, the written evidence is very
scanty (for the most important sources see Festugière 1975;
Jeffreys *et al.* 1986; Whitby 1986), and Downey's researches only

turned up a few, scattered references in general chronicles before his closing date at the time of the Arab conquest in 641. Of the state of the city during the reign of Phocas (602–10), the Persian occupation (611–28) and the Heraclian reconquest, we know virtually nothing. This is not to say that Antioch is not mentioned in the general and military histories of the time, but rather that these notices tell us very little of urban life. If the chronicles are disappointing, the hagiography is not much more helpful, and the one major work from this period, the life of St Simeon Stylites the Younger (Van den Ven 1962–70) portrays a saint who had little to do with urban life. His monastery, although near the city, was a largely self-sufficient community and the saint's visits to Antioch were infrequent and fraught. This suggests that the self-sufficient monastery was as much a feature of Syria at the end of the sixth century as it was of western Europe and hints at the decline of the city as the major focus of economic and social activity (Kennedy 1985b, 24–5).

The Muslim conquest of Antioch is recorded without elaboration in the main Arab chronicles (Downey 1961, 577–8). Although Baladhuri does say that the city had to be subdued three times because the inhabitants broke the initial treaty (Hitti 1916, 226–7), there is no indication of a prolonged siege. Apart from Damascus and Caesarea, the Muslim conquest of Syria does not seem to have been actively opposed by the towns, but it is striking that Antioch put up so little resistance. Some of the inhabitants left, but others remained and land was later distributed to Muslims from Baalbek and Homs to encourage them to settle (ibid., 22); there was some change of population but no wholesale transfer. Antioch is frequently mentioned in the early Arab chroniclers in connection with the conquests and the subsequent campaigns against the Byzantines, but beyond the fact that it was, at least in the early stages, an important military base and later became the home town of a number of learned men, little can actually be discerned of the city itself. More illuminating, although tantalizingly brief, are the accounts of the Arab geographers conveniently collected and translated into English by Guy Le Strange (Le Strange 1890, 367–77).

There are two longer works from the Arab period which throw some light on affairs in the city. One is the Life of the Melkite Patriarch Christophoros who was martyred by the Muslims in the period immediately preceding the Byzantine conquest of 969. This life was written in Arabic in the mid-eleventh century by Ibrahim b. Yuhanna and edited with a French translation (Zayat 1952). While the topographical references are slight and often confusing, it provides a useful insight into the life of the Christian community of the city at this time. The other work is more problematic. It is a fairly short undated Arabic manuscript which deals with the wonders of Antioch (Guidi 1897). The probability is that it was composed in the early Islamic period, although there are no references to Islam in it. It is mostly concerned with the legend of the building of the city by 'Antiochus, King of Rum' and the wonders and talismans of the city. Particularly in its attempts to explain the significance of classical statuary whose real purpose had long since been forgotten, it relates to other Arabic works in the genre, but it also reflects genuine memories of the classical city like the aqueducts, the hippodrome outside the city walls and the streets that were wide enough for two carts to pass without bumping into each other. For the historical geographer it is disappointing, and specific references to known monuments are few, but it is an interesting exposition of the thoughts of those who lived surrounded by the relics of an antiquity they had long ceased to understand.

The Byzantine re-occupation produced few literary remains apart from the Arabic 'Life' noted above and the Arabic chronicle of Yahya b. Sa'id al-Antaki, a Melkite refugee from Fatimid Egypt (Arabic text and French translation up to 1015 in Kratchkovsky and Vasiliev 1932; Arabic text of the complete work up to its conclusion in 1034 in Cheikho 1960). This work is an invaluable source of information for the political history of the period, but provides little in the way of local detail. For further detailed descriptions we have to wait for the coming of the Crusaders. The prolonged siege and counter-siege of 1097–8 are recounted at length in a number of sources, some of which give geographical details (see especially Babcock and Krey 1976, i.199–297), and there is also a body of charter evidence dating from the Crusader occupation which contains some details of urban geography. Some of this information was collected by Claude Cahen in his famous work, *La Syrie du nord* (Cahen 1940), but it has not been seriously re-examined since. It may be objected that this evidence is very late, but, in the absence of contemporary data, I believe it can be used cautiously to shed useful light on questions of continuity and discontinuity in the history of the city. Such then is the patchwork of literary evidence on which we are obliged to rely.

The archaeological evidence is equally erratic. The excavations conducted by the Princeton team in the years immediately before World War II produced some exciting results, especially in the recovery of some of the finest antique floor mosaics ever discovered in the Near East, but in terms of urban history the results were rather disappointing, not through any fault of the excavators but rather because their labours were cut short by political events and they were not able to bring them to a proper conclusion (Elderkin 1934; Stillwell 1938 and 1941; Lassus 1977). We do have records of some individual buildings, including the Church of St Babylas (Stillwell 1938, 5–48), and of some sections of the main colonnaded street. No new archaeological evidence of importance has emerged since and it is notable that even the city walls and the citadel, considerable fragments of which still remain, have not been the subject of any scientific study, nor is the dating of the existing fabric by any means certain.

Having discussed the sources, or lack of them, I want now to turn to the central issue of continuity and discontinuity in urban life, both in its fabric and its institutions.

Apart from the walls, the most important physical features of the antique city to survive beyond the classical period were the churches. It is logical to start our survey with the cathedral or great church. This was constructed on the island between the two branches of the Orontes. The large octagonal church was begun by Constantine and completed in the reign of Constantius (Downey 1961, 342–7). Its sixth-century history is a lamentable record of destruction and decay: in 526 it was shaken by the first of the sixth-century earthquakes in Antioch and subsequently destroyed by fire (ibid., 522), but by 537–8 it had been rebuilt and re-dedicated, the dome being constructed of cypress trees from Daphne (unlike Haghia Sophia, but like most Syrian churches and, indeed, the Dome of the Rock in Jerusalem, the great church at Antioch clearly had a wooden dome). Subsequent earthquakes in the terrible series which did such harm to the city, in 551, 557 and 587, tilted the dome to the north and the *coup de grâce* came in 588 when the whole church was destroyed by an earthquake

Mediaeval Antioch

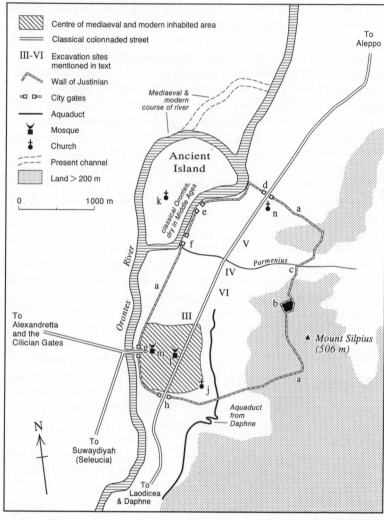

	Centre of mediaeval and modern inhabited area
	Classical colonnaded street
III-VI	Excavation sites mentioned in text
	Wall of Justinian
	City gates
	Aquaduct
	Mosque
	Church
	Present channel
	Land > 200 m

0   1000 m

a	City walls as rebuilt by Justinian	h	Daphne Gate or Bab Muslim or Gate of St George
b	Citadel	j	Approximate position of round church of the Virgin
c	Iron Gate	k	Approximate position of Great Church of Constantine
d	Eastern Gate or Bab Faris or Gate of St Paul	l	Mosque of Habib al-Najjar
e	Gate of the Dog	m	Modern Great Mosque
f	Gate of the Duke or Gate of the Gardens	n	St Paul's Monastery
g	Gate of the Bridge or Bab al-Bahr		

except for the dome which, curiously, settled back on an even keel (Downey 1961, 568; Festugière 1975, 452–3). There is no record of any subsequent rebuilding.

This tottering relic did not survive to become the chief church of the mediaeval period. This seems clear from the fact that it was on the island, an area far from the centre of the mediaeval town and by then largely uninhabited, while the most important mediaeval church, the building known at first as the church of Cassianus and later as the church of St Peter, was basilical, not octagonal, and in the heart of the inhabited part of the town. It seems then, that the ancient cathedral had fallen out of use some time before the Muslim conquest. Professor Liebeschuetz has convincingly suggested to me that the abandonment of the cathedral is connected with the abandonment of other official buildings like the palace and the hippodrome in the same area when Antioch ceased to be an occasional capital of the Empire (for the late antique history of the palace, see Downey 1961, 646–7). Whatever the reasons, it is clear that the ruin of the cathedral and its replacement by a more modest and conveniently situated structure marked an important shift in the urban geography.

More fortunate was the church of the Virgin, built in 527 and rebuilt in 552 by the new *agora* in the Epiphaneia quarter of the city (Downey 1961, 525 and 552). In 582 the Emperor Maurice worshipped there before his accession, perhaps because the cathedral was ruinous. This church seems to have survived both Persian and Muslim conquests, and al-Mas'udi, writing in about 940, speaks of the round church of St Mary being much venerated and of great beauty, despite the fact that the Umayyad Caliph al-Walid b.'Abd al-Malik (705–15) had carried off some of its columns for the mosque in Damascus which he was then constructing (Le Strange 1890, 368). A round church is also noted by the German traveller Willibrand of Oldenburg in 1211, so it would seem to have survived throughout the period under discussion (Cahen 1940, 130).

The church of Cassianus presents a different sort of problem. We have only incidental references to it in antiquity: in 459 St Simeon Stylites' body is said to have rested there on its way to the Great Church, and in about 530 a jewelled robe presented by Justinian was displayed in the church of Cassianus so that it would be acceptable to the people (Downey 1961, 481 and 551).

This interesting comment suggests that the Great Church may already have been considered too far away from the centre of population for convenience. Despite the lack of information from antiquity, the church of Cassianus became the most important church in early Islamic Antioch. al-Mas'udi describes it, using the Arabic form of the ancient name, al-Qusyan, as the most venerated of the churches and the centre of the Easter celebrations (Le Strange 1890, 368). Ibn Butlan, writing in about 1051, explains that it was in the centre of the city and that it acquired its name (otherwise unexplained) because it was built on the site of the palace of King Qusyan whose son St Peter restored to life. It was a rectangular structure, 100 paces by 80 paces, resting on an undercroft (Le Strange 1890, 371). The author of the *Life of Christophoros* mentions that the Muslims who killed the Patriarch pillaged the treasury of the church of Cassianus and the nearby cell of the Patriarch (Zayat 1952, 352). After the Byzantine reconquest of 969, the body of the martyred Patriarch was buried with due ceremony. His first resting place was in a marble 'table' in the western part of the big church (presumably a sarcophagus in the narthex), but in the time of Patriarch Nicolas II (1025–30) he was moved into the 'house' of St Peter to join other relics (ibid., 358–61). It seems likely that the 'big church' mentioned here should be identified with the church of Cassianus and the cathedral of St Peter of Frankish times. According to Ibn Butlan, the church of Cassianus was the principal church of Byzantine Antioch, with innumerable servants and ten or more accountants to administer its revenues (Le Strange 1890, 372), a far cry from the impoverished late Muslim treasury described in the *Life of Christophoros*. It survived to impress the Crusader conquerors of 1098 who were convinced that St Peter's chair was still found in it, and the narthex again became a place of burial (Babcock and Krey 1976, i.263).

Downey records a number of other churches mentioned in late antiquity which seem to have disappeared by mediaeval times (Downey 1961, 656–9). The archaeological evidence supports the idea that a number of churches were lost, notably the splendid *martyrion* of St Babylas (Stillwell 1938, 5–48). It seems, though, that it was the devastating earthquakes of the sixth century and the Persian invasions of 540 and the early seventh century, rather than the Muslim conquest, which caused the most serious losses.

This is especially clear in the case of suburban buildings, where the archaeological evidence suggests no rebuilding in the late sixth century (Kennedy 1985a, 154–5), and Theophylact (Whitby 1986, 87–8) states that all the buildings outside the city walls were ruined by the Persian invasion of 573. A similar pattern can be observed at Jerusalem where it seems that none of the extra-mural churches survived the Persian invasion of the early seventh century.

However, there were a number of churches noted by the Arab geographers which were not recorded in antiquity. The most important of these seems to have been the church of St Paul, also known in Arabic as Dayr al-Baraghith, the Monastery of the Fleas. It was already in existence in the tenth century and was situated by the north-east gate of the city, which the Arabs called the Bab al-Faris and the Franks St Paul's Gate, and a long way from the nucleus of the mediaeval town which lay near the south-west gate (Le Strange 1890, 368; Cahen 1940, 131). There was also a church called the Ashmunit, an ex-synagogue, possibly to be identified with the synagogue which became the church of the Maccabean martyrs in 380 and was still in use in Crusader times (Guidi 1897, 148–9 and 160; Cahen 1940, 131; Downey 1961, 448). Mas'udi in the tenth century notes a church of St Barbara, not previously recorded, which survived into the twelfth century.

New churches were founded after the Byzantine reconquest: the *Life of Christophoros* mentions a church of St John Chrysostom and another church whose largely indecipherable name seems to read Azkas'utis (Zayat 1952, 336–7), and William of Tyre (Babcock and Krey 1976, i.207) mentions a basilica of St George, which gave its name to the nearby southern gate of the city (the dedication suggests a Byzantine rather than a Latin origin). The foundations of an early eleventh-century basilica were found on the line of the main street just north of the Parmenius torrent on a site where there was no sign of previous ecclesiastical building (Lassus 1972, 54–5), but there is no evidence by which we can identify the remains with any of the churches mentioned in the literary sources.

Muslim religious building seems to have been very limited. Mas'udi (Le Strange 1890, 368) talks of the great mosque but, beyond the fact that there were the substantial remains of a Greek temple on its right side, nothing is known of it, and there is no record of any church being taken over for Muslim worship as happened at Damascus or Hims. It is likely that it lay in the southern, inhabited quarter of the ancient *enceinte*. The principal mosque of the modern city lies near the bridge and the suqs (see the map in Weulersse 1934, 41): there is no evidence that it occupies the site of the early mediaeval mosque save that that too was said to be close to the suqs.

In later times and down to the present day, the most important shrine is that of Habib al-Najjar (the Carpenter), a largely mythical Muslim holy man of pre-Islamic origin (Vajda 1971). It is tempting to associate this with the site of St Peter's church, especially as it has deep ancient vaults adjacent and is in the same part of the town as the old church must have been, but such a possibility seems to be ruled out because Yaqut, who was writing at the beginning of the thirteenth century, when Antioch was still under Frankish rule, mentions the shrine of Habib as a place of Muslim pilgrimage (Yaqut al-Rumi 1979, i.269). Aerial photographs make it clear that the mosque was partly built over the line of the ancient street, causing the road to bend to go round it (Downey 1961, plates 6–8). It is possible therefore that this, rather than the modern mosque, is on the site of the early Islamic mosque.

A church is more than the buildings in which its worshippers gather, and we must next examine the institutional continuity of the church in Antioch. The late Byzantine period was marked by notable and continuing theological feuds between the Dyophysite Chalcedonians and the Monophysite Jacobites, which tore apart the church in Syria. The city of Antioch itself, however, remained firmly Chalcedonian even after the Muslim conquest, for the titular Jacobite patriarchs of Antioch did not really establish themselves in the city. Another threat to the integrity of the Chalcedonian church came from the Monothelite doctrine espoused by the Emperor Heraclius in an effort to heal the self-inflicted wounds of the church.

The aftermath of the Islamic conquest saw the evacuation of the Patriarchate to Constantinople where a series of Monothelite titular patriarchs was appointed until the Monothelite creed was abandoned in 681. In the city itself, the Chalcedonian community survived and re-emerged as the Melkite church (for the survival of the Melkite church in Syria and Palestine see Kennedy 1986). The Melkites rejected Monothelitism, and this along with the barriers imposed by the Muslim conquest led to the development of an independent, Arabic-speaking church which in 742 chose a local man as Patriarch. From then on there was a continuous succession of Melkite Patriarchs who, apart from one schism, exercised their office without much difficulty.

The *Life of Christophoros* shows us a Patriarch, chosen in this case from the Melkite church in Iraq, exercising considerable influence in the city, both in his political dealings with the Hamdanid emirs of Aleppo and in his charitable works in the city itself. Christophoros was martyred as a result of the strains imposed by the collapse of Hamdanid rule and the growing Byzantine threat, which meant that when the Byzantines did reconquer the city in 969 there was no incumbent. Immediately after the reconquest, John Tzimisces sent one Theodore, a monk from Colonea, to take over as Patriarch (Zayat 1952, 358–9). The Melkite community in Antioch no doubt benefited from imperial protection, but they lost their right to appoint their leaders, and, when the chartophylax of Hagia Sophia was appointed Patriarch by Basil II in 996, he was ordered to bring the customs of the Church of Cassianus into line with those of Haghia Sophia (Kratchkovsky and Vasiliev 1932, 445). The Byzantine reconquest certainly increased the size of the Melkite community by immigration from Egypt and other parts of the Near East (ibid., 519). William of Tyre notes that in 1097, after fifteen years of Muslim occupation, the population was almost entirely Christian, employed in trade and crafts but politically and militarily quite powerless (Babcock and Krey 1976, i.241).

Monastic continuity is very hard to pinpoint. There seems to be no evidence of any continuing monastic community within the city. It is clear, however, that the monastery of St Simeon Stylites the Elder, in the countryside between Antioch and Aleppo, functioned at least until the mid-eleventh century, and there was a monastic presence on the Mont Admirable, once home of Simeon Stylites the Younger, into Crusader times. By the north-east gate of the city stood the monastery of St Paul which is known from the time of the Byzantine reoccupation and from Crusader sources, but not from antiquity.

The boundaries of the city were defined by its walls. This vast circuit had already been reduced somewhat after Justinian's rebuilding of the city in the aftermath of the Persian invasion of

540. It seems that the circuit remained intact throughout the early mediaeval period, even though the population was too small to provide the men to garrison it. In the tenth century the geographer Istakhri mentions 'fields, gardens, mills, pasture lands and trees' within the circuit of the walls (Le Strange 1890, 369). Continuity in the walls is matched by the continuity of the gates. The gates recorded in mediaeval times seem to have been used in classical times as well. The eastern gate of the ancient city, known as the Bab al-Faris (Gate of the Horseman) to the Arabs and the Gate of St Paul to the Franks, continued to be used and fortified even though it lay well away from the centre of population. Along the river side of the walls lay the Gate of the Dog, the Gate of the Gardens (Bab al-Jinan) or of the Duke (both these seem to have been comparatively unimportant), the Gate of the Bridge, also called the Suwaydiyah Gate in mediaeval times, and to the south-west the ancient Daphne or Golden Gate, known to the Arabs as the Bab Muslim after an early Islamic hero said to have been killed there and to the Franks as the Gate of St George. The citadel high on Mount Silpius overlooking the city is said to have been built by Leo Phocas in 989 (Kratchkovsky and Vasiliev 1932, 427): there is no record of such a castle in antiquity or in the Muslim period. Despite the various invasions, there was a remarkable continuity in the fortifications of the city: in fact there was no significant alteration between Justinian's reduction of the circuit after the Persian conquest of 540 and Baybars' destruction of the city after 1268.

Further evidence of continuity is provided by the street plan. The built structure of the ancient city has almost completely vanished, but its traces linger in the layout of the thoroughfares (Downey 1961, plates 6–8). The bridge across the Orontes is the much-repaired and rebuilt Roman structure. Although the inhabited area is much reduced in size, the main street still follows the line of the colonnaded street of antiquity, and many of the other streets of the ancient grid pattern can be traced in the same area. The suqs of the modern town are on approximately the same site as the original Seleucid *agora*, though whether this represents real continuity or is simply a function of the proximity of the site to the bridge across the Orontes is impossible to say. Weulersse (1934, 59) notes the resemblance between the ancient *insulae* and the small quarters of the modern city. All this bespeaks a significant continuity of settlement in this area.

The fate of the great colonnaded street, which was the main artery of the ancient town, in the sixth century and after has provoked considerable discussion (on which see Kennedy 1985a, 152–4). We know that it was destroyed by earthquake and Persian invasions, and Procopius (*Buildings* 2.10.20–2) recounts its rebuilding after 540. It seems that it never recovered its former glory and the surface was soon built over by smaller structures, as happened to antique streets in so many other parts of the Near East, obliging the roadway to thread a winding, almost path-like course along the ancient sidewalk. The continuity of settlement noted above is matched by the adaptation of the built environment to changing needs and resources.

A series of excavations conducted along the line of the great street give us some further idea of urban life (for the sites see the map, p. 186). In the centre of the modern city it was possible to conduct a very small excavation which showed a continuity of use from ancient times through to 1268 (Elderkin 1934, 93–100; Lassus 1977, 13–14). At site III there were traces of late antique or early Islamic as well as twelfth-century structures on the surface of the Justinianic street, suggesting that this area was inhabited for at least part of the mediaeval period (ibid., 26). Further out at site IV the excavations showed the same late antique/early Islamic building activity, but by the eleventh century the road was bordered by tombs (ibid., 101–6). The major excavations at site V show a somewhat similar pattern of building on and beside the colonnaded street, which can be assigned to the sixth to eighth centuries, followed by an apparent interruption and then by the appearance of an early eleventh-century cemetery and church (ibid., 62, 66–7, 81). Some of the Byzantine gravestones are reused Muslim stones of around the ninth century, suggesting that there may have been a Muslim cemetery in the area (Stillwell 1938, 166–9; Lassus 1977, 54–5). The evidence here seems to show a continuity of habitation in this area, at least along the main street, into the Umayyad period, followed by a period of severe contraction, perhaps after *c.* 800. The presence of tombs at sites IV and V suggests that these areas were outside the settlement in the eleventh century and probably earlier. The evidence of site III is less clear, but it may point to a sixth- to eighth-century occupation, followed by a gap and reoccupation in the twelfth century.

All this suggests that the city contracted in the ninth and tenth centuries to the area which was inhabited in the 1930s when the geographers and archaeologists recorded it. Perhaps it is no coincidence that the inhabited area was the one closest to the entry of the aqueduct from Daphne into the city, suggesting that the area of settlement in this period was determined by the availability of the water-supply. The fragmentary information from the colonnaded street in Antioch ties in well with what we know from other sites in the Near East, notably from Jerash (Kraeling 1938, and my own observation of recent unpublished excavations) and Palmyra, where there are many signs of rebuilding on or beside the colonnaded streets and other public areas in late antiquity and Umayyad times, but no evidence of any significant activity after the end of the eighth century.

Ancient cities were characterized by the efficiency of their water-supplies, and Antioch was no exception. Water was certainly gathered from the springs and streams which ran down from the mountains immediately behind the city, but these were inadequate for all the demands of the metropolis. Water was brought by long aqueducts from Daphne some five miles south of the city. In western Europe, the end of antiquity usually led to the decay of such ancient water systems and the reliance on wells and rivers, but it seems that in Antioch, as in other Near Eastern towns, at least part of the ancient system was maintained. We have no explicit testimony that any of the aqueducts from Daphne continued in use after the middle of the sixth century, until William of Tyre in the twelfth century mentions that water was brought from Daphne to the city by aqueduct at certain specified times. However, Evagrius mentions winter and summer bath-houses at the end of the sixth century (Festugière 1975, 453), and the Arab geographers lay great stress on the excellence of the water-supply. According to Istakhri, writing in the mid-tenth century, 'there is running water in all the markets, the streets and the houses and also in the Jami' mosque' (Le Strange 1890, 369). Ibn Butlan in the eleventh century speaks of the abundant water-supply of the bath houses, and both Istakhri and Idrisi (mid-eleventh century) mention (water) mills within the city. Benjamin of Tudela (Wright 1848, 78) comments on the running water in the twelfth century, and baths were a feature of the Crusader city (Cahen 1940, 132). There is some archaeological evidence to support this. One of the aqueducts bringing water from Daphne shows signs of use and repair well into mediaeval times (Stillwell 1938, 49–56). Water pipes were found in the sixth- to eighth-century level on the colonnaded street sites (Lassus 1977, 66–7). The traces of a fountain were found near the mosque of Habib al-Najjar which from its position was plainly post-antique (ibid., 13–15). Lassus assigns it quite arbitrarily to the Byzantine reoccupation, but it is just as likely to have been Islamic.

The evidence suggests that an organized public water-supply continued to be a feature of city life throughout the first period of Muslim rule. In some ways this is surprising, for Muslim government did not normally reckon to take a direct hand in organizing civic life, which resulted in the evolution of the unplanned cities typical of the Near East. There were, however, two exceptions to this general lack of concern: any Muslim government had to ensure that its subjects could be secure from attack by the infidel and could perform the rituals of their faith. In order to pray properly the Muslims needed to wash and in order to wash they needed water. The provision of a reliable water-supply was essential, not just for convenience and pleasure but for the proper performance of religious rites.

Unlike the water-supply, the evidence from Antioch is scanty, often running in thin trickles and disappearing completely, but a consistent picture does seem to emerge. After the disasters of the second half of the sixth century, Antioch survived and thrived. It is true that it was much smaller than the classical city at its zenith and had lost many of the public buildings, theatres, hippodromes and the like which a changing culture no longer saw as necessary for a civilized lifestyle. There is also evidence that, while the early Islamic period was one of modest rebuilding along the main streets, the ninth and especially the tenth centuries represented the nadir of the city's fortunes. The Byzantine reconquest saw Antioch becoming once again an important administrative centre and the scene of renewed church-building. Despite these ups and downs there were significant elements of continuity. In the walls and the streets, two important churches remained in use throughout and a water-supply system was maintained. On an institutional level, the Melkite church continued its rituals and its succession of Patriarchs. It is in this light that we should view Downey's verdict that 'the real greatness of the city must have come to an end in AD 540' (Downey 1961, 559), for that was the end of one era and the beginning of another which was to last through the various political upheavals to the destruction of 1268.

The urban history of Antioch compares interestingly with that of other cities of the Near East. These can be divided into a number of different groups. Firstly there are those which survived and flourished after the Muslim conquest: Damascus, which became the capital of the Umayyad Caliphs and almost certainly increased its inhabited area (although it too suffered a major urban crisis in the bleak tenth century); Aleppo, which emerged from small-centre status to become the metropolis of northern Syria; Emesa/Hims, already becoming more important in the sixth century; and Jerusalem, which acquired a new cultic importance in Umayyad times with the building of the Dome of the Rock and associated shrines. There is no common thread here: Damascus was important for political reasons, but Aleppo expanded for economic ones and only gradually took over political power as the centre of local government from Chalcis/Qinnasrin, which became a dead town, while Jerusalem's survival was based on its political and religious status. Apart from Hims, all these cities retained important elements of their classical street plans and traces of the classical urban fabric.

A second group of cities had declined well before the Muslim invasions and remained dormant thereafter. I have argued elsewhere (Kennedy 1985a, 168–9) that this included most of the coastal cities, including Tyre, Sidon, Beirut and Laodicaea (Lattakia). Not until the period of Fatimid rule after 969, when the coastal areas were controlled by sea from Egypt, did the coastal towns revive. In some cases this long period of stagnation meant that the plan and the fabric of the classical period were lost. In contrast to Damascus, Aleppo and Antioch, none of the coastal cities (except, partially, Lattakia) retains its ancient street plan.

There was a third group of largely inland towns which seem to have survived as urban centres for the first 150 years of Islamic rule but declined to vanishing point in the ninth and tenth centuries: Gerasa/Jerash, Philadelphia/Amman, Chalcis/Qinnasrin and probably Apamea are among these. Unlike the cities of the coast, none of these sites enjoyed a revival in the eleventh and twelfth centuries.

Antioch falls between the second and third groups, marked as it is by late antique decline and survival on a reduced scale in the early Islamic period with evidence of further decline in the ninth and early tenth centuries. From the Byzantine reconquest of 969, however, Antioch shows signs of joining in the revival experienced by the coastal cities, to take its place once again in the twelfth century as one of the most important cities of the Levant.

Bibliography

Babcock, E.A. and Krey, A.C. (1976), *William of Tyre, History of Deeds done Beyond the Sea*, trans. 1941, repr. 1976 (New York).

Cahen, C. (1940), *La Syrie du nord à l'époque des Croisades* (Paris).

Cheikho, L. (1960), *Eutychii Patriarchae Alexandrini Annales ii: accedunt annales Yahia ibn Said Antiochensis, Corpus Scriptorum Christianorum Orientalium, Scriptores Arabici* vii (Louvain).

Dagron, G. (1976), *Minorities ethniques et religieuses de l'orient Byzantin à la fin du Xe et au XIe siècle, Travaux et Mémoires* vi (Paris).

Downey, G. (1961), *A History of Antioch in Syria* (Princeton).

Elderkin, G.W. (1934), *Antioch-on-the-Orontes* i: *The Excavations of 1932* (Princeton).

Festugière, A.-J. (1975), 'Evagre, Histoire Ecclésiastique', *Byzantion* 45, 187–479.

Foss, C. (1979), *Ephesus after Antiquity* (Princeton).

Guidi, I. (1897), 'Una descrizione araba di Antiocheia', *Rendiconti della R. Accademia dei Lincei, Cl. di scienze morali, storiche e filologiche*, ser. 5, vol. 6, 137–61.

Hitti, P. (1916), *The Origins of the Islamic State* (New York).

Jeffreys, E.M., Jeffreys, M. and Scott, R. (1986), *Chronicle of John Malalas* (Melbourne).

Kennedy, H. (1985a), 'The last century of Byzantine Syria', *Byzantinische Forschungen* 10, 141–83.

Kennedy, H. (1985b), 'From Polis to Madina: urban change in late antique and early Islamic Syria', *Past and Present* 106, 3–27.

Kennedy, H. (1986), 'The Melkite Church from the Islamic

Conquest to the Crusades', *17th International Byzantine Congress: Major Papers* (New Rochelle), 325–44.

Kraeling, C.H. (ed.) (1938), *Gerasa: City of the Decapolis* (New Haven).

Kratchkovsky, I. and Vasiliev, A. (1932), 'Histoire de Yahya-ibn-Sa'id d'Antioche', *Patrologia Orientalis* 23, 247–520.

Lassus, J. (1977), *Les Portiques d'Antioche* (Princeton).

Le Strange, G. (1890), *Palestine under the Moslems* (Cambridge).

Liebeschuetz, J.H.W.G. and Kennedy, H. (1989), 'Antioch and the villages of northern Syria in the fifth and sixth centuries AD: trends and problems', *Nottingham Medieval Studies* 32, 65–90.

Stillwell, R. (1938), *Antioch-on-the-Orontes* ii: *The Excavations, 1933–1936* (Princeton).

Stillwell, R. (1941), *Antioch-on-the-Orontes* iii: *The Excavations, 1937–1939* (Princeton).

Tate, G. and Sodini, J.-P. (1980), 'Déhès, recherches sur l'habitat rural', *Syria* 67, 1–303.

Tchalenko, G. (1953–8), *Villages antiques de la Syrie du Nord*, 3 vols (Paris).

Vajda, G. (1971), 'Habib al-Nadjdjar', *Encyclopaedia of Islam, New Edition* (Leiden), iii.12–3.

Van den Ven, P. (1962–70), *La vie ancienne de S. Syméon Stylite le jeune 521–592*, *Subsidia hagiographica* 32 (Brussels).

Weulersse, J. (1934), 'Antioche: essai de géographie urbaine', *Bulletin d'études orientales* 5, 27–79.

Whitby, M. (1986), *Theophylact Simocatta* (Oxford).

Wright, T. (1848), *Early Travels in Palestine* (London).

Yaqut al-Rumi (1979), *Mu'jam al-Buldan* (Beirut).

Zayat, H. (1952), 'La Vie du patriarche melkite d'Antioche Christophore', *Proche Orient Chrétien* 2, 11–38 and 333–66.

Index